ENCYCLOPEDIA OF THE

Animal Kingdom

Vineyard
BOOKS

ENCYCLOPEDIA OF THE
ANIMAL KINGDOM

Consultant Editor: Graham Bateman
Managing Editor: Lionel Bender
Art Editor: Ben White
Designers: Malcolm Smythe, Ben White
Text Editors: Miles Litvinoff, Madeleine
    Samuel, Barbara Taylor-Cork
Production: Nicolette Colborne

Planned and produced by:
Andromeda Oxford Ltd
11-13 The Vineyard,
Abingdon
Oxon, OX14 3PX

Copyright © 1991 Andromeda Oxford Ltd

Copyright © 1984 Priscilla Barrett

ISBN 1-86199-007-3

Printed and bound by Poligrafici Calderara
S.p.A., Bologna, Italy

10 9 8 7 6 5

Reprinted 1992, 1994, 1996, 1997, 1999

Authors:
Robin Kerrod
Martyn Bramwell
Steve Parker
John Stidworthy
Christopher O'Toole
Jill Bailey

CONTENTS

INTRODUCTION

There are 4,015 species of amphibians, 6,547 species of reptiles, 8,805 species of birds and some 4,030 species of mammals worldwide. How can we understand these tens of thousands of unique animals? By arranging them, as scientists do, into large groups that share important characteristics and behaviours, such as whether they are covered with feathers or fur, or have slimy or scaly skin. Or whether they give birth to live young or lay eggs

The Encyclopedia of the Animal Kingdom presents a vast panorama of animal life in a stunning collection of portraits, a gallery of the most exciting, most representative, most beautiful and most fascinating animals of the world. Reading an entire section, or simply looking at the charts, pictures, captions and graphics, provides a rich overview of an entire class of animal.

The smallest scientific "group" of animals is a genus, which can consist of one or more species. A species is a unique population of animals that generally breeds only with itself. Wolves, coyotes and dogs, for example, belong to a genus (*Canis*) of animals that includes several different species. Pure white Arctic wolves live in the far north, where there are few trees, and have much in common with the coyotes of the open lands of North America and the Red wolves of Texas and the South Carolina bayous, yet they are all different species in the same genus.

Vulpine foxes belong to another genus (*Vulpes*) that comprises several species. The sandy-coloured Fennec foxes that blend into desert landscapes in North Africa have much in common with the Red foxes that slink around the chicken coops of Europe and North America, but they are separate species. The domestic dog is just one species in the genus *Canis*, yet exists in a vast range of forms from the tiny Yorkshire terrier to the gigantic Irish wolfhound and the athletic greyhound.

Dogs, wolves and foxes, nevertheless, obviously share many characteristics. For example, they all have long, sharp fangs, wet noses, conspicuous ears and intelligent eyes. Such similarities among different genera of animals qualify them as a family. Dogs, wolves and foxes belong to the Canidae, or dog family. The family Canidae, in turn, belongs to the order known as Carnivora – the meat eaters. This order also includes cats and weasels, civets, raccoons

and bears. Whales belong to the order Cetacea, bats belong to the order Chiroptera. As different as bats and whales and wolves may seem, they have important things in common – they give birth to live young and feed them with milk, they have hair or fur, warm bodies and large brains. These basic characteristics make the 20 metre whale and the three centimetre bat more alike than they seem, for these traits are shared by a large group of orders that make up the next largest category of animals – the class. Dogs, wolves and bats are members of the class Mammalia, which with all other classes of animals, combine to form the sum total of all animal life – the Animal Kingdom.

How to Use This Book

The Encyclopedia of the Animal Kingdom surveys the higher forms of animal life – amphibians, reptiles, birds and mammals. These groups of animals differ sufficiently enough that each requires a special introduction. People talk, for example, about warm-blooded mammals and cold-blooded reptiles, when, in fact, the blood of reptiles is often far warmer than that of mammals. The four introductory sections in this encyclopedia clarify the major differences among the classes of higher animals. The introductions present broad overviews of vastly different groups of animals; they present concisely the essential characteristics and suggest the variations among species within the group.

Each introductory section ("What is a Bird?", "What is a Mammal?" etc.) is followed by a series of visual and verbal portraits. There are fascinating facts about all sorts of creatures – a frog that swallows its hatching tadpoles, incubates them in a sac in its mouth and then spits them out as tiny froglets; whales that feed all summer in the Bering, Beaufort and Chuckchi seas and eat nothing all winter in the Sea of Cortez; the three hundred thousand llamas that worked in the Inca silver mines; a falcon that dives at 400 kilometres an hour; an alligator that lines its nest with rotting vegetation so the heat of decay will incubate its eggs.

Fact Panel

The "Fact Panel", overleaf consists of 25 symbols that appear throughout the book. These symbols, some of which appear in each section of the book, summarize key characteristics of a species or a group of species. A black circle, for example, indicates an animal or group of animals that is active primarily at night, such as bats; whereas a red circle indicates an animal or group of animals that is active during the day; hawks for example.

Other symbols describe such characteristics as "Group Size", "Conservation Status", "Habitat", "Diet" and "Breeding". Range maps indicate where the particular animals dwell.

These symbols and maps give readers an immediate grasp of the key elements of an animal's behaviour and its chances of surviving in today's world. One can tell at a glance whether to expect a particular species to appear in a swamp or on a mountaintop, in a forest or an open field, in daylight or in darkness, alone or among thousands. The "Fact Panel" symbols are a form of naturalist shorthand, a way of organizing animals by their habitats and, in terms of their relationship to the world's environment, by their probable fate.

Comparison Silhouettes

In addition to the descriptive symbols in the "Fact Panel", the encyclopedia suggests the relative size of animals by comparing them to an average-size human being, or a part thereof. It is difficult to imagine how big an eagle is, or a leopard, or a White whale. But when you look at a picture of a frog sitting next to a human foot, you can tell immediately how big a frog is. Comparison silhouettes appear in the upper right hand corner of many pages in this encyclopedia. Using these symbols gives you an immediate grasp of the relative size of hummingbirds and eagles, whales and tigers, pythons, bats and camels – the relative size, that is, of the vast panorama of animal life.

The Animal Experience

Each entry in the encyclopedia begins with a dramatic story that describes a telling moment in the life of an animal. These stories create a mood, and evoke the power and mystery of the animal world:

FACT PANEL: Key to symbols denoting general features of animals

SYMBOLS WITH NO WORDS

Activity time	Conservation status	◢ Tundra
● Nocturnal	☠ All species threatened	◢ Forest/Woodland
● Daytime	♔ Some species threatened	● Grassland
◗ Dawn/Dusk	No species threatened (no symbol)	≋ Freshwater
○ All the time	SYMBOLS NEXT TO HEADINGS	Diet
Group size	Habitat	■ Other animals
◪ Solitary	◤ General	▨ Plants
◪ Pairs	◢ Mountain/Moorland	◿ Animals and Plants
◼ Small groups (up to 10)	◢ Desert	Breeding
■ Large groups	▱ Sea	◉ Seasonal (at fixed times)
◪ Variable	▭ Amphibious	◡ Non-seasonal (at any time)

"It is a pitch dark night out on the prairie. A mouse scurries about intent on finding seeds. In a hollow lies a rattlesnake. It cannot see the mouse, but it senses the presence of its warm body. It turns its head towards the mouse, waits until it is close, then strikes. It stabs and injects venom, then settles back to wait for its victim's death".

These miniature stories evoke the drama of the Animal Kingdom, the everyday tragedies and triumphs of tiny birds and great whales.

Fact Box

Each entry contains a Fact Box which uses the symbols that appear in the "Fact Panel" in the front of the book. The symbols denoting habitat, activity time and diet, for example, appear in the Fact Box which also includes a range map, a list of species mentioned in the text and comments on such considerations as size. The entry about Frogs and Toads, for example, notes that they range in size from about one centimetre to more than 30 centimetres. in the entry about Swans and Geese we learn that these birds can have wingspans of two metres and weigh more than 14 kilograms.

Our Goal

The Encyclopedia of the Animal Kingdom was designed to deliver vast amounts of information in a very limited space, and yet still have about it an open, airy, expansive feel, rather like the wilderness itself.

Our editorial goal has been to provide a wide range of readers, especially young ones, with a rich assortment of images and concepts of and about the Animal Kingdom. We have tried, too, to bring to the text and its illustrative material a sense of the drama, beauty and fragility of things – a sense, in short, of reality. More than any other generation, today's children are maturing into a natural world that they recognize as a responsibility.

The children of today might never see certain highly endangered animals, unless they fight for their survival. We hope that by instilling a sense of wonder and a sense of diversity, *The Encyclopedia of the Animal Kingdom* will inspire today's children to become tomorrow's environmentally responsible adults.

Graham Bateman

WHAT IS AN AMPHIBIAN?

Most amphibians spend part of their lives in water and the rest of the time on land. The name amphibian comes from a combination of two Greek words, *amphi* and *bios*, meaning a double life. They include frogs, toads, newts and salamanders. Most have fish-like young called tadpoles.

Amphibians are vertebrates – they have a bony internal skeleton built around a backbone – the vertebral column. They are also "cold-blooded" or more correctly ectothermic; their body temperature depends upon the temperature of their surroundings. They are not able to produce their own body heat, and so cannot easily control the speed with which their body systems work. In cold weather, amphibians become cold and lazy, but in warm weather they are warm and very active. If their surroundings become too hot, they must retreat into the shade to cool down.

The skin of most amphibians is usually soft and moist. Some species have claw-like scales on the fingers and toes. Glands in an amphibian's skin produce a slimy mucus to keep the skin moist. The skin is not water-proof, so amphibians are generally found in moist places, which helps prevent their bodies drying out.

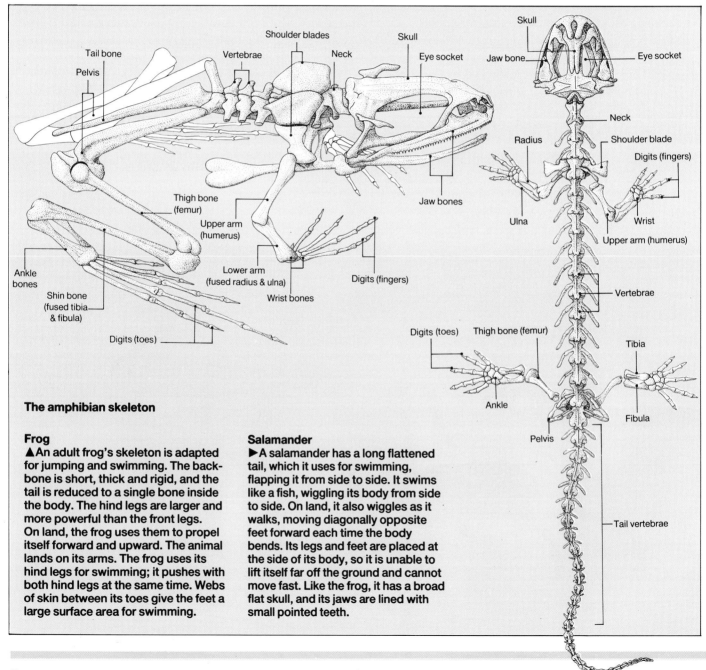

The amphibian skeleton

Frog
▲An adult frog's skeleton is adapted for jumping and swimming. The back-bone is short, thick and rigid, and the tail is reduced to a single bone inside the body. The hind legs are larger and more powerful than the front legs. On land, the frog uses them to propel itself forward and upward. The animal lands on its arms. The frog uses its hind legs for swimming; it pushes with both hind legs at the same time. Webs of skin between its toes give the feet a large surface area for swimming.

Salamander
▶A salamander has a long flattened tail, which it uses for swimming, flapping it from side to side. It swims like a fish, wiggling its body from side to side. On land, it also wiggles as it walks, moving diagonally opposite feet forward each time the body bends. Its legs and feet are placed at the side of its body, so it is unable to lift itself far off the ground and cannot move fast. Like the frog, it has a broad flat skull, and its jaws are lined with small pointed teeth.

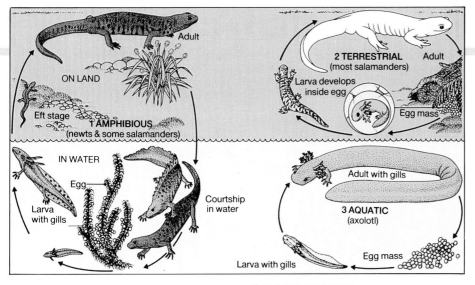

▲ All salamanders and newts produce fish-like larvae that breathe using feathery external gills. Many are truly amphibious: the adults return to water to breed, and the larvae live and feed in the water until they develop lungs and are ready to live on land. Some spend their whole lives on land. The larvae of these species develop inside the egg until they can breathe air. The axolotl spends all its life in water. The adult is like a giant larva: it still has external gills.

▼ Most frogs return to water to mate and lay their eggs. The fish-like tadpoles develop in the water. They crawl out on to land when their lungs are fully formed and their mouths are ready to start eating insects.

A DOUBLE LIFE

Young amphibians do not resemble their parents. They are called larvae. As they develop, they undergo a dramatic change in body shape, diet and life-style. This change is called metamorphosis, which means change of shape. Many amphibians return to water to breed, sometimes travelling several kilometres overland to reach their favourite breeding ponds. Those species that live in hot moist climates may breed at any time of the year. In tropical regions with a distinct wet and dry season, breeding often takes place as the rains begin. In temperate regions, breeding is usually in spring.

Male frogs and toads attract the females by croaking. Once a male frog or toad finds a mate, he climbs on her back and clings to her until she is ready to shed her eggs in the water. Then he sheds his sperm over the eggs to fertilize them. Frogs lay from 1 to 25,000 eggs at a time. Each egg has a layer of jelly. In some species the eggs (spawn) are glued together in bubbly masses. In others the eggs are laid in long strings of jelly. The spawn tends to float near the surface of the water.

The salamanders' courtship relies on smell and visual displays. In a few species of salamander the males shed their sperm into the water as frogs do. However, most male salamanders and newts produce small packets of sperm which the female picks up during courtship. The eggs are fertilized inside the female's body.

In many amphibians the eggs hatch into aquatic larvae with gills. In others, the larvae develop inside the egg until they have developed lungs. These tadpoles do not need to be in water. Sometimes, in caecilians, the young develop inside the mother's body and are born as tiny adults with lungs.

▼ When the amphibian egg is released, it is surrounded by a thin layer of jelly. This swells in water, and sticks the eggs together. The jelly is slippery, and any animal wishing to eat the eggs must swallow all or none. The embryo's belly is swollen by the yolk on which it feeds.

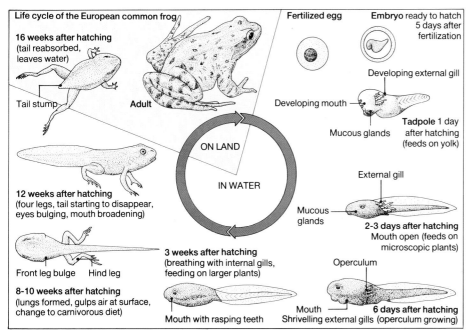

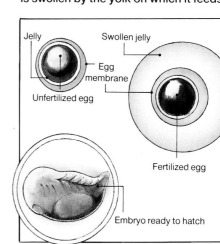

HUNTERS AND GRAZERS

Salamanders and newts feed on small invertebrates, such as insects, slugs, snails and worms. Usually they stalk their prey or lie in wait for it, then seize it in their jaws. Several salamanders can flick out their tongues to capture their prey.

Frogs and toads feed mostly on flying insects, especially gnats, mayflies, dragonflies and moths, and rely on a rapid flick of their long sticky tongue to capture food. The tongue is attached to the front of the mouth. Some species also eat large quantities of insect larvae, slugs, snails – eating the shell as well – and earthworms. The majority of adult amphibians are most active at night, when the air is moist. At night they are also less easily spotted by their enemies.

Amphibian larvae have a very wide variety of diets. Newt and salamander larvae are fierce underwater hunters, attacking smaller invertebrates. Most frog and toad tadpoles start life as vegetarians. Some filter particles of food from the water. Others scrape algae from the surfaces of underwater plants with their tiny horny teeth. As the tadpoles grow, they shed these teeth and the mouth grows wider. They gradually change to a meat diet, scavenging on dead animals or hunting smaller water animals.

HOW AMPHIBIANS BREATHE

Most adult amphibians have lungs for breathing air. They also take in oxygen through their moist skins and through the moist lining of their large mouths. Some salamanders rely entirely on this method and do not have lungs. Amphibian larvae breathe through their gills. These are fleshy feathery outgrowths with a large surface for absorbing oxygen from the water.

▲ The Paradoxical frog, from Trinidad and the Amazon, gets its name because its tadpole grows up to 25cm long, four times as long as the adult frog.

▼ The Green salamander lives in damp crevices on rock faces. Its green coloration gives it good camouflage against a background of lichens.

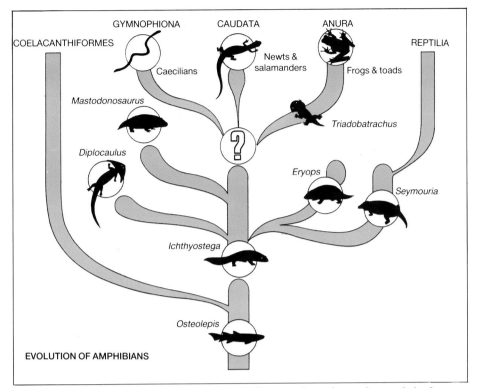

GYMNOPHIONA   CAUDATA   ANURA

COELACANTHIFORMES

Caecilians

Newts & salamanders

Frogs & toads

REPTILIA

Mastodonosaurus

Diplocaulus

Triadobatrachus

Eryops

Seymouria

Ichthyostega

Osteolepis

EVOLUTION OF AMPHIBIANS

▲Amphibians evolved from lobe-finned fishes, relatives of the present-day coelacanth, about 370 million years ago. Modern frogs, salamanders and caecilians are different from primitive amphibians, and from each other, but the fossil record is incomplete, and we do not know exactly how they evolved.

POISONOUS PROTECTION

Amphibians have a large number of enemies. With their soft bodies they are ideal food for small mammals, birds, lizards and snakes, turtles and even larger amphibians.

The skin of most adult amphibians has poison-producing glands which make them taste bad, and may even poison a predator. Highly poisonous amphibians usually have bright warning colours so predators can learn to recognize and avoid them.

If threatened, frogs and toads may raise themselves on tiptoe and puff up their bodies so that they look much bigger than they really are. Or they may escape by diving into the water. Their bulging eyes and nostrils are situated on the top of their heads, so they can breathe and see while the rest of the body remains hidden from view under the water.

TYPES OF AMPHIBIANS

There are three living orders and some 4,015 species of amphibians: salamanders, newts and mudpuppies (Urodela 358 species), frogs and toads (Anura 3,494 species) and caecilians (Gymnophiona 163 species).

The salamanders are the most fish-like of the amphibians. They have long flattened tails and rather small legs. Some species of salamander spend almost their entire lives in water. Others spend most of their adult lives on land.

Frogs and toads crawl over land in the same way as salamanders, but they can move much faster by leaping. They have long hind legs with large webbed feet, and they have no visible tails. Most adult frogs and toads spend most of the time on land.

Caecilians are strange worm-like amphibians with no legs. They live underground, and are almost blind.

ANCESTORS OF AMPHIBIANS

About 370 million years ago a group of fish, the lobe-finned fish, developed bony supports for their fins and lungs for breathing air. They were able to haul themselves out of the water on to land. Here, there were new sources of food – the insects now flourishing around the edges of the swamps. There were no large land predators to attack them, or to compete with them for food. These were the ancestors of the amphibians.

FROM WATER TO LAND

The oldest amphibian fossils are 360 million years old. Early amphibians like *Ichthyostega* show many features related to living on land instead of in water. Their skeletons had hip girdles and shoulder girdles to support the developing limbs. The skull was separated from the rest of the back by a flexible neck, allowing the head to turn when catching prey. Ribs protected the animal's soft parts as it rested on the ground. The amphibians had ears that could hear in air, eyelids to keep the eyes moist, and tongues to moisten and move food.

Some of these ancient amphibians were very large. The largest, *Mastodonosaurus*, had a skull 125cm long, and was probably about 4m long. For millions of years the amphibians ruled the world, until they were finally overcome by a newly evolved group of animals, the dinosaurs.

SALAMANDERS

It is a dark, rainy evening. From beneath a mossy log a tiny salamander emerges. Tonight the salamander is unlucky. It is seized by a small snake. But the salamander's skin produces so much sticky slime that the snake lets go.

SALAMANDERS Order
Urodela: 6 families (*336 species*)

● ◱ ⚶

▦ Habitat: water or land; breeding usually in water.

▪ Diet: small animals.

○ Breeding: internal or external fertilization. Most lay eggs; some produce live young.

Size: smallest from about 4cm; largest (giant salamanders): up to 180cm long.

Colour: varies, from dull browns and greys to vivid reds and yellows.

Species mentioned in text:
Alpine salamander (*Salamandra atra*)
Axolotl (*Ambystoma mexicanum*)
Cave salamander (*Eurycea lucifuga*)
Grotto salamander(*Typhlotriton spelaeus*)
Hellbender (*Cryptobranchus allegeniensis*)
Redback salamander (*Plethodon cinereus*)
Spotted salamander (*Ambystoma maculatum*)
Texas blind salamander (*Typhlomolge rathbuni*)
Two-lined salamander (*Eurycea bislineata*).

▲The axolotl usually spends all its life in water, and keeps larval features such as the feathery gills. Some forms are albino.

Salamanders, newts, and their relatives make up the amphibian order Urodela. They have long bodies, long tails, and two pairs of legs of roughly similar size. Most are found in temperate climates in North America, Europe and Asia, but some live in the tropics of Central and South America.

There are nine different families of the Urodela. Six are dealt with here. Other families are the Congo eels and the sirens, in North America, and the 5 North American and 1 European species of mudpuppies. A few species of salamander are commonly called "newts."

WATERY HOMES
Salamanders live in a wide variety of habitats. Some species live entirely on land, some live entirely in water, while others divide their time between land and water. The skin of a salamander allows water to pass through quite easily. Because of this, even the land types need to live in damp places. If they are exposed to hot dry conditions, they soon lose water and die. Land-living species commonly live under rocks and logs or burrow in damp earth. In very hot weather, salamanders retreat into damp refuges, emerging only during the cool of the night. But, like other amphibians, they are a similar temperature to their surroundings. If temperatures are too low, they hide away and become inactive.

BREATHING SKINS
Many salamanders breathe air using lungs. A salamander may also use the damp inner surface of its mouth to get oxygen. Often the soft skin under the salamander's throat can be seen pumping rapidly, helping to change the air in the mouth.

Even when these two methods are used, quite a large part of a salamander's oxygen is obtained through the damp skin. The largest family of salamanders, with over 200 species, do not have lungs at all. They breathe just through the mouth and skin.

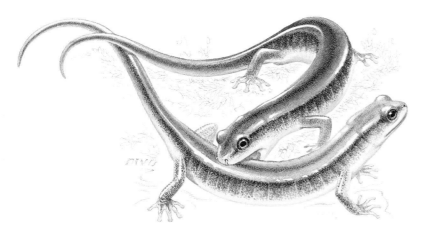

▼The Cave salamander spends all its life on land. It lives in the twilight zone near cave entrances.

▲Many male salamanders bite or grasp the female during courtship, as do Two-lined salamanders.

REPULSIVE SKINS

In a salamander's skin there are many glands. Some of these help to keep it moist and slimy. But some species have other glands that secrete substances which are poisonous or taste nasty. These can deter enemy attacks.

Poisonous salamanders are often very brightly coloured to warn predators to leave them alone. Several species, such as the Spotted salamander, have glands on the back of the neck. When attacked, they crouch to present their bad-tasting neck to the enemy. Others with glands on the neck actually butt an enemy with their heads. Some of the American mole

salamanders do this. It seems effective against small predators such as shrews. Some lungless salamanders have many glands on the tail. When attacked, they wave the tail at an enemy. They may be able to shed their tails, leaving behind a distasteful morsel which thrashes wildly and distracts the predator. The salamanders can then escape and grow a new tail.

SMALL APPETITES

All salamanders are carnivores. They feed on small living animals such as insects, slugs, snails and worms. Some kinds can flick out the tongue to catch prey. Salamanders can be quite ferocious for their size, but because of their slow pace of life and periods of inactivity they do not consume huge amounts of food. The slow pace of their lives may also help them become long-lived. Quite small species may live 25 years, and some individuals are known to have lived 50 years.

HIDDEN MILLIONS

Salamanders are secretive. Most are small (few are more than 15cm long), live in cool shady places, and become active at night, so they usually escape human attention. But in some places they can be very abundant. In the forests of eastern USA, it has been calculated that there is probably a greater weight of salamanders than all the birds and mammals put together.

BIGGEST AMPHIBIANS

Some salamanders are the biggest of all living amphibians. These are the giant salamanders of eastern Asia. As much as 1.6m in length, they never leave the water, which supports their weight. They breathe with lungs and through the skin.

▲ Species of salamander *Bolitoglossa schizodactyla* (1) is a lungless species with webbed feet. The Red salamander (*Pseudotriton ruber*) (2) burrows into mud near streams. The Tiger salamander (*Ambystoma tigrinum*) (3) is a close relative of the axolotl. *Batrachuperus pinchonii* (4) and *Onychodactylus japonicus* (5) live in Asia. *Tylotriton taliangensis* (6) has a warty skin.

◄ The Spotted salamander of North America lives on land as an adult, but returns to water to lay its eggs.

EGGS AND NESTS

Salamanders have three main types of life cycle. Some breed entirely on land. Some have a "typical" amphibian life cycle, with eggs and larvae in the water and adults on land. (Newts are a good example of this.) Then there are species that spend all the stages of their life cycle in water.

The Redback salamander, found in woodland areas of eastern North America, is a wholly land-living species. After mating, the female lays 20-30

eggs in a rotten log. The eggs are large, and the embryos inside them develop fast. The whole larval development is passed within the egg so the hatching salamander is just a tiny version of the adult. In some salamanders, such as the Alpine salamander of Europe, the egg develops inside the mother, who gives birth to live young.

In salamanders that live entirely in water, the number of eggs laid is often high. The hellbender of America lays up to 450 eggs. The male hellbender digs out a nest and guards it. He allows females to lay their eggs in the nest, then he fertilizes them, and guards them for the 10-12 weeks they take to develop into larvae. The larvae leave the nest and fend for themselves.

STAYING YOUNG

In various species of some families, such as the mole salamanders, gills and other larval features can be kept throughout life. Sometimes populations of the same species develop

differently in different environments. One population may progress to the adult in the normal way. Another population may keep large, frilly gills and a flattened tail. It seems to depend on the living conditions. But these "larval" forms may be able to reproduce. The most famous example is the axolotl of Mexico, which is typically larval looking, but can change to an "adult" if given the chemical iodine. Other species will change into adults if the water they are living in dries up.

▲ The hellbender is the largest of the North American salamanders, reaching 70cm from snout to tail.

BLIND CAVE-DWELLERS

Some of the lungless salamanders live in underground water in caves. The Texas blind salamander is white, with tiny eyes. The Grotto salamander, of the Ozarks in the USA, has a grey or brown larva which lives in streams, but the adult retreats into caves and loses its colour and the use of its eyes.

FROGS AND TOADS

It is a rainy night in early spring. From a pond comes a sound like small motor-bike engines – male frogs calling to advertise their presence. Other frogs hop to the pond from all directions. The large females, full of eggs, are seized by males as they enter the water. Next morning, the pond is full of round masses of frogspawn.

Frogs and toads are the most numerous amphibians. They are found on most islands and on all continents except Antarctica. The great majority occur in warm areas of the world, but many are found in cool climates. Two species, the European common frog and the Wood frog of North America, can even live within the Arctic Circle. Most frogs and toads live both in water and on land, at least for part

FROGS AND TOADS
Order Anura: 17 families
(*2,609 species*)

Habitat: adults live mostly on land. Some burrow or climb. Some live entirely in water.

Diet: insects, worms, snails, some small vertebrates.

Breeding: typically external

fertilization, laying eggs in water where tadpoles develop. Many variations and exceptions.

Size: smallest (*Sminthillus limbatus*): 1.2cm snout to vent; largest (Goliath frog): 30cm.

Colour: from dull browns and greens to vivid reds, yellows, blues.

Species mentioned in text:
Darwin's frog (*Rhinoderma darwinii*)
European common frog (*Rana temporaria*)
Golden toad (*Bufo periglenes*)
Goliath frog (*Rana goliath*)
Malaysian horned toad (*Ceratophrys dorsata*)
Midwife toad (*Alytes obstetricans*)
Red-and-blue poison arrow frog (*Dendrobates pumilio*)
Surinam toad (*Pipa pipa*)
Western spadefoot toad (*Scaphiopus hammondii*)
Wood frog (*Rana sylvatica*)

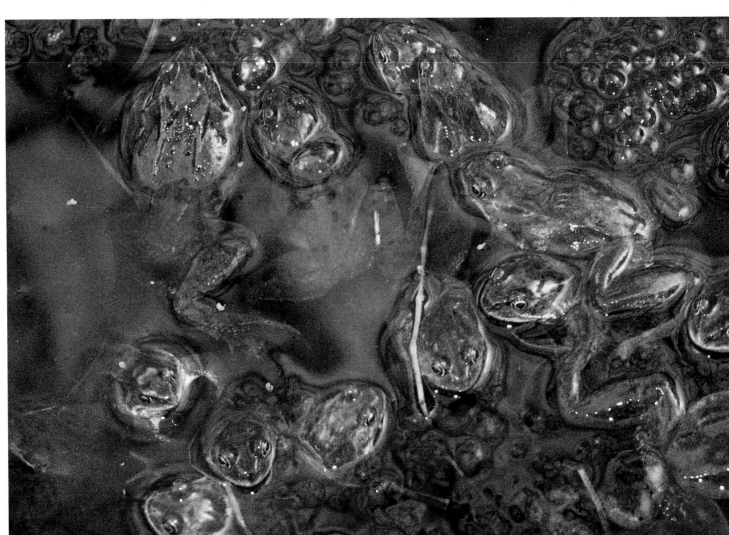

of their lives, but some live entirely in water and others entirely on land. Some succeed in living in places that seem at first sight unsuitable, such as savannahs and deserts.

FROG OR TOAD?

How can frogs be told from toads? "Frogs" are smooth-skinned, long-limbed and live in or close to water. "Toads" are stout-bodied with short limbs, and have warty skins. They live in damp places away from water. The word frog or toad really describes the look of the creature. There is no special scientific difference. Some scientific families contain both "frogs" and "toads." It would appear that either the frog form or the toad form has evolved a number of times to fit the two ways of life. Unless a particular type is specified, the term "frog" includes toads as well.

LONG JUMP EXPERTS

Frogs have a much shorter body than other amphibians. They have nine bones or less in the backbone, which makes it short and rigid. Frogs do not have a narrow neck so the head joins straight on to the body. They do not have a tail either.

These adaptations are connected with the way frogs jump. The long back legs fold into three sections, thigh, shin and foot, of almost equal length. When the leg is suddenly straightened, the frog shoots forward. The short front limbs cushion the landing. The direction of jump is not always very well controlled, but it makes an effective means of escaping an enemy. The record for a single leap by a large frog is over 5m; most jumps are much shorter. The long back limbs are also good for swimming. They are pushed backwards in an action similar to the human breaststroke, and the webbed feet push on the water.

Some species of frog are good burrowers. They dig themselves down backwards using a sideways shuffle of the hind feet. The heel in these species has a special hard projection that acts as a scraper and shovel.

BIG EYES AND EARS

A frog's eyes are usually large. They are at the side of the head, so the frog can watch all round for danger. Some kinds of frog have eyes that are specially adapted to detect small moving objects which might be prey. The eyes have lids to protect them, and

▼Many species of frog gather in large numbers at spawning sites. These are spawning European common frogs.

▼Mating Golden toads. During mating, the male clasps the female and fertilizes the eggs as she lays them.

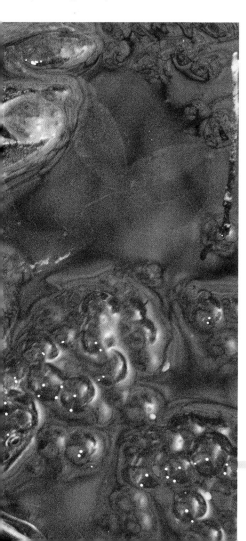

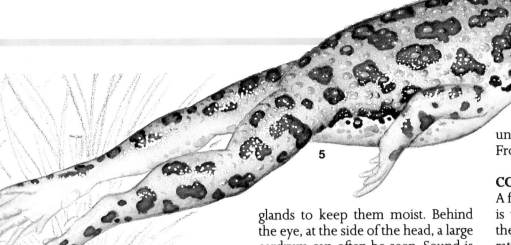

◀▼**Frogs and toads from around the world** Tailed frog (*Ascaphus truei*) **(1)** from North America. Oriental fire-bellied toad (*Bombina orientalis*) **(2)** of Asia. Iberian midwife toad (*Alytes cisternasii*) **(3)** from Portugal and Spain. Surinam toad **(4)** of South America. Eastern spadefoot (*Pelobates syriacus*) **(5)** of eastern Europe and south-west Asia. Couch's spadefoot (*Scaphiopus couchii*) **(6)** of North America. Burrowing toad (*Rhinophyrnus dorsalis*) **(7)** of Central America.

glands to keep them moist. Behind the eye, at the side of the head, a large eardrum can often be seen. Sound is important to many species in finding mates and avoiding rivals. Gatherings of frogs during the mating season can be very noisy. In some places in the tropics, as many as 20 species of frog may call at the same time; some calls carry for more than a kilometre.

Each species has its own particular call. It may be clicks, croaks, whistles or trills. Sounds are usually produced by vibrating the vocal cords in the voicebox (or larynx). Many frogs have vocal sacs which are blown up with air and help in the production of sound. These sacs are generally in the throat region, and may be single or double. The male's "song" attracts females and frightens away males.

Some species also have aggressive calls. Mainly these are made by males about to attack others. Sometimes they are given by an individual of either sex when grabbed by a male, unless it is a female ready to lay eggs. Frogs may scream if a predator attacks.

COLOURS AND CHEMICALS
A frog's skin is generally kept damp. It is used for breathing, in addition to the lungs. The skin lets out water rather easily; even the warty skin of toads is not very waterproof. Some, though, can put up with a surprising amount of water loss. The Western spadefoot toad of North America can survive losing 60 per cent of its body water. However, most frogs that live in very hot or dry climates try to avoid water loss by burrowing during the day and coming to the surface at night.

A few species of toad can absorb water through the skin of the belly just by sitting on damp ground. Some burrowers store water in the bladder, to be used when needed. Several frogs can store half their own weight in water. Using these methods, some of the burrowing frogs can stay underground for weeks, or even years if necessary, until rains appear again.

A frog's skin contains glands of various kinds. Some frogs secrete substances which taste bad or are mildly, or very, poisonous. Many of

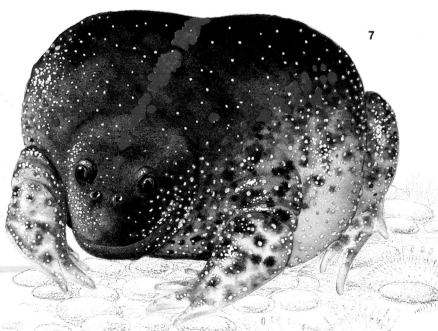

the most poisonous frogs, such as the poison arrow frogs of Central and South America, are decked out in brilliant colours that may serve to warn off enemies. Other frogs may have "flash" colours that suddenly show when they jump, and may confuse a predator. Most frogs, though, have subdued colours which work well to camouflage them. Some, such as the Malaysian horned toad, go one stage better by having bodies which imitate the shape and colour of dead leaves on the forest floor where they live.

MASS BREEDING

Most frogs are scattered over a wide area for much of the year, and must migrate to a suitable breeding site when conditions are right. Hundreds, or even thousands of individuals, may congregate in one spot. Frogs will often return to the same pond or lake again and again, often the one in which they grew up. They may even pass other apparently suitable water on the way there.

Many kinds of clues and landmarks seem to be involved in this navigation. Unfortunately, frogs may continue to return to places ruined as breeding sites by man. They may also cross roads and railways and be killed in large numbers. In some places in Britain "toad tunnels" have been built under roads so they can cross the road in safety.

FROM EGG TO FROG

The typical frog lays large numbers of eggs coated with jelly in the water. The tadpoles that hatch from the eggs have a rounded body containing feeding organs, with a long, coiled gut for digesting plant food. They have gills to breathe, and a long tail which they wriggle to help them swim. After some weeks growing, they "metamorphose". Legs grow. The tail is lost. Gills disappear. Lungs form. The long gut becomes much shorter, and now copes with a diet of insects and other small animals. They are now frogs, and live mainly on land. This is the typical frog life cycle.

Many species of frog have more unusual ways of growing up. Some frogs lay their eggs on vegetation in a nest of frothy foam that hardens like meringue. At hatching time, the foam softens, and the tadpoles drop into the water below.

Some species produce fewer eggs, but look after them so that they stand a better chance of survival. In the Midwife toad, the male winds the string of eggs round his hind legs and carries them about. He takes the eggs to water for hatching. Some species of poison arrow frog put a single tadpole into a tiny pond formed at the leaf base of a plant. The mother lays a clutch of unfertilized eggs to act as food for the tadpole.

The female Surinam toad keeps the eggs embedded in the skin of the back until they develop into tiny toads. Perhaps the oddest of all is Darwin's frog, in which the male swallows hatching tadpoles into his large vocal sac. When they have completed their development there, he spits them out as froglets.

◀Oriental fire-bellied toads are camouflaged above, but display the bright belly colours when attacked.

▶Warning colours are found in many frogs, such as these Red-and-blue poison arrow frogs.

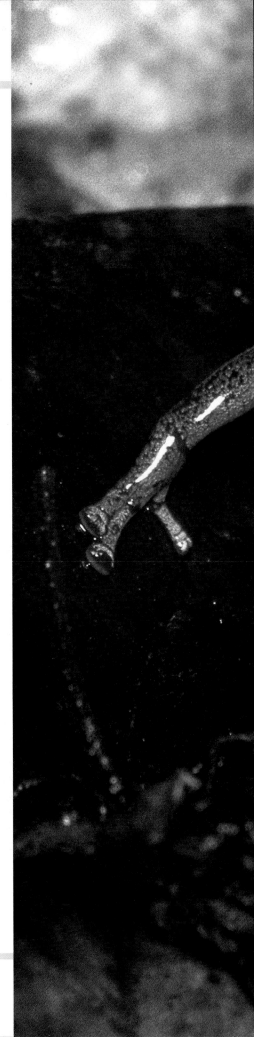

WHAT IS A REPTILE?

Snakes, crocodiles, lizards, tortoises and turtles are all reptiles. Their skin is covered in horny scales, and they are vertebrates: they have an internal bony skeleton with a central backbone. Most species spend all their lives on land. Reptiles are ectothermic (cold-blooded); their body temperature depends on the temperature of their immediate surroundings.

Reptiles are better adapted to life on land than amphibians. Their scaly skin prevents their bodies from drying out. Even more important, they reproduce by laying eggs protected by shells, or by giving birth to live young. There is no free-living larva stage. Reptiles excrete uric acid – a solid waste that does not require water in order to be eliminated from the body.

TYPES OF REPTILES
There are four main categories, or orders, of reptiles:

Turtles are covered in a heavy shell. They have a horny beak instead of teeth, and there are no openings in the back of the skull (244 species).

Lizards, snakes and worm-lizards all evolved from ancestors that had two pairs of legs, and some still have pelvic girdles in their skeletons. They all have a movable bone linking the lower jaw to the skull, which allows for relatively free movement of the jaw. Snakes have very long backbones, and can unhinge their jaws to swallow large prey. Worm-lizards live underground, and have no legs. They have heavy skulls for burrowing, and are almost blind (lizards, 3,751 species; snakes, 2,389 species; worm-lizards, 140 species).

Crocodiles and alligators spend much of their lives in water, where they use their powerful flattened tails for swimming. They are covered in horny plates strengthened with bone,

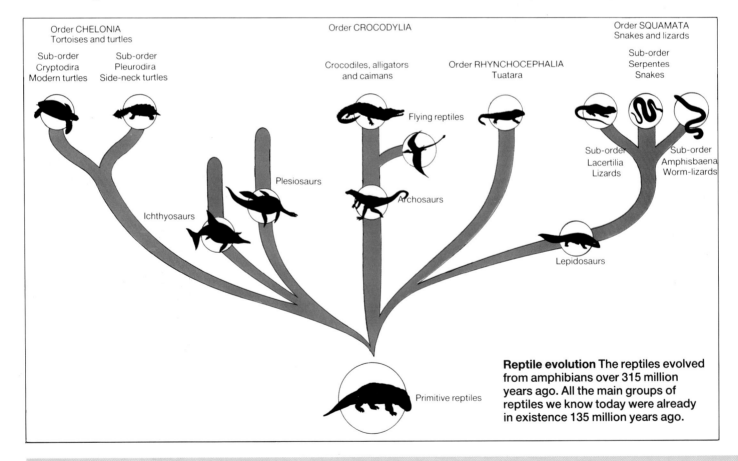

Order CHELONIA
Tortoises and turtles

Sub-order Cryptodira
Modern turtles

Sub-order Pleurodira
Side-neck turtles

Order CROCODYLIA

Crocodiles, alligators and caimans

Order RHYNCHOCEPHALIA
Tuatara

Order SQUAMATA
Snakes and lizards

Sub-order Serpentes
Snakes

Sub-order Lacertilia
Lizards

Sub-order Amphisbaena
Worm-lizards

Flying reptiles

Plesiosaurs

Ichthyosaurs

Archosaurs

Lepidosaurs

Primitive reptiles

Reptile evolution The reptiles evolved from amphibians over 315 million years ago. All the main groups of reptiles we know today were already in existence 135 million years ago.

which extend all around their bodies, and a crest of horny plates on their tails. Their eyes and nostrils are raised so that they can protrude above the water while the rest of the animal is submerged (22 species).

The tuatara is the only living member of an ancient order of reptiles. It has a third "eye" on the top of the head, which is sensitive to light. It has two upper rows of teeth, one row on the upper jaw and one row on the palate. The lower teeth fit between these two rows. A crest of horny plates runs along its back (1 species).

AGE OF REPTILES
Reptiles evolved from amphibians millions of years ago, by slowly developing eggs with shells and a waterproof covering of scales. The earliest fossil reptiles have been found in rocks of the Carboniferous period, about 315 million years old. By this time many different types of reptiles had evolved, including the dinosaurs, so they probably arose even earlier.

Their shelled eggs allowed them to live far away from water, and by the Permian period, 280 million years ago, they were found in large numbers almost all over the Earth.

In this Age of Reptiles, these animals were the dominant creatures on the Earth. Dinosaurs ruled the land, huge sea reptiles (plesiosaurs and ichthyosaurs) and giant turtles ruled the oceans, and flying reptiles (pterosaurs) dominated the air. Then, over a relatively short period of geological time, around 65 million years ago, most of these reptiles, including all the dinosaurs, disappeared. Mammals began to take over as the dominant life forms. No-one knows exactly what killed the dinosaurs.

PARENTAL CARE
Reptiles usually make nests of plant material in damp places or dig holes in the soil in which to lay their eggs. Some reptiles guard their eggs until they hatch. Pythons coil around their eggs to keep them warm and speed

▲ Young lizards and snakes use a special egg tooth on their snout to chisel a way out of the eggs. Once the animals have hatched, this tooth is shed.

▼ Inside the egg, the reptile embryo lies in a water-filled sac, the amnion. Blood vessels from its belly spread over the yolk sac to absorb food. The allantois stores the embryo's liquid waste. Oxygen passes into the egg through tiny holes in the shell, and waste gases from the embryo pass out.

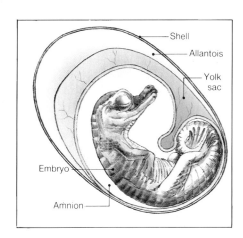

up hatching. The American alligator builds a nest of rotting vegetation. Heat from the decaying plants incubates the eggs.

Tortoises, crocodiles and geckos lay hard-shelled eggs, but most reptile eggs have soft, leathery shells. In many lizards and snakes the eggs develop inside the female, and the young are born alive.

COURTSHIP AND MATING

Most male reptiles display to attract a mate. Male lizards often have crests of skin on their heads or flaps of skin beneath their throats (dewlaps) which they can inflate to make themselves look bigger and more attractive to females, or more threatening to rival males. Dewlaps are often brightly coloured. Male turtles bite the females to excite them, and courting snakes tickle each other with their scales prior to mating.

Reptiles have internal fertilization – the male has a tube-like organ to inject his sperm into the female. Thus they do not need to enter water to ensure that sperm reaches the eggs.

GROWING UP

From the moment they are born, most young reptiles are quite independent of their parents. Alligators may carry their young to nursery

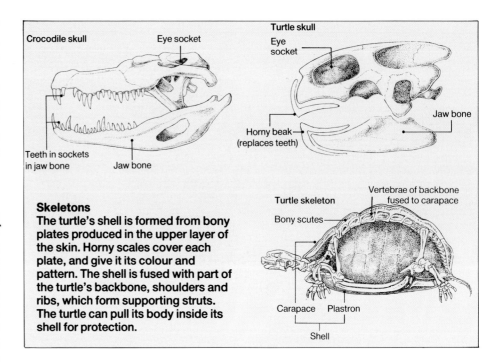

Skeletons
The turtle's shell is formed from bony plates produced in the upper layer of the skin. Horny scales cover each plate, and give it its colour and pattern. The shell is fused with part of the turtle's backbone, shoulders and ribs, which form supporting struts. The turtle can pull its body inside its shell for protection.

pools and guard them for a time, but they do not feed them.

As a reptile grows, its scaly skin must also stretch. Most reptiles shed the outer, keratin-containing layer of the skin from time to time. A new layer of keratin forms underneath, then the old skin flakes or peels off. Reptiles with bony scales (scutes) add rings of new material to each scute as they grow. In snakes, skin-shedding may occur several times a year, being most frequent in young animals.

REPTILE FACTS
Heaviest Leatherback turtle, usually up to 680kg; record 865kg.
Smallest Gecko (lizard) *Sphaerodactylus parthenopion*, 18mm long.
Longest snake Reticulated python, 10m long.
Largest lizard Komodo dragon, 160kg.
Largest crocodile Salt water crocodile, 520kg.
Largest dinosaur *Seismosaurus* ("earthshaker") from New Mexico, USA, was 36m long and weighed 80 tonnes.
Longest lifespan Marion's tortoise, over 152 years.

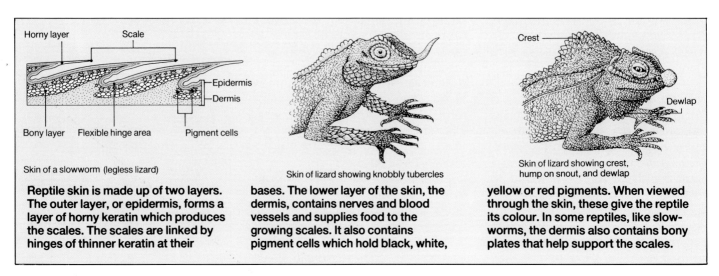

Skin of a slowworm (legless lizard)

Skin of lizard showing knobbly tubercles

Skin of lizard showing crest, hump on snout, and dewlap

Reptile skin is made up of two layers. The outer layer, or epidermis, forms a layer of horny keratin which produces the scales. The scales are linked by hinges of thinner keratin at their bases. The lower layer of the skin, the dermis, contains nerves and blood vessels and supplies food to the growing scales. It also contains pigment cells which hold black, white, yellow or red pigments. When viewed through the skin, these give the reptile its colour. In some reptiles, like slowworms, the dermis also contains bony plates that help support the scales.

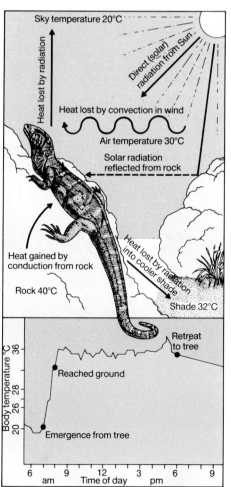

▲A chameleon lies in wait for a passing insect. This reptile can change its colour to match its background – a perfect camouflage.

◄Heat flows from warm to cold objects. Reptiles use special behaviour to control their body temperature. They are always losing heat to the air by radiation and convection. When they need to warm up to get active, they bask in the Sun, often on a hot rock. Here, they absorb heat from the Sun and from the rock. If they get too warm, they retreat to a shady place.

The graph shows how the lizard's body temperature is closely related to its behaviour during the course of a day.

HUNTERS AND GRAZERS

Many tortoises and turtles, and some lizards, graze on plants. Most meat-eating reptiles rely on stealth and ambush to capture prey. They seize prey in their jaws. Many snakes have fangs which inject poison to paralyze or kill their prey or their enemies.

HOW REPTILES MOVE

Four-footed reptiles such as lizards and crocodiles are much more agile than amphibians. This is because their legs are placed almost under their bodies, so they can lift the body well clear of the ground. Despite this, the fastest reptile on land is a snake.

Snakes have several ways of moving. Usually they push the curves of the body against small bumps in the ground to thrust themselves forward. Some snakes can move in a straight line by using their scales as levers. Many snakes climb trees this way, hitching their scales into tiny ridges in the bark.

Lizards have claws on their feet, which help them to climb. Some curl their tail around twigs like an extra limb. Geckos have layers of microscopic projections armed with tiny bristles on their feet. These allow them to walk up smooth surfaces like glass window panes, and crawl upside down on the ceiling.

Crocodiles and lizards are good swimmers. Crocodiles swim like fish, wiggling through the water. The flattened tail is used as the main means of propulsion. Many turtles have flippers instead of legs, and can swim quite fast. The world's fastest reptile, at 22kph, is a swimming sea turtle.

TURTLES AND TERRAPINS

On a mudbank in a slow tropical river dozens of turtles bask in the Sun. Some turtles walk over the others as if they were part of the ground. The shadow of a large bird passes over them. Many turtles plunge into the water. With frantically paddling limbs they dive to the river bottom. Later, when all is quiet, their heads reappear one by one.

Of the 244 species of tortoise-like animals (chelonians) nearly 200 live in and around fresh water. At first sight an animal with a shell seems an unlikely design for the water, but it works well for a whole range of freshwater turtles. In most species the shell has become flatter and lighter compared with that of a land tortoise. It is also a more streamlined shape for swimming. Some turtles have no outer horny plates and the bony part of the shell has large spaces inside it.

These so-called soft-shell turtles have very flat shells which allow them to hide in the mud at the bottom of the water.

In many freshwater turtles the limbs are flattened and paddle-like. This is usually most obvious in types that rarely leave the water, but some pond tortoises that spend most of their time in water still have rounded limbs just like their land cousins.

BREATHING IN A BOX
The turtle's ribs make up part of the bony box of the shell. A turtle cannot move its ribs in and out to pump air in and out of its lungs as we can. Instead, muscles above the tops of the legs and in the abdomen provide the pumping action. Many aquatic turtles have extra ways of getting the oxygen they need. They may take in oxygen through their skin. The thin lining of the throat, or even special thin-walled sacs in the cloaca (the single posterior opening of the body), can also act as a kind of gill (an underwater breathing

structure). In well-oxygenated water some turtles can remain underwater almost forever. Some species hibernate underwater for weeks without needing to surface to breathe.

FINDING A MATE
In many turtle species the sexes look similar, but some species have markings which distinguish males from females. In the Carolina box turtle, males have red eyes, while those of females are yellow. In some turtles the males are smaller than the females. There may be other clues, such as a longer, thicker tail, or an incurved underside to the shell, which show that a turtle is a male. But in most species it seems to be behaviour, rather than appearance, that allows the sexes to recognize one another.

To attract females, males use a variety of means, from biting and butting with the head, to special ways of swimming and stroking the female with their claws. In some turtles, such as the slider, where the male is much

TURTLES AND TERRAPINS Order Chelonia
(families except those of sea turtles and land tortoises) (*196 species*)

○ ■ ⚮

▨ Habitat: rivers, lakes, swamps, estuaries; a few always on land.

◪ Diet: mainly meat, including insects, crustaceans, fish, molluscs, other animals; some species partly or wholly plant-eating.

○ Breeding: lay eggs. Depending on species: round or long, soft or brittle-shelled, clutch from 1-100.

Size: smallest (Bog turtle): 11.4cm long; longest (softshell turtles): up to 1.15m long; heaviest (Alligator snapping turtle): weight 91kg or more.

Colour: mostly drab – brown, olive, grey; some have brightly coloured markings.

Species mentioned in text:
Alligator snapping turtle (*Macroclemys temmincki*)
Australian snake-necked turtle (*Emydura macquarii*)
Bog turtle (*Clemmys muhlenbergii*)
Carolina box turtle (*Terrapene carolina*)
Florida redbelly turtle (*Pseudemys nelsonii*)
Giant snake-necked turtle (*Chelodina expansa*)
Matamata (*Chelus fimbriatus*)
Slider or Red-eared turtle (*Pseudemys scripta*)

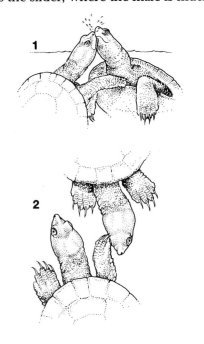

▲A male Australian snake-necked turtle courts a female by nudging her head above water (1), and by stroking her with his foot (2).

▲▼**Species of turtle** This Spiny soft-shell turtle (*Trionyx spiniferus*) **(1)** of North America is "snorkelling". The male Red-eared turtle or slider **(2)** courts a female by fluttering his claws in front of her face. The New Guinea plateless turtle (*Carrettochelys insculpta*) **(3)** is a strong swimmer. The Musk turtle (*Staurotypus salvinii*) **(4)** comes from Central America. Skin flaps and flattened shape camouflage the matamata **(5)** of South America.

▲▼ **More species of turtle** A Yellow-spotted Amazon turtle (*Podocnemis unifilis*) **(1)** takes a breath at the surface. The Yellow mud turtle (*Kinosternon flavescens*) **(2)** digs a special burrow to lay its eggs. The adult Central American river turtle (*Dermatemys mawei*) **(3)**. The Big-headed turtle (*Platysternon megacephalum*) **(4)** is a good climber.

smaller than the female, the male has long claws on his front feet to help in his courtship dance. The male swims backwards in front of the female and fans her with his long claws.

EGG-LAYING

All freshwater turtles lay eggs on land, even if they spend the rest of their lives in the water. Species that live in places where conditions are the same throughout the year may breed at any time. But most turtles breed only at certain times of the year, such as in the early summer in cooler climates, or in time with either the wet or the dry season in the tropics.

Eggs are buried in the ground, or, in species such as the stinkpots, under decaying vegetation. As one might expect, the bigger species of turtle lay bigger eggs. The biggest freshwater turtles, with shell lengths of 80cm, lay eggs 8cm long – about the size of a medium-sized hen's egg.

Apart from choosing a suitable nest, turtles do not look after their eggs or young. The eggs are incubated by warmth from the Sun or rotting vegetation. The warmer the eggs are, the sooner they are likely to hatch. The eggs of some kinds of turtle do not develop straight away so there may be a year between laying and hatching. The shortest time for development is about 2 months. In some species, the temperature during incubation is known to have an effect on the sex of the hatchlings. When temperatures are high more females are produced, and when temperatures are low more males are produced.

HATCHING AT THE RIGHT TIME
The baby turtle has a peg, or "egg-tooth", on the front of its snout, which helps it to escape from the egg. The egg-tooth drops off soon after hatching. The baby turtle hatches with a supply of yolk still in its body, and may not need to feed for some time.

Once they hatch, the babies do not always leave the nest straight away. In the northern USA, some snapping turtles overwinter in their nests as babies. Some Central American sliders have to wait for rain to soften the ground before they can escape from their nests. The longest waiting time on record was for some baby Giant snake-necked turtles in Australia that had to stay in their nest for 664 days until a drought ended.

GETTING WARM
An important part of the day for many turtles is the time they spend basking in the Sun. They come out of the water on to logs or sandbanks, spread their legs, and sunbathe. This helps raise their bodies to a good working temperature, and may also help digestion.

Mid-morning and late afternoon are the main basking times.

Good basking sites may be used by many turtles at the same time. Rich sources of food can also attract a crowd of turtles. But although these animals may sometimes congregate in large numbers, they do not form family or other social groups with any structure. Most turtles seem little interested in one another except as possible mates or rivals. One exception is the cleaning behaviour seen in young sliders. They take it in turns to pull algae from one another's shells.

FEEDING METHODS
Most turtles feed on slow-moving prey, such as shellfish, worms and insect larvae. Many turtles eat some plants too. Diet may change with age. Baby sliders eat insects and other small animals, but adults have much more vegetable matter in their diet. Many turtles eat whatever plant or animal food they can find.

Some turtles have special ways of catching food. Snapping turtles have long bumpy necks and mud-coloured skins. The shell is often covered in

▲ The strong high shell of the Florida redbelly turtle is unlike that of most aquatic species. It is a good defence against the crushing jaws of alligators.

algae. This helps the animals to lie hidden. They suddenly strike out with their powerful jaws at fish or smaller turtles. The matamata has very weak jaws. It catches its prey by opening its mouth wide. Water rushes into its mouth, taking the victim with it.

TOO SLOW AND DEFENCELESS
Populations of many river turtles and terrapins are declining today. Most seriously affected are the large river turtles and species with attractive shells. The main causes are destruction of their habitats, local killing for meat, and the demand from developed countries for luxury items such as turtle shell jewellery, leather goods and pets.

Unfortunately, the turtles' lumbering habits, their predictable nesting behaviour and their passive actions when threatened make them highly susceptible to hunting by people at all times.

LIZARDS

It is a warm day. There is a movement in the heather. A tiny head appears, followed by a long body and an even longer tail. A European common lizard is hunting. It turns its head on one side, listening and watching the vegetation intently. Suddenly it pounces, and snaps up a small spider.

Lizards are found on all continents except Antarctica. Most lizards are found in the tropics, but some live in cooler climates. The European common lizard lives as far north as the Arctic Circle in Scandinavia. There are 16 families of lizards. This article deals with the broad category of lizards. As well as the species mentioned here, lizard families include chameleons, iguanas, geckos, skinks and monitors.

LIZARDS Sub-order Sauria
(3,751 species)

● ▢ 🦎

■ **Habitat:** all types of habitat from wet forest to desert; on all continents and many islands where temperature not too low.

■ **Diet:** usually small animals, but some are plant-eaters.

◎ **Breeding:** typically lay eggs after internal fertilization. Some give birth to live young.

Size: smallest (Virgin Islands gecko): total length 3.6cm; largest (Komodo dragon): length 3m, weight up to 160kg.

Colour: highly variable including green, brown, black and some bright colours.

Species mentioned in text:
Armadillo girdle-tailed lizard (*Cordylus cataphractus*)
Australian frilled lizard (*Chlamydosaurus kingii*)
European common lizard (*Lacerta vivipara*)
Flying dragon (*Draco volans*)
Komodo dragon (*Varanus komodoensis*).
Sharp-snouted snake lizard (*Lialis burtonis*)
Slow-worm (*Anguis fragilis*)
Sri Lanka prehensile-tail lizard (*Cophotis celanica*)
Sungazer (*Cordylus giganteus*)

◀▲ Species of lizard Granite night lizard (*Xantusia henshawi*) **(1)** of California. Sharp-snouted snake lizard **(2)** of Australia. Common tegu (*Tupinambis teguixin*) **(3)** of South America. Colorado checkered whiptail (*Cnemidophorus tesselatus*) **(4)**. Flat lizard (*Platysaurus intermedius*) **(5)** of South Africa. Ocellated lizard (*Lacerta lepida*) **(6)** of western Mediterranean area.

A TYPICAL LIZARD

As may be expected in a group with nearly 4,000 species, lizards come in many different shapes and sizes. But a typical lizard is a fairly small animal, perhaps 10 to 20cm long; about half this length is the tail. A lizard has four legs, and its body is covered in small scales. It has good eyesight, and can see colours. The eyelids are usually movable. At the back of the head are small ear openings.

A lizard uses its tongue to help it "taste" the surroundings. It is a hunter, ambushing or hunting down small animals, often insects. To reproduce a typical lizard lays eggs.

OVER AND UNDERGROUND

Some lizards have become especially good at climbing, and a few, such as the Sri Lanka prehensile-tail lizard, even use their tail to hold on to branches. The Flying dragons of Asia are small lizards that have taken to the air. They climb trees and then jump from one tree to another, gliding on "wings" of skin. The skin is stretched over very long ribs, which stick out from the sides of the body.

At the other extreme are lizards that live underground. Many of these lizards have either very small legs or no legs at all. Their eyes may be tiny or even beneath the skin. When the eyes still work, each may be covered by a transparent "spectacle" instead of eyelids. The "spectacle" helps to protect the eye from damage or injury.

Some lizards, such as the water dragons of the Far East, are good swimmers. Others, such as the Australian frilled lizard, are able to run fast on their hind legs for a short distance if they need to escape an enemy.

RITUAL FIGHTS

Most lizards live on their own, but some species do react to other lizards. A few lizards are territorial, and the males threaten any rivals which enter their territory. This may be done by rituals such as head-bobbing, rather than actual fighting. Lizards with this type of behaviour are often brightly coloured to increase the impact of the display. Colours may also be used to attract a mate.

DEFENCE AND ESCAPE
Lizards have many ways of protecting themselves from other animals that may eat them. They often keep very still, and their colours may allow them to blend into the surroundings. Some have specially tough scales. The plated lizards of Africa have bone underneath their scales. Other lizards have long spiny scales, which makes them difficult for an enemy to swallow. The sungazer will lash its spiny tail at an attacker. The Armadillo girdle-tailed lizard often simply wedges itself in a crevice for protection.

▼ **More species of lizard** The Southern alligator lizard (*Elgaria multicarinata*) (1) of America has strong limbs, but is related to the slow-worm. The Chinese xenosaur (*Shinisaurus crocodilurus*) (2) lives along streams. The sungazer (3) uses its spiny tail for defence. The Bornean earless lizard (*Lanthanotus borneensis*) (4) is a good swimmer. The Gila monster (*Heloderma suspectum*) (5) is venomous, with fangs in its bottom jaw. The Asian blind lizard (*Dibamus novaeguineae*) (6) lives underground. It has eyes under the skin.

Quite a different way of using the tail for defence is shown by wall lizards and slow-worms. By contracting some tail muscles, these lizards can make the tail break off at special weak areas in the tail bones. If it is attacked, the lizard drops its tail and leaves it behind, wriggling, as a decoy. The tail may continue to wriggle for several minutes. The lizard escapes; later it grows a replacement tail. Some lizards have specially coloured tails that attract additional attention.

The greatest threats to such lizards, however, are not natural predators, but humans. Especially in sub-tropical regions, the lizards' habitats are being altered or destroyed such that their populations are unlikely to recover.

EGGS OR LIVE YOUNG?

Most lizards lay eggs. A clutch of about 20 is very common. But some lizards produce live young. In most of these live-bearers, the mother lizard keeps the eggs inside her body until they are ready to hatch. The yolk inside the egg nourishes the young in the usual way. In a few lizards, such as the night lizards, a placenta forms so the babies can obtain some nourishment from the mother.

Live-bearing may be useful in difficult conditions, such as in places where summers are cool. The European common lizard produces live young in the north of its range, but lays eggs in the south, where summers are warmer. Strangest of all are a few lizard species in which no males are known. Females are able to produce a new generation of "identikit" lizards on their own.

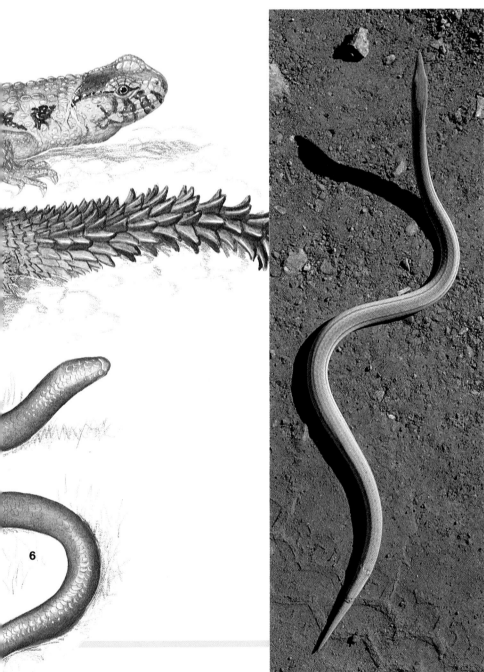

6

The Sharp-snouted snake lizard has no front limbs, and small flaps for hind limbs. It eats other lizards.

33

SNAKES

In the reeds at the water's edge a Water snake waits. It is partly coiled and lies still. Only the occasional flick of the tongue shows that this snake is alert. A frog hops from the water. Stealthily the snake glides forward, so smoothly that the frog doesn't notice. Then the snake strikes. It seizes the frog in its jaws, and begins to swallow it whole.

Snakes are a large and successful group. They occur on all continents except Antarctica and are found in all regions except the very coldest ones. Water snakes, for example, range from Scandinavia to northern Australia. Snakes have even reached many isolated islands, although they do not live on some islands such as Ireland.

SNAKES OF MANY TYPES

About two-thirds of all snake species belong to the large family Colubridae, which includes familiar species such as the European grass snake and the North American garter snakes. Most members of this family are harmless to humans; a few species have poison fangs at the back of the mouth.

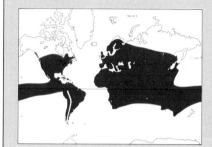

SNAKES Sub-order Serpentes
(2,389 species)

● ◨ ⚜

■ **Habitat:** most ground-living, but many burrow, climb trees, or live in fresh or sea water.

■ **Diet:** other animals, from slugs and insects to mammals, fish, other reptiles, birds and eggs.

◎ **Breeding:** internal fertilization, usually followed by egg-laying. Many species bear live young.

Size: most 25cm-1.5m. Shortest (West Indian thread snake): 12cm; longest (Reticulated python): 10m.

Colour: mostly brown, grey or black. Some bright colours or vivid markings.

Species mentioned in text:
African egg-eating snake (*Dasypeltis scaber*)
Boomslang (*Dispholidus typus*)
Costa Rican parrot snake (*Leptophis depressirostris*)
European grass snake (*Natrix natrix*)
Flowerpot snake (*Rhamphotyphlops braminus*)
Milk snake (*Lampropeltis triangulum*)
Redbelly snake (*Storeria occipitomaculata*)
Toad-eater snake (*Xenodon rabdocephalus*)
West Indian thread snake (*Leptotyphlops bilineata*)

▼**Snake species of several families**
Texas blind snake (*Leptotyphlops dulcis*) **(1)**. Shieldtail snake (*Uropeltis ocellatus*) **(2)**. Montpellier snake (*Malpolon monspessulanus*) **(3)**. Cuban Island ground boa (*Tropidophis melanurus*) **(4)**. Malaysian pipe snake (*Cylindrophis rufus*) **(5)**. Schlegel's blind snake (*Typhlops schlegeli*) **(6)**.

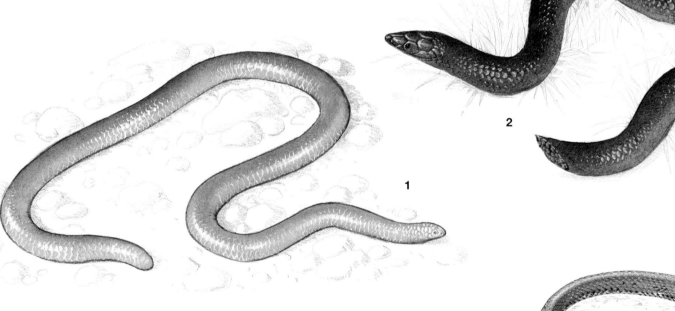

Other types of snake include the primitive pythons and boas, which suffocate their prey, the very poisonous cobras and sea-snakes, and the vipers and rattlesnakes (pages 38-41).

PIPES AND THREADS

There are also six families of rather odd, mainly small, burrowing snakes, which contain 338 known species.

The 11 species of pipesnake live in the tropical areas of South America and Asia. They are all less than 1m long and burrow in damp soil. They feed on other snakes and eels. To fool enemies, many pipesnakes hide their head and wave the tail, which is red underneath.

The thread snakes number 78 species and include some of the smallest snakes; several are less than 20cm in length and no thicker than a matchstick. They live in tropical rain forests and feed on ants and termites.

FEMALE TRAVELLER

The blind snakes live in the tropics. Their eyes are tiny and hidden under the scales of the head. They are burrowers and most of the 163 species also feed on ants and termites.

One species of blind snake, the Flowerpot snake, has spread from Asia to Europe by being carried in the earth in flowerpots. It is able to colonize a new area easily because the females can produce young on their own; there are no males.

6

5

3

4

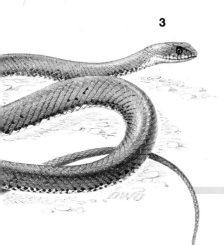

A NARROW SQUEEZE

Like other reptiles, snakes have a head, body and tail, but the body, and sometimes the tail, are extremely long and narrow. The long body is supported by a very long backbone; some snakes have more than 400 vertebrae in the backbone. In such a body, it is difficult to fit in all the organs the snake needs. Often a pair of organs are one behind the other; the kidneys are positioned like this. Sometimes, only one of a pair of organs remains. Most snakes have just one lung.

◄The Costa Rican parrot snake is harmless, but can use its brightly coloured mouth to frighten enemies.

SENSES

A snake is always staring and cannot shut its eyes because it has no eyelids. Instead the eyes are covered with a transparent scale. Burrowing snakes can usually just tell the difference between light and dark. In several daytime species, the eyesight is very sharp, although they find it much easier to see moving prey.

Night-time snakes frequently have vertical slit pupils which can open very wide in dim light to let in as much light as possible.

▼Snakes detect prey with their long forked tongues. This Toad-eater snake hunts on the forest floor in Costa Rica.

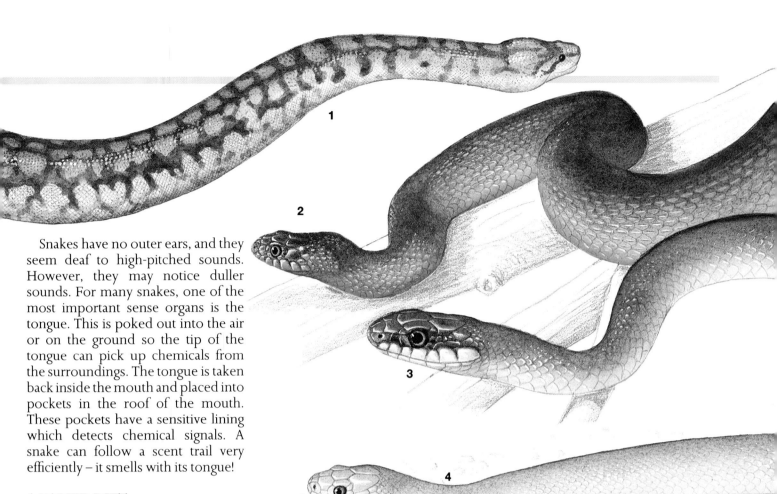

Snakes have no outer ears, and they seem deaf to high-pitched sounds. However, they may notice duller sounds. For many snakes, one of the most important sense organs is the tongue. This is poked out into the air or on the ground so the tip of the tongue can pick up chemicals from the surroundings. The tongue is taken back inside the mouth and placed into pockets in the roof of the mouth. These pockets have a sensitive lining which detects chemical signals. A snake can follow a scent trail very efficiently – it smells with its tongue!

A VARIED DIET

All snakes eat other animals. The prey depends to a certain extent on the size of the snake. Many eat mammals, birds or other reptiles, but some have a very special diet.

The tropical cat-eyed snakes and the Asian snail-eaters eat nothing but snails. They can pull a snail out of its shell. The African egg-eating snake eats eggs and can swallow an egg twice the size of its head. Part of its backbone sticks into its throat. To crack an egg, the snake squeezes it against this bone. The snake then swallows the contents of the egg and spits out the shell. The Redbelly snake of North America feeds exclusively on slugs. American green snakes eat caterpillars and grasshoppers. Perhaps a more typical diet, however, is that of the American garter snakes, which eat anything from worms and insects, to fish and mammals.

SWALLOWING DINNER

When snakes do feed, the meal is nearly always large compared with the size of the mouth. Food is always swallowed whole. A snake's teeth are sharp and point backwards.The teeth are good at holding food, but cannot bite off chunks of flesh. Instead, a snake has an amazingly flexible skull and jaws. It can open its mouth very wide. The bottom jaw can be swung down from the skull, and the two halves of the bottom jaw will swing apart, held together only by elastic tissue. The jaws can be "walked" around the prey, gradually edging it more and more into the throat, until contractions of the gullet can carry the food down to the stomach.

Those snakes of the family Colubridae that have fangs at the back of the mouth often "chew" on the prey. This probably helps them work in their poison, or venom. The most poisonous of these species includes the boomslang, an African tree snake. A

▲ **Harmless snakes** Arafura wart snake (*Acrochordus arafurae*) **(1)** from rivers in New Guinea and Australia. Red-bellied water snake (*Nerodia erythrogaster*) **(2)** and the racer (*Coluber constrictor*) **(3)** from North America. The African house snake (*Lamprophis fuscus*) **(4)**.

bite from this snake has proved fatal to a person in 24 hours.

A LONG SLOW LIFE

For much of the time, a snake's body works at a slow rate. Perhaps this is why they live for a long time. Even a small snake, such as a Milk snake, has been known to live for 18 years. Species of snake from cool areas may hibernate during the winter months. During this time they may be scarcely breathing and do not need to feed at all. Even during their active periods snakes are often still and can survive for long periods without a meal.

VIPERS AND RATTLESNAKES

It is a pitch-dark night out on the prairie. A mouse scurries about, intent on finding seeds. In a hollow lies a rattlesnake. It cannot see the mouse, but it senses the presence of its warm body. It turns its head towards the mouse, waits until it is close, then strikes. It stabs and injects venom, then settles back to wait for its victim's death.

Vipers and rattlesnakes have the best-developed fangs of all the snakes. Members of this family live in all parts of the world that are warm enough for snakes, except for Madagascar and the Australian region. There are two main groups. The 45 species of true viper live in Africa, Europe and Asia. The 142 species of pit viper (including rattlesnakes) live in the Americas and southern Asia.

Instead of the big head shields seen in most other snakes, snakes of this family usually have triangular heads covered with many small scales. The body is thick, and often rather short. The eyes have slit-like pupils.

BIG FANGS

Vipers have a pair of very long fangs. In a Gaboon viper 1.7m long, the fangs can be 5cm long. When a viper is at rest, the fangs are folded back against the roof of the mouth. When it strikes, the mouth is opened wide and the fangs are swung down into a stabbing position.

Many vipers and rattlesnakes stab their prey, give a quick injection of powerful venom, then let go. There is no need to hang on. The prey soon dies, and even if it has moved a little way away, the snake can track it down and find it. Because of their shape and

▶ On the Wyoming prairie, a Western rattlesnake hides in low brush, ready to strike a passing lizard or hare.

VIPERS AND RATTLESNAKES
Viperidae (*187 species*)

○ ◼ ☠

◼ Habitat: all types, from tropical rain forest, to grassland, desert, mountain and moors.

◼ Diet: other animals.

◎ Breeding: most give birth to small number of live young. Some have up to 50 per litter. Some lay eggs.

Size: most 0.6-1.2m. Smallest (Peringuey's viper): 0.30m long; longest (bushmaster): up to 3.7m long.

Colour: generally dull colours, brown or blackish, often with dark blotches on lighter background. Some with bright colours or markings.

Species mentioned in text:
Bushmaster (*Lachesis muta*)
European adder (*Vipera berus*)
Gaboon viper (*Bitis gabonica*)
Hog-nosed viper (*Bothrops nasutus*)
Peringuey's viper (*Bitis peringueyi*)
Pygmy rattlesnake (*Sistrurus miliarius*)
Side-winder rattlesnake (*Crotalus cerastes*)
Western diamondback rattlesnake (*C. atrox*)
Western rattlesnake (*C. viridis*)

the way their fangs work, vipers are best suited to ambushing their prey rather than chasing it.

DEADLY POISONS

The venom of vipers is not so strong as that of some snakes in the cobra family, but it is made in such quantities, and is so efficiently injected, that it does its work well.

Many vipers are capable of killing a person, but they are less aggressive than cobras and are often slow to anger. Some small species, such as the European adder, have a bite that is painful to people, but is rarely fatal. Viper venoms act mainly on the blood and muscle systems, causing pain, swelling, severe bruising, discolouration and other acute symptoms. Recovery may be slow.

HEAT DETECTORS

The major difference between pit vipers and true vipers can be seen in the face. Pit vipers have a pair of large pits below the eyes. Each pit has a membrane inside which can detect heat; it can detect a heat difference of just 0.2°C.

Warm-blooded prey can be sensed with these pits. The snake can line up its head on prey, even in complete darkness, by turning the head so that the same amount of warmth is detected by each pit. A rattlesnake can detect and strike a mouse nearly a metre away with deadly accuracy, even in total darkness.

RATTLE AND BUZZ

Rattlesnakes are found in the Americas. The rattle on the tip of the tail is

▲ After injecting venom for the kill, the two fangs of the Hog-nosed viper help to pull a frog into the snake's mouth.

▲ Below the eye and nostril of this rattlesnake can be seen the large pit which acts as a heat detector.

made of a series of hollow, horny tail-tips. Like other snakes, a rattlesnake sheds its skin at intervals, but the horny tip of the tail remains permanently in place.

Each time the snake sheds its skin, a new segment is added to the rattle. Many snakes shake the tail if they are alarmed or annoyed; this may make a sound by hitting against and rustling leaves or dry plants. But, if rattlesnakes are disturbed, the tail itself makes a loud, angry buzzing noise. The snake cannot hear the noise, but it can scare off enemies and is a useful method of defence. A rattlesnake's main enemies are foxes and birds of prey.

SPRINGING SIDEWAYS
Several vipers and rattlesnakes are adapted to living in deserts. These snakes are often a sandy colour, and may bury themselves in the sand so that only their eyes show above the surface. Many of these desert-living snakes have "horns" over their eyes, which may help to keep the sand out of their pupils.

Some of these desert vipers, and the Side-winder rattlesnake, have a special way of travelling over the sand. It is hard for the snakes to grip the sand to pull themselves along, and, in the middle of the day, the sand may be burningly hot. So the snakes move by "side-winding", which allows them to touch the sand as little as possible.

A side-winding snake makes an arc with the front part of its body and "throws" its head sideways for some distance before it touches the sand. The rest of the body is then thrown forward in another arc, clear of the ground, so it lands in front of the head. The tail curves over and lands last, but by this time the head has already been thrown to a new position and the body follows. The effect is rather like a spring rolling sideways.

Side-winding is weird to watch, but is an effective, and quite speedy, way of travelling across sand. It is mostly used by vipers of African and North American deserts. A very characteristic series of marks, each shaped rather like a "J", is left behind by the snake as it "side-winds" over the sand.

◄Peringuey's viper of southern Africa leaves characteristic parallel tracks as it moves swiftly across the sand by "sidewinding".

▼Rattlesnakes, such as this Western diamondback, strike prey or an attacker with the mouth wide open and the long fangs erect.

CROCODILES

At the water's edge a group of antelope are drinking. A few metres out in the water, a pair of eyes and a nose are the only signs that a crocodile is hunting. Gently it glides towards the bank. With a sudden lunge, it grabs an antelope by the leg, and pulls it into the water. The crocodile holds the antelope underwater until it drowns, then tears off chunks of flesh to eat.

Crocodiles are fearsome predators. Some 14 species live in Africa, tropical parts of Asia and Australia, and in America from southern Florida to northern South America.

One species, the gharial, is found only in the great river systems of northern India. It is also the odd one out among these reptiles on account of its extremely long, narrow snout and weak legs. It is grouped in a separate family of its own, Gavialidae.

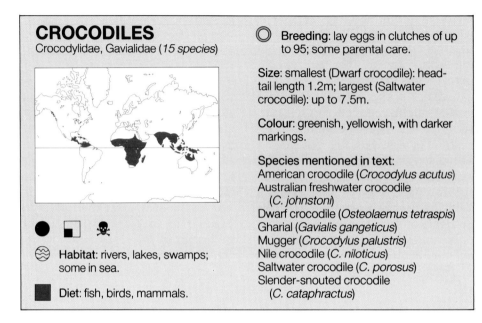

CROCODILES
Crocodylidae, Gavialidae (*15 species*)

⊖ **Breeding:** lay eggs in clutches of up to 95; some parental care.

Size: smallest (Dwarf crocodile): head-tail length 1.2m; largest (Saltwater crocodile): up to 7.5m.

Colour: greenish, yellowish, with darker markings.

Species mentioned in text:
American crocodile (*Crocodylus acutus*)
Australian freshwater crocodile
   (*C. johnstoni*)
Dwarf crocodile (*Osteolaemus tetraspis*)
Gharial (*Gavialis gangeticus*)
Mugger (*Crocodylus palustris*)
Nile crocodile (*C. niloticus*)
Saltwater crocodile (*C. porosus*)
Slender-snouted crocodile
   (*C. cataphractus*)

● ◼ ☠

🌊 **Habitat:** rivers, lakes, swamps; some in sea.

◼ **Diet:** fish, birds, mammals.

MEATY MENUS

Crocodiles with long snouts, such as the Slender-snouted crocodile, feed mainly on fish.

Species with broader snouts, such as the mugger, tackle bigger prey, including deer and cattle. The Nile crocodile may feed on all sorts of animals from fishes to zebras. In fact, the diet of a crocodile often varies through its lifetime. Newly hatched crocodiles feed on small items such as grasshoppers, but as they grow they start to eat frogs and small fish. Eventually they move on to larger fish, and mammals such as antelopes.

1

The long, thin jaws of the gharial, which are full of pointed teeth, are ideal for snapping at fish in the water. The gharial specializes in eating fish.

HIDDEN KILLERS

Crocodiles usually take their prey by surprise. Most crocodiles are well camouflaged, and will stay completely still, or move slowly towards their prey without being detected.

Crocodile teeth are good for seizing and holding, but not so good at cutting up or chewing prey. To pull apart large prey, which cannot be swallowed whole, crocodiles make twisting movements of the whole body to tear off chunks of meat. Crocodiles may often lose teeth while dealing with prey, but this does not matter, as they are constantly growing new ones. A Nile crocodile 4m long is probably using its 45th "set" of teeth.

Crocodiles swim using their powerful tails, which have flattened sides. On land they often slither along on their bellies, but can also walk with the body lifted clear of the ground.

▼Species of crocodile Dwarf crocodile (1) of forest areas of West Africa and the Congo. The False gharial (*Tomistoma schlegeli*) (2), a fish-eater of swamps and rivers in Malaya, Borneo and Sumatra. The gharial (3) from northern India. The Slender-snouted crocodile (4) of African tropical forests. The mugger (5) of India lives in rivers, pools and marshes. American crocodile (6).

Some crocodiles can even gallop, reaching speeds of 13kph. They are all most active at night. Much of the day may be spent basking. When crocodiles are hot they open their jaws and lose water from the skin inside the mouth to cool themselves. The Nile crocodile, when it is basking open-mouthed, will allow birds to pick over its teeth for scraps of food.

SEA-GOING CROCODILES

Crocodiles of several species may venture into estuaries or the sea. The American crocodile often lives in brackish swamps, and may swim out to sea. The Nile crocodile is found in estuaries in parts of Africa. But the most sea-loving of all crocodiles is the Saltwater crocodile, which is found in estuaries and mangrove swamps. Around Indonesia, some individuals may live in the sea all the time. The Saltwater crocodile is a strong swimmer. Stray animals have reached the Cocos-Keeling Islands, 900km from their usual haunts. This species is found from the Ganges delta in India throughout South-east Asia and to as far as northern Australia.

The Saltwater crocodile is also the largest living species, some specimens reaching 6m in length. One skull, owned by an Indian rajah, probably came from a crocodile 7.46m long.

▲A baby Australian freshwater crocodile breaks out of its eggshell.

▼A female Saltwater crocodile sits on guard on top of the huge nest mound in which she has laid her eggs.

Other large crocodiles include the American crocodile at 7m, the Nile crocodile at 6.7m, and the gharial at 6.5m. Nowadays it is difficult to find a crocodile of anything like this size.

LAST OF THE LINE
Crocodiles are an ancient group. They lived alongside the dinosaurs and have changed little in the last 65 million years. But for some species, the chances of surviving for even another 10 or 20 years are poor. Even as recently as 1950, there were large numbers of crocodiles in some parts of the world. But in the 1950s and 60s a demand for crocodile skins for leather bags and shoes led to the deaths of untold numbers of crocodiles.

All species are now on the danger list. Large crocodiles were killed first. Mothers guarding nests made easy targets. Then hunters moved on to smaller specimens. Young animals were not allowed to grow old enough to breed and, with the breeding animals gone, populations crashed.

Although crocodiles produce large clutches of eggs, many eggs and young are taken by predators, floods and other hazards. Even in good conditions, only a tiny percentage of young survives. Most crocodiles take several years to grow into adults. The Saltwater crocodile, for example, may be 10 years old before it breeds for the first time. All species need help if they are to survive.

USEFUL CROCS
It may seem unimportant that a big, sometimes dangerous, animal such as a crocodile does survive. But crocodiles form a vital part of the balance of nature. In some lakes in Africa where crocodiles have disappeared, human fishermen have suffered. The crocodiles ate large fish which fed on the small fish that the fishermen were catching. With the crocodiles gone, more large fish survived and ate more of the small fish.

CROCODILE CONSERVATION
The gharial was nearly hunted to extinction. In 1974, fewer than 60 adults survived in India. But now, large sanctuaries have been created. Eggs are collected and then incubated artificially so more baby gharials will hatch out. Babies are reared until they are about 1.2m long. Then they can be released into the wild. Several thousand gharials now live in sanctuaries, but until they are breeding well we cannot say they are safe. In some places, the mugger and other crocodiles have similar protection.

▼Crocodiles often wait at water holes to ambush their prey. This Nile crocodile has caught an impala.

WHAT IS A BIRD?

Birds, with their powers of flight, are found in almost every part of the globe. A few birds, such as ostriches and penguins, cannot fly. Instead, the ostrich can run very fast, up to 50kph, and the penguin uses its wings as flippers for swimming.

All birds lay eggs with hard, water-proof shells and a good supply of yolk as food for the developing embryo.

Birds are warm-blooded animals with bodies covered in feathers. They are vertebrates, having an internal bony skeleton with a central back-bone or vertebral column for support. The forelimbs are highly modified and take the form of wings. Birds walk on their two hind legs. The hind legs and feet are covered in scales. The mouth is a horny beak or bill.

▼The bird's smooth, streamlined shape helps it move swiftly through the air. The skeleton is very light – many of the bones are hollow. The breastbone has a large keel to which the powerful flight muscles are attached. The body and wings are covered in feathers, which are light but strong. The lungs lead into a series of air sacs which improve the bird's oxygen supply when flying, as well as making its body lighter. In some birds the air sacs even extend into the legs.

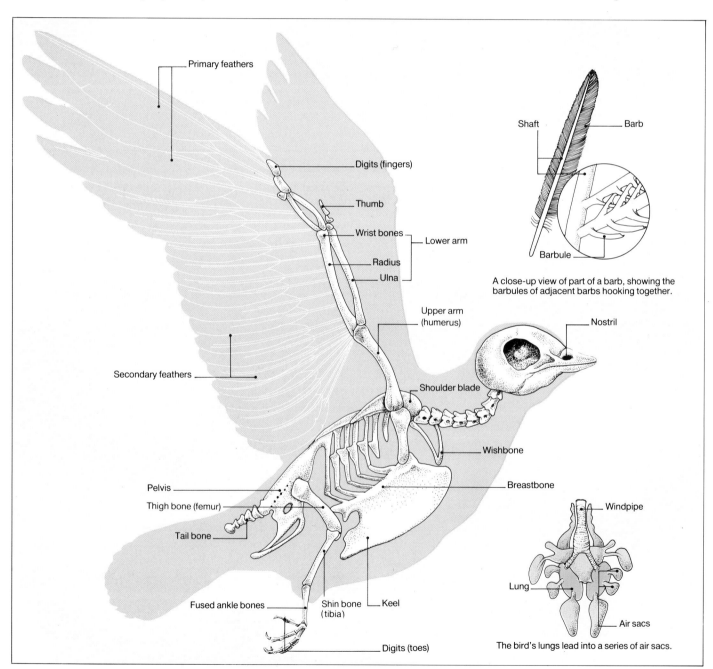

A close-up view of part of a barb, showing the barbules of adjacent barbs hooking together.

The bird's lungs lead into a series of air sacs.

FEATHERS

Birds are the only animals that have feathers. The feathers are of different shapes and sizes according to their position on the body and therefore their function. The wing feathers, for example, are long, stiff, and slightly curved to improve the bird's streamlining. A chick's down feathers have no definite shape. A very small bird, such as a hummingbird, may have about 900 feathers, while a large bird like a swan may have over 25,000.

Feathers are made of keratin, the same material that forms hair, nails and, in reptiles, scales. Each feather has a stiff hollow shaft with hundreds of side branches called barbs. Each barb has two rows of barbules. The hooks of one row lock into furrows on the next row. This keeps the feather stiff and flat. Feathers are lightweight because of all the air spaces between the barbules.

Feathers also help to keep the bird warm. Air trapped between them prevents the bird's body heat escaping. Baby birds have soft fluffy down feathers for extra warmth. Some adult birds that live in cold regions also have an underlayer of down.

When preening, the bird runs its beak along its feathers to "zip up" the barbules. It rubs oil on the feathers from a special gland under the tail to make them waterproof. Once or twice a year, birds shed their old, worn feathers and grow new ones. This is called moulting.

▶ The feet of some birds are adapted for swimming, with flaps of skin called webs to give a bigger area for pushing against the water. In ducks, the web stretches right across the foot, while in moorhens it is just a flap along the base of the toes. Grebes have lobed toes instead. Penguins use their wings as flippers, as if they are flying underwater.

▼ Beaks come in many shapes and sizes. Birds have no teeth. The hawk, however, can tear up pieces of meat. The parrot uses its beak like an extra foot when climbing. The flamingo has tooth-like edges to its bill for sieving food from the water. The finch can crack open hard seeds, while the pelican can store several fish in its throat pouch.

BEAKS GALORE

A bird's beak is often a special shape and size to deal with a particular kind of food. Some birds feed on meat or fish, others on leaves, flowers, seeds or fruit. Hummingbirds sip liquid nectar from flowers. A few birds, like flamingos, sieve food from the water of lakes and rivers. Several birds, such as seagulls, will eat almost anything.

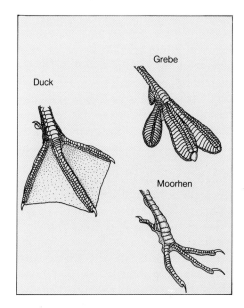

▼ The young chick grows inside a little bag of fluid, the amnion. The yolk and albumen are a source of food for the chick. Its blood vessels spread out over the yolk sac to absorb the food. The chick's waste is stored in another little bag, the allantois, until hatching.

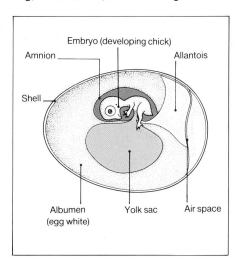

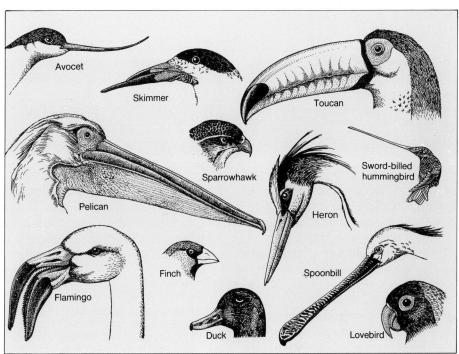

BIRD SENSE

Birds have excellent eyesight, often better than human sight. They have an extra transparent eyelid to protect their eyes from dust and rain while flying. Most birds have a poor sense of smell, but excellent hearing. A bird's ears are hidden under feathers at the side of its head.

COURTSHIP AND BREEDING

Birds usually become interested in courting only at a time of year when there is going to be plenty of food around to feed to the young. First, the male bird looks for a mate. He shows off to any females he meets, dancing, calling and fluffing out his feathers. Male birds are often more brightly coloured than the females, and their displays show off their plumage. The female is usually dull coloured so that she will be camouflaged while she is sitting on her nest.

Many male birds defend a special feeding area – a territory – during the breeding season. This makes sure they can feed their family. For small birds, the territory may be just the area immediately around the nest, but large birds of prey may defend an area of 20sq km.

FROM EGG TO ADULT

Birds usually build nests in which to lay their eggs. The nest may be just a scrape in the ground lined with grass and leaves, or a cup of twigs or moss high in a tree or on a cliff ledge, out of reach of predators.

The baby birds grow inside the eggs for several weeks before hatching. During this time, the eggs must be kept warm, so the parent birds must sit on the nest to "incubate" them.

Birds such as chickens, which nest on the ground, usually have well-developed young. They hatch already covered in fluffy down, and can run around and feed themselves almost at once. But the young of many birds hatch naked and blind, and have to be fed by their parents for several weeks. Gradually, they grow a warm fluffy coat of down, and later a coat of proper feathers.

LIVING FLYING MACHINES

The bird's wings are really forelimbs: they have the same bones as the human arm, but some bones in the wrist and fingers are fused together for extra strength. Some of the bones of the back are also fused together to withstand the beating of the wings.

There is more than one way of flying. Small birds, with plump bodies and rather short wings, have to flap a lot to stay airborne, but larger birds with long, narrow wings can make greater use of air currents and gliding.

LONG-DISTANCE TRAVELLERS

Some birds spend the summer in one part of the world and the winter in another to take advantage of seasonal food supplies. Swallows, for example, rear their families in northern Europe and North America in summer, when insects are plentiful, but fly south in autumn as the insects disappear. Such journeys are called migration.

▶ *Archaeopteryx* was part bird, part reptile. Its body was covered in feathers, but it had a long tail, jaws with teeth, a small breastbone, and claws on its wings. It probably lived in trees, using its claws for scrambling among branches.

▲As the Blue tit beats down with its wings, the force of the air spreads and bends its feathers.

ANCESTORS OF BIRDS

Birds are believed to be descended from small dinosaurs. Today, the most obvious clue to their reptile ancestry is the scales on their legs and feet. Some of their ancestors had large overlapping scales to help keep them warm. These scales may well have evolved into feathers. There are very few bird fossils. The oldest is *Archaeopteryx*, 150 million years old.

BIRD FACTS
About 8,805 species
Weight Smallest, Bee hummingbird,
1.6g; largest, ostrich, 156.5kg.
Eggs Largest, ostrich, 20cm long,
1.78kg; smallest, Vervain hummingbird,
9.9mm, 0.37g.
Most feathers Whistling swan, 25,216.
Fastest flying bird White-throated
spine-tail swift, 170kph.
Longest lifespan Sulphur-crested
cockatoo, 80+ years.

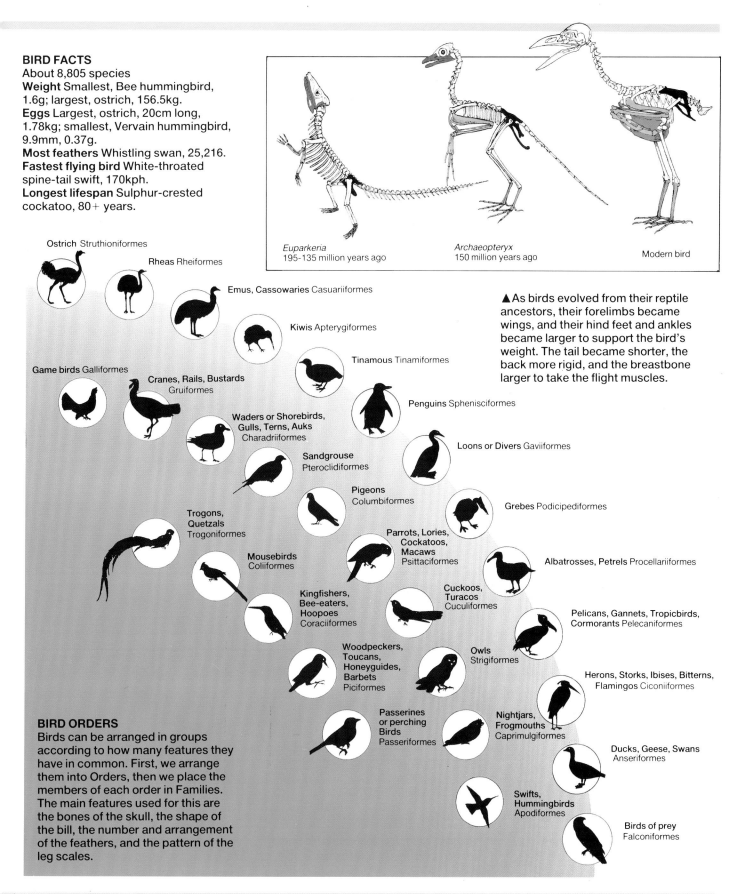

Euparkeria
195-135 million years ago

Archaeopteryx
150 million years ago

Modern bird

▲As birds evolved from their reptile
ancestors, their forelimbs became
wings, and their hind feet and ankles
became larger to support the bird's
weight. The tail became shorter, the
back more rigid, and the breastbone
larger to take the flight muscles.

Ostrich Struthioniformes

Rheas Rheiformes

Emus, Cassowaries Casuariiformes

Kiwis Apterygiformes

Tinamous Tinamiformes

Penguins Sphenisciformes

Game birds Galliformes

Cranes, Rails, Bustards
Gruiformes

Waders or Shorebirds,
Gulls, Terns, Auks
Charadriiformes

Loons or Divers Gaviiformes

Sandgrouse
Pteroclidiformes

Pigeons
Columbiformes

Grebes Podicipediformes

Trogons,
Quetzals
Trogoniformes

Parrots, Lories,
Cockatoos,
Macaws
Psittaciformes

Albatrosses, Petrels Procellariiformes

Mousebirds
Coliiformes

Kingfishers,
Bee-eaters,
Hoopoes
Coraciiformes

Cuckoos,
Turacos
Cuculiformes

Pelicans, Gannets, Tropicbirds,
Cormorants Pelecaniformes

Woodpeckers,
Toucans,
Honeyguides,
Barbets
Piciformes

Owls
Strigiformes

Herons, Storks, Ibises, Bitterns,
Flamingos Ciconiiformes

BIRD ORDERS
Birds can be arranged in groups
according to how many features they
have in common. First, we arrange
them into Orders, then we place the
members of each order in Families.
The main features used for this are
the bones of the skull, the shape of
the bill, the number and arrangement
of the feathers, and the pattern of the
leg scales.

Passerines
or perching
Birds
Passeriformes

Nightjars,
Frogmouths
Caprimulgiformes

Ducks, Geese, Swans
Anseriformes

Swifts,
Hummingbirds
Apodiformes

Birds of prey
Falconiformes

49

DIVERS OR LOONS

A long wailing cry drifts across the lake. It is echoed by others from different directions. These are the calls of Red-throated divers declaring their territory. Here and there pairs are noisily performing an aggressive display as neighbours enter their territory. With bodies half-submerged and necks thrust stiffly forwards, they chase the intruders away.

DIVERS OR LOONS
Gaviidae (*4 species*)

Habitat: freshwater lakes in summer, usually sea coasts in winter.

Diet: fish, crustaceans, frogs.

Breeding: usually 2 eggs; 24-29 days incubation.

Size: smallest (Red-throated diver): length from 53cm, weight 1kg; largest (White-billed diver): length up to 93cm, weight 6.4kg.

Plumage: black or brown back and white belly; often white stripes on neck and white spots on back. Red-throated diver has red throat in summer.

Species mentioned in text:
Black-throated diver (*Gavia arctica*)
Great northern diver (*G. immer*)
Red-throated diver (*G. stellata*)
White-billed diver (*G. adamsii*)

The Red-throated diver always has its head tilted slightly upwards. This is one way it can be distinguished in winter from its slightly bigger relative, the Black-throated diver. In winter both have similar plumage, brown on the back and white on the belly. So also do the other two species of diver, the Great northern and the White-billed divers.

The divers, called loons in North America, breed in the far north. The Great northern diver, or Common loon, breeds only in arctic North America; the White-billed diver only in arctic Europe and Asia. But the other two species breed in all these locations. All species migrate south for the winter, a few even as far as southern Europe and the southern United States.

GOING FISHING
Divers are superb swimmers; they have streamlined bodies and strongly webbed feet set well back. They spend little time on land, where they can move only clumsily. They feed underwater, chasing and catching fish with an easy grace. As well as fish, they take frogs, crustaceans and worms. They dive regularly to depths of 10m and

▲**Summer plumage** Red-throated diver (1): rust-red throat, grey head and brown back. Black-throated diver (2): grey head, black back and white stripes on neck and wings. Great northern diver (3): glossy green-black head and neck, neck patch of black and white bands and white-spotted black back. At times divers swim with their bodies almost submerged (4).

occasionally much deeper. They can adjust their buoyancy – the way they float in the water – by adjusting the amount of air in their feathers, air sacs and lungs. They can stay submerged for up to several minutes.

The food divers catch is being greatly affected by pollution, in the form of pesticides and acid rain. And this is causing them to alter their feeding sites and range. In many parts of Europe and North America their numbers are also declining as their habitats are disturbed or destroyed by human development. Large numbers are also at risk because of oil pollution at their coastal wintering sites.

NESTING
Divers are usually solitary nesters, although the Red-throated and arctic divers sometimes nest in colonies. They nest on bare lake shores or

low-lying islands, where they are safe from most predators. They lay their eggs on the ground or in a crude nest of water-weed. The eggs are olive green to dark brown in colour and are incubated by both parents.

The chicks emerge well developed and leave the nest within a day of hatching. They often ride on their parents' backs. Their parents catch food for them and feed it to them fresh, not regurgitated. The chicks begin catching prey for themselves before they are 2 weeks old.

▶The Great northern diver swims with powerful thrusts of its webbed feet. At the end of one stroke (top) it streaks through the water like a dart. As it brings its feet forward for another thrust, its head stays more or less still in the water. This allows it to detect prey more easily. It then extends its neck as it gives another thrust (bottom).

▼The beautiful head of the Black-throated diver, showing its neck stripes. It is well streamlined for swimming efficiently underwater.

PENGUINS

Just off shore what look like porpoises are rippling through the icy water, first leaping into the air and then diving. As they come closer one can see that they are not porpoises at all. They are penguins swimming fast, performing what is called "porpoising".

Penguins are the most common of all the flightless birds, but unlike most of the others they are skilled swimmers. They are found most widely along the coast of Antarctica and in the surrounding waters of the Southern Ocean. Some species, however, live farther north, even as far as equatorial regions.

Four of the best-known species are the Emperor, Adelie, Chinstrap and Rockhopper penguins. The first three always stay in the Antarctic, while the

Rockhopper ranges farther north to more temperate regions.

The Emperor, the largest of the penguins, is almost twice as big as the other three species. It has distinctive orange-yellow patches on the sides of its head and throat. Its close, but slightly smaller relative, the King penguin, has similar markings.

The Chinstrap penguin is so-called because of a black band around its throat. The Adelie has a sharp head and white eye-rings. To most people

PENGUINS Spheniscidae
(*16 species*)

○　■　🐟

| Habitat: open sea, coastal waters and islands.

■ Diet: fish, squid, krill.

◎ Breeding: usually 2 eggs, white to whitish green; 1 or 2 months incubation.

Size: smallest (Little blue penguin): height 30cm, weight from 1kg; largest (Emperor penguin): height up to 1m, weight 40kg.

Plumage: black or grey on back, white on front: some species have coloured patches on face and neck.

Species mentioned in text:
Adelie penguin (*Pygoscelis adeliae*)
Chinstrap penguin (*P. antarctica*)
Emperor penguin (*Aptenodytes forsteri*)
Galapagos penguin (*Spheniscus mendiculus*)
Gentoo penguin (*Pygoscelis papua*)
King penguin (*Aptenodytes patagonicus*)
Rockhopper penguin (*Eudyptes crestatus*)

▼▶**Species of penguin and their activities** Two nearly full-grown chicks stand with an adult Yellow-eyed penguin (*Megadyptes antipodes*) (1). Rockhopper penguin (2) parents with young. Note their distinctive head crests. Two male King penguins (3) incubating eggs under a flap of skin near their feet. One is using its bill to arrange the position of the egg.

▲A Gentoo penguin carries grass back to its nest. Like most penguins it nests in huge colonies, often some way inland.

the typical penguin, it is found widely in zoos. The Rockhopper is named for its comical-looking hopping walk. It is one of the crested penguins, with long yellow tufts on the sides of the head.

SUPREME SWIMMERS

On land, penguins move very awkwardly and, to humans, comically. Their feet are set well back on the body, and they walk with a clumsy waddle or a hop. Going downhill on ice and snow, they often slide on their bellies to move faster. This is called "tobogganing". Penguins cannot fold away their short stubby wings like ordinary birds, so these constantly flap about.

However, when penguins enter their natural element, the sea, they become graceful and swift movers. They have a beautifully streamlined body and use their wings, or flippers, as paddles to propel themselves through the water. They use their webbed feet as a rudder to change

▲Two Adelie penguins greet each other (4). Adelies often "toboggan" in the snow (5). When swimming, the Adelie may skim the surface like a porpoise (6). Then it leaps out of the water (7). The Jackass penguin (*Spheniscus demersus*), pictured standing (8) and swimming ashore (9), is named after its braying call.

direction and also as a brake to slow them down.

The penguin's body is covered with a dense coat of three layers of short oily feathers. This keeps the body dry underneath and acts as insulation to keep in the body heat. A layer of fat, or blubber, beneath the skin also helps protect the bird from the ice-cold water.

FEEDING TIME

All species of penguin feed in the water. Some, including the Gentoo penguin, feed mainly on fish near the surface. Others, including the King and Emperor penguins, often dive deep for prey such as squid. Emperors have been known to remain underwater for over 15 minutes and to dive deeper than 250m. It is not known how these birds can dive to such a depth, where the water pressure is high, without suffering from "the bends". This is a painful and often dangerous condition human divers experience if they surface too quickly after a deep dive.

Most penguins do not feed at all times of the year. When they are breeding they may go for weeks or, in the case of the Emperor penguin, months without feeding. So before the breeding season begins, penguins feed constantly to build up a reserve of fat. During the fasting period they may lose nearly half their body weight.

BREEDING TIME

Penguins that live in warmer climates sometimes breed twice a year. These species include the Galapagos penguin of the Galapagos Islands on the equator. But the majority of penguin species breed in the spring, which in the Southern Hemisphere means during the months of September and October.

The Adelie penguin, for example, returns to its nesting grounds in October. Like most other species, males and females usually pair up with their partner of the previous year. They build a nest of pebbles and the female lays two eggs. After about 40 days of incubation, the chicks are hatched. Both parents feed them by regurgitation – swallowing food and bringing it up again. By February or March the chicks have moulted their thick downy coat and acquired adult plumage. Then they head for the sea and become independent.

Curiously, the Emperor penguin breeds in Arctic midwinter, when the temperature drops to −50°C and below, and winds blow at speeds of up to 80kph. Breeding colonies form in the autumn (mid-May). The female lays a single egg on the ice. The male incubates the egg, tucking it under a flap of skin on its belly. Emperors keep warm themselves by huddling together. In some colonies as many as 6,000 birds may do this. When the chick hatches, one of the parents carries it on its feet to keep the chick off the frozen ground.

◀The only time penguins "fly" is when they dive into the sea. Here Adelie penguins launch themselves from the edge of the ice.

▶A colony of King penguins. Each incubates an egg under its bulging lower belly for about two months.

PELICANS

The Great white pelicans are swimming on the lake looking for a meal. Finding a shoal of fish, they arrange themselves into a horseshoe formation and swim quickly forwards. This drives the fish in a panic towards the centre. Then, as if by a secret signal, the pelicans all plunge their bills into the water to catch their herded prey. The birds swallow their food before flying off.

▼ Great white pelicans may live and nest in huge colonies of tens of thousands. The doubled-back neck position in flight is typical of pelicans.

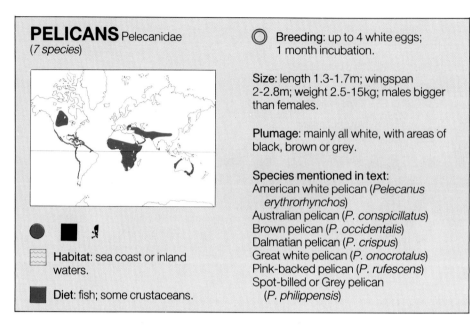

PELICANS Pelecanidae
(*7 species*)

○ Breeding: up to 4 white eggs; 1 month incubation.

Size: length 1.3-1.7m; wingspan 2-2.8m; weight 2.5-15kg; males bigger than females.

Plumage: mainly all white, with areas of black, brown or grey.

Species mentioned in text:
American white pelican (*Pelecanus erythrorhynchos*)
Australian pelican (*P. conspicillatus*)
Brown pelican (*P. occidentalis*)
Dalmatian pelican (*P. crispus*)
Great white pelican (*P. onocrotalus*)
Pink-backed pelican (*P. rufescens*)
Spot-billed or Grey pelican (*P. philippensis*)

● ■ 🦅

Habitat: sea coast or inland waters.

Diet: fish; some crustaceans.

Pelicans are among the largest flying birds, with a bulky body and sturdy webbed feet. But their most outstanding feature is their bill. It is flat, very long and straight, with a hook at the end. Beneath the lower jaw is a fold of elastic skin which can expand into a deep pouch. The pelican does not use this enormous pouch ("which can hold more than its belly can") to store food, as some people think. It uses the pouch for fishing.

As the pelican thrusts its bill into the water to catch a fish, the pouch opens up to form a large scoop. The bird sweeps up the fish in its pouch, together with 10 litres or more of water. It then closes the bill and raises its head from the water. At the same time the skin of the pouch contracts, forcing the water from the pouch, but not the fish. The pelican then lifts up its bill and swallows the fish whole.

In several species, groups of pelicans often fish together, forming a so-called "scare line" to herd schools of fish. The exception is the Brown pelican, which feeds by itself by diving at its prey from the air.

TAKING FLIGHT
Pelicans live only in temperate and tropical regions of the world. Their bodies are not well insulated from the cold, which forces the northern species to migrate south in winter.

Although they are large and ungainly birds which move awkwardly on land, they are skilled flyers. They have many air sacs in their bodies, which makes them exceptionally light for their size. And they can soar effortlessly on the air currents and cover long distances with ease. Some species often travel hundreds of kilometres daily between remote nesting sites and their lake feeding grounds.

▼The Brown pelican of the Americas has more distinctive colouring than the others, which becomes more intense in the breeding season. It feeds mainly on sea coasts, rather than inland.

▲The Brown pelican dives for its food from the air. After sighting its prey (1), it draws in its wings and dives fast (2, 3). As its bill enters the water, its wings and legs are thrust back (4). It captures its prey in its open bill and greatly expanded pouch (5).

NESTING SITES

All pelicans nest in colonies, often in huge numbers. The four mainly white species (American white, Australian, Dalmatian and Great white) all nest on the ground. They build simple nests of mud, twigs and weeds. The remaining species (Spot-billed, Brown and Pink-backed) which are mainly brown in colour, nest in low trees. They build platforms of twigs and branches.

In temperate regions pelicans breed seasonally, in the spring. But in the tropics they may breed at any time of the year. On average they lay only one or two eggs. Both sexes help in incubating and in feeding the chicks when they hatch. The parents feed the chicks by regurgitating partly digested fish into the pouch. The chicks put their heads inside the pouch to eat.

If the parents cannot supply sufficient food for all the nestlings, it is usually the last birds to hatch – and therefore the smallest of the brood – that starve. Nevertheless, the majority of the young do not survive their first year out of the nest.

DISTURBING NEWS

In general pelicans are very sensitive to disturbance. Whole colonies numbering thousands can forsake a nesting site if it is disturbed. Human disturbance and the destruction of habitats have in some regions led to a drastic decline in the numbers and range of some species. Severely at risk at the present time are the Dalmatian pelican of eastern Europe and China, and the Spot-billed pelican of India and Sri Lanka. Both species have been reduced to fewer than 1,500 breeding pairs. A decline in food availability due to over-fishing by humans, and pesticide poisoning, are additional threats to these, and all, pelicans.

▶ A group of Australian pelicans expecting a feed. Like white pelicans the world over, they nest in colonies on the ground.

STORKS

On the East African savannah vultures have gathered around the carcass of an antelope. They squabble as they tear at its flesh. Then two larger birds, with bald heads and large fleshy throat pouches, fly in. These are marabous. They harry the vultures and steal the food from their mouths.

Marabous, the largest of the storks, feed a lot on carrion. They also eat anything else around that is edible – eggs, young birds and mammals, insects and scraps. The adjutant storks of India and South-east Asia are closely related to the marabous and are also scavengers. Both marabou storks and adjutants have a bald head and a strong straight bill.

DIFFERENT FEEDING METHODS

The White and Black storks of southern Europe are more typical in their eating habits and behaviour. The White stork can often be seen walking slowly across the fields on its long legs, with its long neck stretched out and its head down looking for insects and worms. The Black stork tends to remain near the water, wading in the shallows to catch fish.

The wood storks, such as the American wood stork, also feed while wading. But they use touch rather than sight to locate their prey, just as spoonbills do. The open-bills, for

▲A threatening bill-clattering display (1). "Head-shaking crouch" performed by male as mate approaches (2). Part of an "up-down" courtship display (3).

▼Black stork (1), and Whale-headed stork (2), noted for its broad, hooked bill.

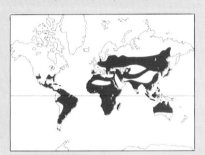

STORKS Ciconiidae, Scopidae, Balaenicipitidae (*19 species*)

● ■ ☠

⊗ Habitat: lakes, marshes, savannah.

■ Diet: fish, insects, crustaceans, amphibians, small birds and mammals.

◎ Breeding: 1-7 white or bluish eggs depending on species; 30-50 days incubation.

Size: length 75-150cm; wingspan 1.5-3.2m; weight 2-9kg.

Plumage: mainly white, grey and black; hammerhead dark brown.

Species mentioned in text:
African open-bill stork (*Anastomus lamelligerus*)
American wood stork (*Mycteria americana*)
Black stork (*Ciconia nigra*)
Hammerhead (*Scopus umbretta*)
Marabou (*Leptoptilos crumeniferus*)
Whale-headed stork (*Balaeniceps rex*)
White stork (*Ciconia ciconia*)
Yellow-billed stork (*Ibis ibis*)

▲Gaping is one of the displays special to wood storks, like this Yellow-billed stork. Wood storks also have a bare head and a slightly down-curved bill.

▼White storks often nest on buildings, as here on a Spanish church.

instance the African open-bill stork, are touch-feeders too.

LONG-DISTANCE FLIGHT
On their long legs, storks walk with body upright and a purposeful stride. They can also run well. They fly powerfully with their long broad wings, the neck extended and feet straight out behind.

When flying, they usually alternate powered flapping flight with soaring on warm air currents. In this way they can travel long distances with ease while foraging and when migrating. The European White and Black storks migrate south each winter to southern Africa. There are also resident populations of these two species in Africa and eastern Asia.

GREETING DISPLAY
During courtship and nesting, storks put on some fascinating displays. Most common is the "up-down" display, performed as a greeting when one bird rejoins its mate on the nest. The birds raise and lower the head in a stiff characteristic way, clattering the bill at the same time. Some species may also whistle, hiss or scream.

Other interesting displays include, in wood storks, gaping and pretend preening. Male open-bills have an "advertising" display in which they lower the head between the legs and shift their weight from one foot to the other.

Nesting success depends on availability of food and on the weather; storks do not nest well in rainy areas.

SWANS AND GEESE

A family of Mute swans is swimming sedately among the reeds in a still backwater. In front is the male, ever on the look-out for danger. The female follows, one cygnet on its back, four more swimming behind. As the male comes out of the reeds, it spies a rival male close by. Arching its wings and drawing in its neck, it surges towards the intruder at high speed. The rival takes fright and flees. The proud father rears out of the water and flaps its wings in triumph.

▼ Snow geese in their thousands gather to feed. Within the flock, family groups usually stay together.

SWANS AND GEESE

Anatidae (tribes Anserini, Anser-anatini) and Anhimidae (*25 species*)

  🦢

 Habitat: sea coasts, estuaries, lakes, rivers.

 Diet: fish, molluscs, crustaceans, insects, vegetation.

◯ Breeding: 4-14 white, bluish or greenish eggs; 18-39 days incubation.

Size: length up to 1.5m; weight up to 15 kg; wingspan up to 2m (Mute swan).

Plumage: often white or black and white; also grey, brown.

Species mentioned in text:
Barnacle goose (*Branta leucopsis*)
Bewick's or Whistling swan (*Cygnus columbianus*)
Black swan (*C. atrata*)
Black-necked swan (*C. melanchoryphus*)
Canada goose (*Branta canadiensis*)
Emperor goose (*Anser canagicus*)
Magpie goose (*Anseranas semipalmata*)
Mute swan (*Cygnus olor*)
Pink-footed goose (*Anser brachyrhyncus*)
Red-breasted goose (*Branta ruficollis*)
Snow goose (*Anser caerulescens*)
Trumpeter swan (*Cygnus buccinator*)
Whooper swan (*C. cygnus*)

Mute swans are naturally quarrelsome and become extremely aggressive in the breeding season when they are defending their territory. They are powerful creatures, which by flapping their wings hard can inflict severe injuries on any humans who disturb them. They are the largest of the swans, easily recognizable by their graceful curved neck, their orange bill and the knob at the base of the bill.

WHITE AND BLACK SWANS
The plumage of the Mute swan is all white. So is that of the other swans in the Northern Hemisphere. These include the Whooper and Bewick's swans. The Whooper is almost as large as the Mute swan, but can be distinguished by its straight neck and by its bill, which is black and yellow. Bewick's swan is similar, but rather smaller, with less yellow on the bill.

▲A male Canada goose races up to a rival and threatens with an aggressive mouth-open display.

▼A male Black swan incubating on the nest. It shares this chore with the female, which is unusual among swans.

Both species are noisier than the Mute swan. The Whooper swan has a trumpeting call, like the even louder Trumpeter swan, which is another northern species. The Mute swan is noisier in flight, however. Its slow wing beats produce an unmistakable wheezy, buzzing sound.

Two of the most distinctive swans live in the Southern Hemisphere. The Black swan of Australia is all black with a red bill. The Black-necked swan of South America has a black head and neck, which contrast with its otherwise white plumage. There is a red knob on its blue bill, and its feet are pink. A white stripe around its eyes and head is only sometimes distinct.

BIRDS OF THE NORTH

The 15 species of geese are found only in the Northern Hemisphere. Geese show a much wider variation in plumage than swans. One of the most colourful is the Red-breasted goose of Siberia, which has black, white and chestnut-red markings. It is one of the black geese, so-called for their generally dark plumage. They belong to the *Branta* genus. Other black geese include the quite similar Barnacle and Canada geese, which have a black head and neck and pale breast. The Barnacle goose has a white face, and the Canada goose a white chin patch. The Barnacle can be identified by its yapping call, like that of a small dog.

▼Species of swan and goose and some aspects of their behaviour Bar-headed goose (*Anser indicus*) (1). Aggressive posture of the Red-breasted goose (2). Magpie goose (3). Crested screamer (*Chauna torquata*) (4). Triumph displays of male Hawaiian goose (*Branta sandvicensis*) (5) and Whooper swan (6). Emperor goose nesting on the tundra (7). Pink-footed goose (8). Black-necked swan and cygnets (9).

65

The paler-coloured grey geese belong to the *Anser* genus. They include the Emperor goose and the Pink-footed goose. Palest is the beautiful Snow goose. Its plumage is all white, except for the wing tips, and it has a red bill and pink legs.

GOOSE STEP
Swans and geese are well adapted for their life on or near water. The body is well insulated, and the plumage is waterproof. The legs are powerful, and the toes webbed for swimming.

The bill of swans and geese is quite broad and is usually open at the sides, where there are fine comb-like "teeth" ("lamellae"). These are used to help filter food particles from the water. But geese in particular also feed by grazing at water margins and on pastureland.

Swans are more aquatic than geese. Their legs are short and placed well back on the body. They cannot walk well on land. Geese, with longer legs placed further forward, are able to walk readily and even run quite fast. Some walk lifting their feet high, with an exaggerated "goose step".

MAGPIES AND SCREAMERS
The Magpie goose of Australasia has especially long legs. Its toes are only slightly webbed. Unusually, it often perches in trees.

Screamers (family Anhimidae) are other birds related to, but different from, true geese. Like the Magpie goose they have scarcely any webbing on their long toes. They have a short hooked bill. All three species of screamer, which live in South America, are noted for their loud penetrating call. Their "scream" is different from the "honking" of true geese.

PAIRED FOR LIFE
The male and female in a pair of swans or geese usually remain together for life. They often preen each other and display together. These activities help cement their relationship. One typical display is the "triumph ceremony", performed when they have driven away an intruder. Waving the head and lifting the wings, they call loudly as if saying, "Let that be a lesson!"

Swans and geese usually nest away from other birds, sometimes defending a wide territory around the nest. In most cases only the female builds the nest and incubates the eggs. It builds the nest from plant material and usually lines it with down from its breast. It covers over the eggs with the down when leaving the eggs to feed.

Both sexes feed and look after the chicks when they hatch, remaining with them throughout the first winter. The juveniles have different plumage from the adults. Young Mute swans, for example, look ordinary ("ugly ducklings") in their dull-brownish plumage, until suddenly they grow into graceful adulthood.

Many swans and geese breed in far northern regions – in Greenland, Siberia and Arctic North America. They migrate south to spend winter in warmer climates every year, flying in typical V-formations, or skeins. They return to their breeding grounds in the spring as the snows clear. Their annual migrations are one of the great rhythms of nature, marking the passage of the seasons.

A LEADEN DEATH
Swans and geese are, with ducks, classed as waterfowl. They have been hunted for thousands of years for their eggs, meat and plumage, and more recently for sport. Few species are as yet under threat from shooting. But many birds die as an indirect result of it, from lead poisoning by shotgun pellets they pick up from the ground. Others suffer lead poisoning from the lead weights dropped by anglers.

▶ The beautiful Mute swan thrashing its wings in the water to bathe its plumage. Afterwards it will preen itself.

DUCKS

After fishing on the lake, a female goosander flies up to a tree near the water's edge. It perches near a hole, where several fluffy little heads soon appear. The female flies down to the ground and calls to its young, which are only a few days old. After some hesitation the ducklings jump down from the tree. They land in a heap, but unharmed. Then they follow their mother to the water's edge.

Ducks are among the most widespread and the most colourful of all waterfowl. They are found on all the continents except Antarctica. Many species are shot for sport, while others such as the mergansers are killed by anglers because they take fish.

Ducks are mostly quite small birds, with a short neck and short legs. The body is well adapted for life on the

water. The breast is broad and flat, like a boat-bottom. The plumage is waterproof, and the feet are webbed. The legs are set well back on the body to aid swimming. But this makes walking on land awkward, resulting in the typical duck waddle.

Ducks belong, with the swans and geese (see pages 62-67), to the family Anatidae. They are generally classified

◄When diving, the Tufted duck **(1)** holds its wings close to the body. The Velvet scoter **(2)** has its wings slightly open.

into different tribes according to their body structure, plumage or behaviour. The tribes are whistling ducks (9 species), Freckled duck (1), shelduck and sheldgeese (16), steamer ducks (3), perching ducks and geese (13), dabbling ducks (40), diving ducks (16), sea ducks and sawbills (20) and stifftails (8).

COLOURFUL MALES
In most species the male (drake) is more highly coloured. The female (duck) is generally a dull brown. This inconspicuous colouring acts as camouflage when the duck is sitting on the nest incubating the eggs.

When moulting, the drake sheds its flight feathers and cannot fly for several weeks. During this time it goes into "eclipse plumage", which is dull

▼►**Variation in plumage** The attractive Mandarin **(1)** is a perching duck. The White-faced tree duck (*Dendrocygna viduata*) **(2)**, a whistling duck, also perches in trees. The Red-breasted merganser **(3)** is a sawbill, the Ruddy duck **(4)** a stifftail.

DUCKS Anatidae (9 tribes)
(*126 species*)

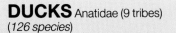

Habitat: freshwater wetlands, estuaries, coasts.

Diet: water weed, seeds, insects, molluscs, frogs, small fish.

Breeding: 6-14 whitish, creamy, bluish or greenish eggs; 3-4 weeks incubation.

Size: length 36-68cm; weight up to 2kg.

Plumage: highly variable in males: mixtures of black, white, brown, chestnut red; usually speckled dull brown in females.

Species mentioned in text:
Common eider (*Somateria mollissima*)
Common or European pochard (*Aythya ferina*)
Common scoter (*Melanitta nigra*)
Freckled duck (*Stictonetta naevosa*)
Goosander or Common merganser (*Mergus merganser*)
Mallard (*Anas platyrhynchos*)
Mandarin duck (*Aix galericulata*)
North American wood duck (*A. sponsa*)
Pintail (*Anas acuta*)
Red-breasted merganser (*Mergus serrator*)
Redhead (*Aythya americana*)
Ruddy duck (*Oxyura jamaicensis*)
Shelduck (*Tadorna tadorna*)
Shoveler (*Anas clypeata*)
Teal (*A. crecca*)
Tufted duck (*Aythya fuligula*)
Velvet scoter (*Melanitta fusca*)

◀The Black-headed duck (*Heteronetta atricapilla*) of South America is a parasite when it comes to nesting. It lays its eggs in the nests of other waterfowl.

brown just like that of the female, for camouflage.

(Except where otherwise stated, the plumage colours mentioned for the different species of duck described below refer to the male.)

THE DABBLERS

Many species of duck feed at the surface by dabbling – constantly dipping the bill into the water and sifting out bits of food. Their bills are edged with lamellae (comb-like teeth) which act like a sieve. Dabbling ducks often up-end themselves for a few seconds to reach weed underwater.

Some of the most common species of ducks are dabblers. They include

the mallard, teal, pintail and shoveler. All these species are widespread and are found right across northern North America and Eurasia.

The mallard can be found on virtually any small pond in the town as well as in the country. It has a dark green head, maroon on the breast and a yellow bill.

The smaller teal has a handsome head of chestnut red, with a glossy dark green eye patch. A patch of yellow beneath the tail shows up in flight. When alarmed, teal take off almost vertically. They fly in tightly bunched flocks.

▼ Four distinctive species of duck Males are shown. The shelduck (1) is heavy-bodied like a goose. Unusually in ducks, the female has similar plumage. But it lacks the knob on the bill. The pintail (2) has an unmistakable tail, an elegant body and long wings. The Common eider (3) has a much plumper body shape. The Tufted duck (4) has a noticeably rounded, purplish black head with a long tuft of feathers on the nape.

The pintail is easy to recognize because of its long, sharply pointed tail. The shoveler's most distinctive feature is its long bill, which broadens at the tip like a shovel.

THE DIVERS

The tribe of diving ducks generally live in freshwater habitats. When diving, they usually keep the wings tight into the body. But some species use the wings to help them steer underwater.

The diving ducks are often called bay ducks or pochards. The Common or European pochard is grey and black with a chestnut-red head. The redhead of North America is similar, but is larger and darker. The scaups are also related and are probably named for their habit of diving for scallops. They often feed along the sea coast.

Stifftails are also very good divers. These small dumpy birds are named after their long spiky tail feathers, which they use for steering underwater. They usually have a chestnut-red plumage, often with a black-and-white head. The Ruddy duck is typical. It lives in North America, unlike most stifftails, which live in the Southern Hemisphere.

▼ Fluffy-feathered mallard ducklings dabble among the duckweed. They scoop up a mouthful of water, then strain out from it seeds, leaves and insects.

SEA DUCKS AND SAWBILLS

Some species of diving duck spend much of their time at sea. A well-known example of these sea ducks is the Common eider. The soft down that the female plucks from its breast during nesting has been gathered for centuries to make eiderdown quilts. The eider is a striking bird, with black belly and flight feathers and black cap; the rest of the plumage is white, with tinges of pink on the breast and green on the nape. It breeds in far northern regions, like another very distinctive sea duck, the Common scoter. This bird is black all over, except for an orange mark on the bill.

The sawbills are close relatives of the sea ducks, but they are usually found on inland waters. They get their name from the saw-tooth edge to their bill, which helps them grasp the fish they catch when they dive. This group includes the mergansers.

GOOSE-LIKE DUCKS

In the United States mergansers are sometimes called sheldrakes. This can cause confusion with the quite different shelduck and sheldgeese. The shelduck is a northern coastal and inland bird with a goose-like body. Sheldgeese are similar in build.

The steamers of southern South America and the Falkland Islands are sometimes classified with shelducks and like them are heavily built. The group name comes from their habit of thrashing their wings like a paddle-steamer when racing over water. Two of the three species are flightless.

WHISTLING IN THE TREES

Most ducks spend their time on the water or on ground close by. A few species, however, have the habit of perching in trees. Among the most attractive of them are the Mandarin duck of Asia and the North Amer-ican wood duck. Most tree-perching species are found in the tropics.

The birds usually nest in hollows in trees. The young have sharp claws and a stiff tail to help them climb out of the nest hole a few days after hatching. A few other ducks nest in trees, including the goosander.

The whistling ducks are another tribe of ducks that often perch in trees. Also called tree ducks, they are found mainly in tropical and subtropical regions in the Americas, Africa and Asia. They are noted for their high-pitched whistling call. Both sexes have similar plumage, which is usually highly patterned.

NESTING AND BREEDING

During courtship, drakes put on displays to attract the females and prepare them for mating. They may jerk back the head and make whistling noises, flick water with the bill or splash with the feet, cock the tail or even "burp".

Most ducks build nests on the ground or in reed beds, with grass, weed, leaves and feathers. Exceptions are the perching ducks and goosander, which are tree-nesters, and the shelduck, which nests in burrows. Most ducks nest away from other birds, though some do nest close together if space is limited.

Only the female builds the nest and incubates the eggs. Incubation begins when the whole clutch is laid, and the young hatch within a few hours of one another. They have their eyes open and are covered in thick soft down. After only a few hours in the nest drying off, they are ready to follow their mother into the water and start to swim. Among sea ducks and shel-ducks several broods often join up to form a nursery group or crèche under the care of a few females.

A pair of ducks usually stay together for only one season. This happens because, after mating, the drake takes little or no part in raising the young.

GULLS

GULLS Laridae (*45 species*)

Habitat: mainly coastal waters.

Diet: fish, crustaceans, molluscs, worms, carrion, eggs, chicks, refuse.

Breeding: 2-3 brownish or greenish, mottled brown or grey

eggs; 3-5 weeks incubation .

Size: smallest (Little gull): length 25cm, weight 0.9kg; largest (Great black-backed gull): length up to 78cm, weight 2kg.

Plumage: white, grey and black.

Species mentioned in text:
Black-headed gull (*Larus ridibundus*)
Bonaparte's gull (*L. philadelphia*)
Common or Mew gull (*L. canus*)
Glaucous gull (*L. hyperboreus*)
Great black-backed gull (*L. marinus*)
Herring gull (*L. argentatus*)
Kittiwake or Black-legged kittiwake (*Rissa tridactyla*)
Laughing gull (*Larus atricilla*)
Lesser black-backed gull (*L. fuscus*)
Little gull (*L. minutus*)

A gull chick has decided to leave the nest and explore. It scuttles over to a nearby clump of grass, then to a pile of stones. Suddenly a piercing call rings out. Looking up, it sees an adult gull – not one of its parents – heading towards it. It has wandered into a neighbour's territory, and in a gull colony the neighbours are not friendly.

Gulls are the most common sea-birds in the Northern Hemisphere. They range widely over the northern Atlantic and Pacific and the Arctic oceans. Only a few species of gull are found south of the equator.

Gulls are very adaptable creatures and have benefited directly from the

▶**Varied plumage** The juvenile Great black- backed gull **(1)** does not have the dark wings and white underparts of the adult, nor the yellow bill. The young kittiwake **(2)** has diagonal bars on its wings and tail and neck rings, unlike the adult. The Ivory gull (*Pagophila eburnea*) **(3)** juvenile is not pure white like the adult. The young Little gull **(4)** has dark spots on its head. Sabine's gull (*Larus sabini*) **(5)** and Ross's gull (*Rhodostethia rosea*) **(6)** are both Arctic breeders. The Swallow-tailed gull (*Creagrus furcatus*) **(7)** is a tropical bird, found in the Galapagos and La Plata Islands of Ecuador.

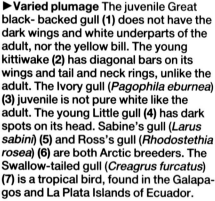

1

activities of people. They are more and more found inland, where they scavenge for food on rubbish dumps and follow the plough on farmland. The larger species steal other birds' eggs and kill their chicks.

Gulls vary greatly in size. The Little gull is typical of the smaller gulls, with a trim body and a slender, pincer-like bill. The Great black-backed gull is a powerfully built bird with a heavy hooked bill. It looks vicious and is a fierce predator.

Most gulls have mainly white plumage underneath and pale or dark grey plumage on the back and wings. The bill and legs may be black, yellow or red. This may be a way of distinguishing gulls that otherwise look very much alike. The toes are webbed, and all the gulls are excellent swimmers. They are equally at home in the air, soaring and gliding with ease on the sea breezes.

BLACK AND WHITE HEADS

The Little gull is one of the group of hooded or masked gulls. In summer it has a black head, moulting in winter to leave just dark patches. Another hooded gull in Europe is the larger Black-headed gull. This is not a good name, because in summer the head is dark brown, not black. Both birds have grey upper parts like most gulls, and the bill and legs are red. American

hooded gulls include the Laughing gull and Bonaparte's gull.

The Great black-backed gull is one of the white-headed group of gulls. This group also includes the smaller Lesser black-backed gull and its close relative the Herring gull. The Herring gull is a very successful species, found throughout the north Atlantic.

The kittiwake is a much smaller white-headed bird. It spends more time at sea than most other gulls. Its

name describes its strident call. The kittiwake is distinguished from the Common gull by its legs, which are black, not yellow. It catches fish by plunge-diving from the air.

SHORE, CLIFFS AND TREES

Most gulls nest in huge colonies, which they return to year after year. The nest sites are varied. The Black-headed gull nests mainly on the ground, often in a shallow scrape lined with grass and seaweed. The kittiwake favours ledges on cliffs to build its cup-shaped nest of seaweed and moss. The Herring gull nests on beach or cliff and even on roofs. Bonaparte's gull is unusual in that it nests in trees, usually conifers. The Common gull may nest in trees too, as well as on walls and buildings.

Both sexes incubate the eggs and look after the chicks when they hatch. The chicks run about as soon as their downy feathers dry. Many are killed by other gulls when their parents leave them to fish or when they wander from the nest.

▼The long call of gulls (1) is a victory display. Throwing back the head (2) shows a bird is begging for food. Grass-tugging (3) takes place on the territory boundaries. Head-flagging (4) shows that the birds do not want to fight. But when they threaten each other (5), fights may break out.

▲Grey and white kittiwakes nesting in a colony on a cliff ledge below a group of black and white guillemots.

►Young Herring gulls peck at the red spot on the tip of their parents' bill to make them regurgitate their food.

TERNS

A Sandwich tern is out hunting, flying about 5m above the waves. Soon it spots a shoal of sprats swimming near the surface. It hovers briefly before plunging into the water. Within seconds it surfaces, a wriggling sprat held in the vice-like grip of its bill. Satisfied with the kill, it flies quickly back to the nest to feed its two hungry chicks.

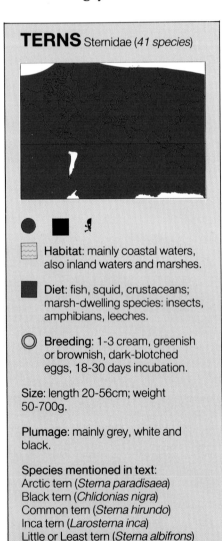

TERNS Sternidae (41 species)

![habitat map]

● ■ 🦴

~~~ Habitat: mainly coastal waters, also inland waters and marshes.

■ Diet: fish, squid, crustaceans; marsh-dwelling species: insects, amphibians, leeches.

◯ Breeding: 1-3 cream, greenish or brownish, dark-blotched eggs, 18-30 days incubation.

Size: length 20-56cm; weight 50-700g.

Plumage: mainly grey, white and black.

Species mentioned in text:
Arctic tern (*Sterna paradisaea*)
Black tern (*Chlidonias nigra*)
Common tern (*Sterna hirundo*)
Inca tern (*Larosterna inca*)
Little or Least tern (*Sterna albifrons*)
Roseate tern (*S. dougallii*)
Sandwich tern (*S. sandvicensis*)
White tern (*Gygis alba*)
White-winged black tern (*Chlidonias leucoptera*)

Closely related to gulls, the terns are among the most graceful of all seabirds. They have slender bodies, long sharply tapered wings and short legs. The head is streamlined and the bill sharply pointed.

The commonest species are the sea terns, noted for their deeply forked tail. This feature gives terns their popular name of sea swallows. The sea terns are among the most widespread of birds, ranging from the Arctic to the Antarctic. Some species, notably the Arctic tern, migrate south tens of thousands of kilometres from their nesting grounds.

BLACK CAPS
The sea terns include the Common, Arctic, Sandwich and Roseate terns. They all have a black cap on the head, a mainly white body and grey wings. In the Roseate tern the breast has a pinkish tinge.

The Common and Arctic terns are at first sight nearly impossible to tell

▲ Tern plumage and bill colour Blue-grey noddy (*Procelsterna cerulea*) (1), Lesser noddy (*Anous tenuirostris*) (2), White tern (3), Inca tern (4), Arctic tern (5), Long-billed tern (*Phaetusa simplex*) (6), juvenile Black tern (7), Sooty tern (*Sterna fuscata*) (8) (named after its sooty-black upperparts), Caspian tern (*S. caspia*) adult (9) and young (10).

apart. They are both the same size and have red legs. But the Common tern has its red bill tipped with black, whereas the Arctic tern's bill is red all over

The slightly bigger Sandwich and Roseate terns can also be identified by their bills. In the first species the bill is black tipped with yellow; in the second it is black with red at the base. The Sandwich tern in addition has a short head crest.

In winter the black cap of these terns recedes slightly to give them a white forehead. A white forehead is shown in summer by the Little tern. It is the smallest of the terns with its tail

◄During courtship, terns perform the spectacular high-flight display (1), in which the female pursues the male to a height of several hundred metres. Later in courtship the male feeds the female (2) for some time before mating (3). After their high-flight display and mating, the birds adopt what is called the "pole stance" (4), with wings drooped and bill pointing upwards.

▼The beautiful White tern has near-transparent wings. It is found around the coasts of tropical and subtropical oceans throughout the world.

only slightly forked. It is one of the most widely distributed of the terns, found in most temperate and tropical regions except South America.

MARSH TERNS AND NODDIES

The sea terns, which belong to the genus *Sterna*, breed inland only occasionally. But species of the genus *Chlidonias* usually nest inland by rivers and lakes and in marshes. These marsh terns include the Black tern and the White-winged black tern.

In the summer the Black tern has a black head and body and smoky grey wings above and below. The White-winged black tern has a black body, but wings that are white above and black and grey below. In winter they both lose the black plumage and become very nearly indistinguishable from the sea terns. But their short tail gives them away.

In tropical regions terns known as noddies are found. They are named after their nodding displays during courtship. They have similar build to the other terns, but different plumage. Another tropical species is the Inca tern, so named because it is native to Chile and Peru, home of the Inca civilization. Its plumage is slate coloured, but its most fascinating features are the yellow mouth wattles and white moustache.

THE LONGEST MIGRATION

Of all the migrations that take place in the animal kingdom, few can rival those of the Arctic tern. The most northerly populations breed in the tundra during the short Arctic summer, then begin to fly south.

The birds that nest in the Canadian Arctic often ride the prevailing winds to western Europe. They travel south down the coast to West Africa. They may then continue down to southern Africa and from there into Antarctic waters. Or they may cross to South America and follow its coastline south to the Antarctic.

As the northern winter ends, the terns make their way back north again to their Arctic nesting sites. By the time they arrive they will have travelled up to 35,000km since they set out the previous year.

FAVOURITE FOOD

Fish is the favourite food of sea terns. They usually catch fish by diving into the sea from the air. They swallow the fish immediately they surface, unless they are feeding young. Then they carry the catch back to the nest site.

The marsh terns eat insects, and larvae, tadpoles, spiders and leeches. They often feed on the water surface by dipping in the bill while flying. They may also dive in to catch frogs and small fish.

Noddies also dip to feed. They often catch flying fish, which are common in their tropical habitats, in mid-air. They swallow the fish and, when feeding young, regurgitate it for them at the nest.

BREEDING AND NESTING

In northern latitudes terns breed seasonally, but in the tropics they may breed at any time of the year. Most terns pair for life. Even though they wander off on their own outside the breeding season, they both return to the same nest site each year to mate.

Most sea terns breed in colonies. Their nests are usually simple scrapes in the ground, lined with a little plant material. Noddies build larger nests of vegetation in trees and bushes and on cliff ledges. Marsh terns often build floating nests anchored to the reeds. The White tern builds no nest at all, laying its single egg on a branch.

Both male and female incubate the eggs and look after the young when they hatch. In crested terns, such as the Sandwich tern, young birds often gather together for safety to form a nursery group or crèche. Parents returning with food recognize their young by voice, and feed only them.

OSTRICH

An elegant, swan-like brown neck curves above the waving grasses, and a pair of large dark eyes surveys the distant scene. More ostriches stop feeding and raise their heads, their eyelashes fluttering in the dust-laden wind. They pick up the scent of danger. With a few leaps they are off, bounding across the plains with a swaying gait, their wings spread to give them extra lift.

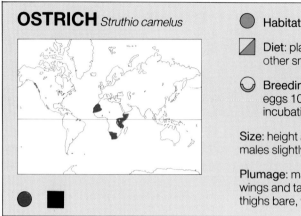

OSTRICH *Struthio camelus*

○ Habitat: semi-desert, savannah.

◩ Diet: plant material, insects and other small animals.

◖ Breeding: nest a scrape in ground; eggs 10-40, 1,100-1,800g; incubation period 42 days.

Size: height about 2.5m; weight 115kg; males slightly larger than females.

Plumage: males black with white on wings and tail; females brown; neck and thighs bare, with skin blue or pink.

The ostrich is the world's largest living bird. A large male may be 2.5m high and can weigh 135kg. Ostriches cannot fly. Their wings are small relative to their size, but their legs are long and powerful. They have long flexible necks and rather small heads with large eyes. Their heads and necks are almost bare, except for some thin fluffy down and a few bristly feathers. The females have pinkish-grey necks,

▼A male ostrich stands guard over his eggs and newly-hatched chicks.

the males pink or blue. The legs are also covered in bare pinkish skin.

RECORD-BREAKING RUNNER

The ostrich's body is adapted for running. A fit male ostrich can run at 50kph and keep up that speed for at least half an hour. His top speed is around 70kph. Each stride lifts the ostrich 3.5m into the air.

Ostriches and other flightless birds such as rheas, emus, cassowaries and kiwis have poorly developed flight muscles, and their skeletons lack the large breastbone which is typical of flying birds. These flightless birds are often grouped together and called ratites. Their wing feathers are soft plumes lacking barbs and barbules. This gives ratites a shaggy appearance.

HOOF-LIKE WEAPONS

The ostrich's thigh muscles are large and powerful. It has only two toes on each foot, one much larger than the other. These toes have fleshy pads and act like the hoofs of horses, providing a small surface area to reduce friction with the ground as the bird runs. The leg bones are solid, without the air chambers found in the bones of other groups of birds.

The powerful legs are used for defence on the rare occasions when the bird cannot outrun its enemies or when it is guarding its chicks. A kick from an ostrich can knock over a man.

STRETCH-A-NECK

Ostriches are omnivores – they will eat almost anything. Their main food is shoots, leaves, flowers and seeds, supplemented by small animals such as insects and lizards. They swallow grit and stones to help break down tough seeds and plant material.

Ostriches feed quickly, pecking at one item after another. They collect a lot of food in their mouth, then form it into a ball (bolus) and swallow it. You can see the bolus passing down the ostrich's neck as a large bulge. Ostriches are attracted to very shiny things and will swallow watches and other metal objects.

FARMED FOR FEATHERS

Ostrich feathers have long been used by Africans and Europeans for decorating clothing. In many parts of South Africa ostriches have been farmed for their plumes for over a century. In some places the eggshells are even believed to have magical properties; the shells are also used to carry water. Ostriches are easily domesticated and trained but do not make good pets – they are too bad-tempered. The main threat to their survival comes from loss of habitat.

COURTSHIP AND PARENTHOOD

Ostriches are polygamous: each male mates with several females. He defends a territory during the breeding

season by displaying aggressively to intruders and by a deep booming call accompanied by inflation of the brightly coloured neck skin.

Ostrich courtship is a very showy affair. The male displays to the hen, flapping first one wing, then the other, showing off his white wing plumes. He throws himself to the ground and beats a hollow in the sand with his wings, as if making a nest scrape. Then he lowers his head and waves his wings, uttering little noises. The hen parades in front of him, lowering her head and quivering her wings.

Male ostriches make good fathers. The male makes the nest scrape, and the hen may lay up to 12 eggs on alternate days. As many as six or more other females may also lay in the nest, until it contains up to 60 eggs. The male shares incubation duty with the dominant hen: the male, relatively conspicuous, sits on the nest at night, the camouflaged female by day.

The ostrich egg is the largest in the world, up to 15cm long and 13cm wide. Yet it is only a fraction of the size of the adult bird, so one ostrich can sit on a lot of eggs.

The young chicks are camouflaged in speckled brown coats. If danger threatens, they lie flat on the ground, their necks stretched out, pretending to be dead. They can run around and feed by themselves as soon as they hatch. Their parents stay with them to guard them from birds of prey, hyenas and other predators. When the family are feeding with heads down among the grasses, each parent keeps looking up to scan the area for signs of danger.

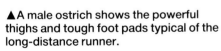
▲ A male ostrich shows the powerful thighs and tough foot pads typical of the long-distance runner.

► With its huge wings, long neck and legs and great flexibility, the ostrich has a wide range of displays. Here a hen attacks with wings full-spread (1), a hen shows a male she is interested in mating (2), a hen pretends to be injured to lure predators away from her chicks (3), and a cock struts about in a threatening posture (4).

HUMMINGBIRDS

The loud whine of a chainsaw shatters the quiet of a Central American forest. Within seconds a tall tree crashes down into flower-laden bushes nearby. A cloud of small, brightly coloured birds rises in fright from the bushes. Many hummingbirds have lost their territories and their nectar-laden flowers (and so probably their lives) to the loggers.

A few species of hummingbird live in North America, as far north as Alaska, while others are found in the far south of South America. However, most species of these tiny, dazzlingly-bright birds live in Central America and northern South America, near the Equator.

A century ago they were caught, stuffed and used to decorate the hats of rich and fashionable women. Fortunately, they are no longer at risk from this sad trade. Today, the main threat to many hummingbirds is the destruction of their natural forest, shrubland and grassland homes, and the raising of crops or livestock in these areas. It is thought that about 40 species of hummingbird are now threatened with extinction.

HUMMING TO THE FLOWERS
The main food of all hummingbirds is nectar – the sweet, sticky "honey" made by flowers. As a hummingbird hovers in front of a flower, its wings beat so fast that they produce the humming noise that gives the birds their name. The long, pointed bill is pushed deep into the flower to reach the nectar, and the bird sucks up the nectar with its long, tube-like tongue. Different species of hummingbird have different shaped bills, which are

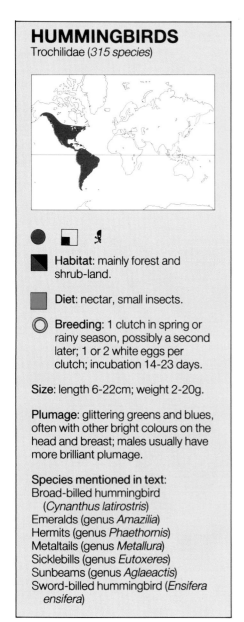

HUMMINGBIRDS
Trochilidae (*315 species*)

● ■ ⌇

■ **Habitat:** mainly forest and shrub-land.

■ **Diet:** nectar, small insects.

◎ **Breeding:** 1 clutch in spring or rainy season, possibly a second later; 1 or 2 white eggs per clutch; incubation 14-23 days.

Size: length 6-22cm; weight 2-20g.

Plumage: glittering greens and blues, often with other bright colours on the head and breast; males usually have more brilliant plumage.

Species mentioned in text:
Broad-billed hummingbird
 (*Cynanthus latirostris*)
Emeralds (genus *Amazilia*)
Hermits (genus *Phaethornis*)
Metaltails (genus *Metallura*)
Sicklebills (genus *Eutoxeres*)
Sunbeams (genus *Aglaeactis*)
Sword-billed hummingbird (*Ensifera
 ensifera*)

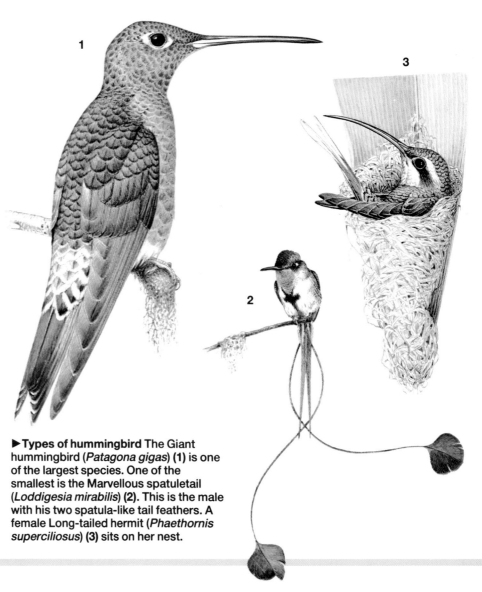

►**Types of hummingbird** The Giant hummingbird (*Patagona gigas*) **(1)** is one of the largest species. One of the smallest is the Marvellous spatuletail (*Loddigesia mirabilis*) **(2)**. This is the male with his two spatula-like tail feathers. A female Long-tailed hermit (*Phaethornis superciliosus*) **(3)** sits on her nest.

suited to flowers of a particular shape. The sicklebills, for example, specialize in feeding from heliconia flowers, which are the identical down-curved shape as the birds' bills.

Hummingbirds are so small that they lose body heat quickly so they need to take in plenty of energy. A hummingbird eats more than half its own weight in food each day. Nectar is rich in energy-giving sugars and is an ideal food for these tiny, busy fliers.

Flowers benefit from a hummingbird's visit. As the bird feeds, it collects pollen dust on its bill and face. When it visits another flower, it may leave the pollen there (cross-pollination),

▶Hummingbirds are the only birds that can hover. The wing twists near the body at the "wrist", pushing air downwards on the "down" stroke (1-5), and swivelling to do the same on the "up" stroke (6-10).

▼More hummingbirds Showing their gleaming colours are a Bee hummingbird (*Mellisuga helenae*) (1), Amethyst woodstar (*Calliphlox amethystina*) (2), Frilled coquette (*Lophornis magnifica*) (3), and Ruby-topaz hummingbird (*Chrysolampis mosquitus*) (4). The Sword-billed hummingbird (5). A White-tipped sicklebill (*Eutoxeres aquila*) (6). A Bearded helmetcrest (*Oxypogon guerinii*) (7).

so helping the flowers to produce seeds and therefore to spread.

As well as feeding on nectar, most hummingbirds occasionally eat small insects and other tiny creatures. They catch them on the wing or pick them off leaves and twigs.

MEETING A MATE

In some hummingbird species, such as emeralds and sunbeams, each bird lives in its own territory, which contains enough flowers to provide food. As the patch of flowers dies away, the bird transfers its territory to another area where there are plenty of fresh flowers. In other species, such as the hermits and the Sword-billed hummingbird, each individual regularly visits groups of long-flowering plants that remain in bloom right round the year.

These habits mean that hummingbirds come together only at breeding time. Males from an area collect in one place, called a "lek". Here they sing their simple, squeaky songs and display their vivid plumage to the watching females. After mating, the female builds a nest and raises the young; the male plays no further part.

Most hummingbirds build deep cup-shaped nests from moss and soft plant material. The nests are usually attached to twigs by cobwebs and hidden deep in the vegetation.

When the nestlings hatch out, the mother feeds them while hovering in front of them. She puts her bill into the youngster's mouth and pumps in a regurgitated mash of nectar and insects. After leaving their nest, the fledgling hummingbirds are still fed by their mother for up to 40 days.

▶A Broad-billed hummingbird approaches a flower to take nectar, its wing-beats "frozen" by high-speed photography. Most hummingbirds can beat their wings up to 80 times a second.

TOUCANS

TOUCANS Ramphastidae
(37 species)

● ■ ☠

△ **Habitat:** mostly rain forest.

■ **Diet:** mainly fruit; some insects and other small animals.

○ **Breeding:** average 1 clutch a year, 2-4 white eggs incubated for 15-16 days.

Size: length 33-66cm.

Plumage: most species black with red, yellow and white, or chiefly green; bills, faces and throats brightly coloured.

Species mentioned in text:
Aracaris (genus *Pteroglossus*)
Channel-billed toucan (*Ramphastos vitellinus*)
Cuvier's toucan (*R. tucanus*)
Mountain toucans (genus *Andigena*)
Toco toucan (*Ramphastos toco*)
Toucanets (genera *Aulacorhynchus, Selenidera*)
Yellow-browed toucanet (*Aulacorhynchus huallagae*)

At dusk in a Brazilian forest, a group of toucans croak and hop among the branches. Their black bodies are almost invisible, but their yellow-and-orange bills glow warmly in the light of the setting Sun. The birds clack bills together and toss pieces of fruit, which they catch in their bill-tips.

Toucans have long been favourite birds of artists, photographers and nature-lovers. The Toco toucan is probably the best known species. It has a bright-eyed expression, huge and colourful bill with the trace of a smile, and white throat patch and black body feathers like a person's dinner suit and shirt.

PLAYING "CATCH" WITH FRUIT?

The toucans' behaviour is also well known – and puzzling. They generally live in straggling groups and when perching together in a tree they sometimes seem to play. They toss a piece of fruit to each other, rather like our game of catch. Or two toucans may clasp bills and then push and "wrestle" until one gives up – but there are no signs of aggression, as when fighting off predators. Whether these activities are play, simply for the fun of it, or whether they help to keep the members of a group together, is not clear.

Toucans live in Central and South America, except for the cold far southwest of the continent. The group

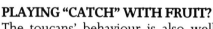
◀The Channel-billed toucan is widespread across northern South America.

▶**Types of toucan** An Emerald toucanet (*Aulacorhynchus prasinus*) **(1)** giving its call. A Black-billed mountain toucan (*Andigena nigrirostris*) **(2)** searches for fruit, a Chestnut-mandibled toucan (*Ramphastos swainsonii*) **(3)** swallows a berry, while a Toco toucan **(4)** stretches to pick food. A Guianan toucanet (*Selenidera culik*) **(5)** examines a possible nest hole. A Saffron toucanet (*Andigena bailloni*) **(6)**. A Collared aracari (*Pteroglossus torquatus*) **(7)**.

includes toucans themselves, which comprise 10 species in the genus *Ramphastos*. These large birds have mainly blackish plumage and are found in lowland rain forests.

The 11 species of aracaris are all smaller and more slender, and they also live in forested lowlands. The 12 species of the mainly green-coloured toucanets vary in size from small to large. Some toucanets live in the cooler Andean rain forests, at heights of about 3,000m, and rarely descend into the warm lowlands. The four species of little-known mountain toucans dwell even higher. They live in the Andes Mountains, from north-west Venezuela to Bolivia.

BERRY-PICKING BILL

All toucans are mainly fruit-eaters, picking food with the bill-tip and tossing it upwards and back into the mouth to be swallowed.

Although the bill looks heavy, it is in fact very light. It is made of a horny outer sheath covering a hollow "box", which is strengthened by slim, criss-crossing rods of bone. The toucan, being a large and weighty bird, has to perch on thicker branches. Yet its bill gives it a long reach, so that it can stretch out to pick berries and other fruits from the thin and delicate outer-most twigs of trees.

The Toco toucan has the largest bill of any toucan; it may be almost one-third of the bird's total length of about 66cm.

WEAPON OR "PERSONAL FLAG"?

Being able to reach out for food may explain the length of the bill, but why is it so thick and brightly coloured? Over the centuries naturalists have suggested many reasons. It may be a conspicuous weapon that frightens smaller birds, so that the toucan can raid their nests and steal their eggs and young. Or it might be a form of identity, a sort of "personal flag". Each individual has a slightly different size, colour and pattern of bill. This would allow each bird to recognize others in its group, others of its species (which is particularly important when look-ing for a mate) and also toucans of other species with which it may compete for food or living space.

TREE-TOP TOUCANS

Toucans spend most of their lives high in the tree-tops. They feed there, bathe there in pools of rainwater that collect in hollow branches, use their long bills to preen each other – and breed there, in holes in tree trunks.

A suitable nest hole has an entrance just large enough for the toucan to squeeze through, but its depth may vary from only a few centimetres to 2m. Most larger toucans use a natural cavity usually resulting from the decay of tree trunks. Some smaller species

◄A Toco toucan delicately holds two berries in its huge, saw-edged bill as its strong feet grip an old tree tunk.

may take over a hole made by a woodpecker, sometimes evicting the owners. The toucan might attempt to enlarge the hole, but its bill is not nearly so strong as the woodpecker's bill, and it usually has little success. A suitable nest hole may be used year after year.

WELL-HEELED BABIES
Toucan parents do not line their nest hole. The eggs are laid on a bed of wood chippings and regurgitated seeds. The male and female take it in

▼The toucan's great bill (this is Cuvier's toucan) is seldom used in battle, except when food-hunting.

turns to incubate the eggs, but they rarely remain at their task for more than an hour at a time. They often leave the eggs uncovered, and if they are disturbed by intruders, they fly away rather than stay on the nest and use their great bills as weapons. When the eggs hatch, the babies have padded, spike-covered heels that protect them from rubbing against the wood and seeds under their feet.

Newly-hatched baby toucans cannot see and have no feathers. They are fed by both parents and after about 6 to 7 weeks, their feathers grow and they learn to fly. In the aracaris, the parents, each night, lead their young back to the nest hole. Even out of the

breeding season, these toucans sleep in holes. In other species, the young roost among the foliage, with their parents and others in the group.

Young toucans have comparatively small, drab bills. As they grow, their bills grow bigger and take on the bright colours of their parents.

UNDER THREAT
Since toucans generally live in remote forests, many species have not yet been studied in detail in the wild. One species, the Yellow-browed toucanet from Peru, is now threatened, and some species are becoming rarer as their forest homes are cut down for timber and to make way for farmland.

AMERICAN BLACKBIRDS

On a midwinter's evening, in the southern USA, it looks as though a dark cloud has suddenly appeared and almost blotted out the Sun. But the black, swirling mass is not a cloud. A gigantic flock of American blackbirds, including Common grackles and cowbirds, is returning to its nightly roost, after a day feeding on winter crops in the surrounding fields.

American blackbirds are common and familiar over much of North and South America. The family includes grackles, blackbirds, the bobolink, oropendulas and cowbirds. Outside the breeding season, many species form enormous mixed flocks – some winter roosts in the southern USA have numbered 50 million birds!

Most species in the family are found in the tropics. In Columbia, for example, there are 27 species. These birds prefer mostly open places – prairie and farmland, scrub, scattered woodland and marshes. The female builds the nest, incubates the eggs and feeds the chicks; in some species the male helps with this last task.

TRANS-AMERICAN FLIGHT
Some American blackbirds migrate each year. A sign of spring is the arrival of the bobolink in grassy areas of central North America, having flown from its southern summer in Argentina. On its autumn return journey, it island-hops across 2,000km of open sea. Females look as they do all year, their buff-brown plumage speckled with darker brown and black. Males have a similar plumage out of the breeding season, but in spring they exchange it for a bright yellow patch on the back of the neck, white patches on the shoulders and rump, and a black body. This patterning gives them their local name of "skunkbird".

▲The Common grackle is sometimes a pest in ricefields and cornfields.

UNWANTED VISITORS
Cowbirds, like cuckoos, are brood parasites. They lay their eggs in the nests of other birds, which are the unsuspecting hosts. The hosts then raise the chicks. Some species of cowbirds choose host species with eggs that look similar to their own. Also, they throw out one of the host's eggs for each egg they lay.

▼Types of blackbird The bobolink (1), Red-winged blackbird (*Agelaius phoeniceus*) (2), Red-breasted blackbird (*Leistes militaris*) (3) and Rusty blackbird (*Euphagus carolinus*) (4).

AMERICAN BLACK-BIRDS Icteridae (*94 species*)

Habitat: grassland, marsh, scrub, patchy wood, forest.

Diet: seeds, fruit, small animals such as insects.

Breeding: 1 or 2 clutches yearly; eggs incubated for 12-15 days.

Size: length 15-53cm; weight 20-454g.

Plumage: males black with patches of yellow, orange or red; some females and grassland species are brownish.

Species mentioned in text:
Bobolink (*Dolichonyx oryzivorus*)
Bay-winged cowbird (*Molothrus badius*)
Common grackle (*Quiscalus quiscula*)
Screaming cowbird (*Molothrus rufoaxillaris*)
Yellow-headed blackbird (*Xanthocephalus xanthocephalus*)

Not all cowbirds do this. The Bay-winged cowbird takes over the nest of another bird, empties it, lays its eggs and rears its own chicks. This species may be visited by a close relative, the Screaming cowbird, which lays an egg and leaves. So one cowbird species raises the chicks of another!

About nine species of American blackbird are thought to be under threat, chiefly in South America and on Caribbean islands. Other species, especially in grain-growing areas of North America, are very common.

▲Like many American blackbirds, the Yellow-headed blackbirds gather in large flocks outside the breeding season.

◄American blackbirds find much of their food by "gaping". The bird pushes its closed bill into a hollow stem or other likely place, and then opens its bill to split the stem. This reveals small creatures such as insects and spiders, which the bird would not otherwise be able to see.

FINCHES

On a warm tropical evening in the Hawaiian Islands, a flock of apapanes flies over. Their dazzling orange plumage matches the rays of the setting Sun. They have spent the day probing flowers for nectar with their long, delicate beaks, and are now flying home to their roost.

FINCHES Fringillidae
(*153 species*)

![world map]

● ■◻ 𝕏

◢ Habitat: woods, forest, shrubland, parks, gardens.

▢ Diet: seeds, nuts and berries, some insects. Some Hawaiian finches suck nectar from flowers.

◎ Breeding: average 1 or 2 clutches per year, each 3-5 eggs; incubation 12-14 days.

Size: length 10-20cm; weight 10-100g.

Plumage: varied in colour, usually with striking wing or tail markings.

Species mentioned in text:
American goldfinch (*Carduelis tristis*)
Apapane (*Himatione sanguinea*)
Brambling (*Fringilla montifringilla*)
Bullfinch (*Pyrrhula pyrrhula*)
Crossbills (genus *Loxia*)
European goldfinch (*Carduelis carduelis*)
Greenfinch (*C. chloris*)
Linnet (*Acanthis cannabina*)
Nihoa finch (*Telespyza ultima*)

A problem with the name "finch" is that it is often given to any smallish or medium-sized bird with a stout, cone-shaped bill used for crushing seeds. Yet not all finches belong to the "true" finch family, Fringillidae, described here. For example, the small seed-eating and insect-eating birds of the Galapagos Islands are known as Galapagos finches, but they belong to the bunting family.

WHAT IS A FINCH?

The true finch family also includes the Hawaiian finches, which live on various islands of the Hawaii group, in the Pacific. Some of these Hawaiian finches are called honeycreepers but birds from other families are also called honeycreepers, such as (once more) certain buntings.

This confusion shows the importance of scientific (Latin) names for species and groups of animals. The scientific name for each species is the same throughout the world, and is unique for that species, so there can be no mix-up.

CROSS-OVER BILL

Some of the strangest bills in the bird world belong to the crossbills. The two parts of the bill cross over at the tip, like a pair of bent pliers. The bill is used to lever open the scales on the cones of various conifer trees, to reach the seeds underneath.

Like many finches, crossbills tend to breed whenever food is abundant. In larch forests, this is mainly in late summer or early autumn. In spruce forests, it is late autumn to winter, and in pine forests it is spring. In areas where various types of conifer grow, crossbills may breed for 10 months of the year – including mid-winter, when hardly any other birds are nesting. Near Moscow, USSR, crossbill nests were found in February, when the air temperature was −19°C! Yet inside the nest, as the female sat on her eggs, it was a snug 38°C.

▼ The chaffinch (this one is a male) is the commonest bird in many parts of Europe and is a familiar sight in woods, gardens and parks.

►▼Heads and bills of finches The hawfinch (*Coccothraustes coccothraustes*) **(1)**, which has a massive bill for cracking large seeds and nuts. The siskin (*C. spinus*) **(2)**, European goldfinch **(3)**, ou (*Psittirostra psittacea*) **(4)** and Two-barred crossbill (*Loxia leucoptera*) **(5)**. The apapane **(6)**, a nectar-eater from Hawaii, has a thin bill for probing into flowers. The Parrot crossbill (*Loxia pytopsittacus*) **(7)** tackles the hard cones of pine trees.

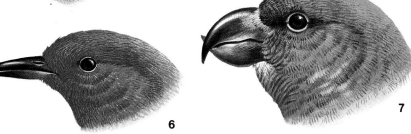

Other finches which breed as food (mainly seeds) becomes available include the greenfinch, linnet and bullfinch. They can nest and raise young from early spring to midsummer. The European goldfinch, which likes the seeds of thistles and similar plants, breeds later in summer. The American goldfinch, which depends even more on thistles, breeds even later in the year. The average start of its breeding season is the latest of all the birds in North America.

THE COMMONEST BIRDS...

The finch family includes such common and well-known species as the chaffinch, greenfinch and European goldfinch, each of which often comes into parks and gardens to feed. These colourful and active birds, with their chirpy, twittering songs, are favourites with birdwatchers, and they are also very familiar to many people who know little about birds.

The chaffinch, in particular, is one of the commonest birds in Europe. In some areas of wood and scrub, one bird in every four is a chaffinch. It is

▼Some finches are common visitors to feeders, and people have devised tests to see if they are "intelligent". After a few tries, this European goldfinch worked out how to lift the string with its bill, hold the loop with its feet, and do this several times in order to lift the food on to the twig.

thought that there are as many as 12 million of these birds in Britain.

Bramblings, too, are common over much of Northern Europe and Asia. They gather in huge flocks where food such as berries, seeds, and especially beechmast (beech "nuts") is plentiful. Some bramblings migrate to Britain in winter, where they join their finch cousins in mixed flocks, foraging for seeds and nuts in woods, hedgerows, parks and farmland.

...AND THE RAREST
At the other end of the scale, some of the Hawaiian finches are among the rarest birds in the world. Of the 28 species identified by scientists in recent times, 8 have died out completely and 16 more are probably threatened with extinction.

Like the Galapagos finches, it is thought that the Hawaiian finches evolved over thousands or millions of years from one original finch species. This "ancestral species" probably resembled the Nihoa finch of today. It crossed more than 3,000km of ocean to reach the Hawaiian Islands. Here it found a lot of different habitats, from coral reefs to lowland woods and mountain rain forests. Also, the islands were remote, and had formed relatively recently, so there were few other birds and animals to compete with the finch for food or nesting sites. In such conditions, evolution could happen rapidly.

Years ago, rabbits were brought to Laysan, one of the Hawaiian Islands. It was hoped they could be farmed for meat. Sadly they ate so much vegetation that by the 1920s they had turned the island almost into a desert. The Laysan honeycreeper, an island sub-species of the apapane, became extremely rare. After a great storm in 1923, which swept sand and dust over

▲ A crossbill male regurgitates a meal of seeds for its young. The nestlings have streaked plumage, while their parents have blotchy feathers.

▶ A Laysan finch perches, its short, tough bill and long tail feathers clearly visible.

the island non-stop for 3 days, this honeycreeper disappeared for ever.

Today, there are several threats to the survival of the Hawaiian finches. These include destruction of their habitats by people and their animals (chiefly cattle, goats and pigs), predators such as cats brought by people, and diseases brought by new animals and birds. These threats have greatly reduced the numbers of all the remaining Hawaiian finch species. It is to be hoped that conservation efforts now under way will protect most of the species still alive, saving these beautiful birds from extinction.

EAGLES

High above the Appalachian Mountains of eastern North America, a Golden eagle hangs almost motionless in a clear summer sky. Far below it sees an ideal hunting spot – a long ridge covered with open grassy vegetation. The eagle glides down, and flies fast and low along one side of the ridge. Suddenly it swoops up and over the crest. Fifty metres away, on the other side of the ridge, a hare is feeding, completely unaware of the danger. It has no chance. Even as the hare turns to run, the aerial hunter strikes, killing it outright with its talons.

The Golden eagle is one of the largest members of a group of 30 species of birds of prey called the booted eagles. These birds get their name from the fact that their legs are covered with feathers right down to the foot, instead of being bare and scaly like those of all the other eagles. They are also known as "true" eagles.

EAGLES Accipitridae (part of family) (*53 species*)

Habitat: all land habitats, also sea coasts, lakes.

Diet: mammals, birds, fish and reptiles; also carrion.

Breeding: most species 1 or 2 eggs, incubated for 32-60 days.

Size: length 40-120cm; weight 0.5-6.5kg.

Plumage: plain grey, brown, or striking combinations of dark brown and white. Forest species often with black and white bars on wings.

Species mentioned in text:
African fish eagle (*Haliaeetus vocifer*)
Bald eagle (*Haliaeetus leucocephalus*)
Bateleur (*Terathopius ecaudatus*)
Booted eagle (*Hieraaetus pennatus*)
Golden eagle (*Aquila chrysaetos*)
Little eagle (*Hieraaetus morphnoides*)
Martial eagle (*Polemaetus bellicosus*)
Vulturine fish eagle (*Gypohierax angolensis*)
White-bellied fish eagle (*Haliaeetus leucogaster*)

The booted eagles are a varied group indeed. The smallest is probably the Little eagle of Australasia, which weighs around 500g. Unlike many of its open-country relatives, this tiny hunter inhabits forests and well-wooded regions. It hunts by dropping on to its prey either from flight about 10m above the ground, or from a perch in a leafy tree. Because of its small size it concentrates mainly on young rabbits, ground-dwelling birds and occasionally lizards.

MAMMAL-KILLER

At the other end of the scale is the magnificent Martial eagle of Africa, which can have a wingspan of well over 2m and weigh up to 6.5kg. It lives in the savannah and thornbush country south of the Sahara Desert, and is even found in semi-desert regions. This eagle spends a great deal of its time on the wing, soaring for hours at a time on the currents of hot air that rise over the Sun-baked hills and plains. Often the bird will fly so high that it appears as little more than a speck from the ground.

Because food is widely scattered over the huge African grasslands, a

◄A European Booted eagle with young. This small eagle, weighing about 600g, inhabits wooded mountains and ravines.

pair of Martial eagles may require a hunting territory of up to 130sq km. The birds usually hunt in one area for a few days and then move on to a new location. In some regions Martial eagles prey mainly on large birds such as guineafowl and bustards. In other regions they take mainly mammals, for example hyraxes. However, these powerful birds will also take prey as big as monkeys and goats.

The Martial eagle may occasionally hunt from a perch, but its main method is to spot a target from high in the sky and then attack in a long fast slanting dive that takes the victim completely by surprise.

WRONGLY ACCUSED?

The most widespread and numerous of the world's large eagles is the Golden eagle. It inhabits mountain country right across Europe, Asia and North Africa, and is the only booted eagle found in North America.

In some parts of Europe and North America the Golden eagle has been persecuted by people, mainly because

▲An adult Golden eagle in Finland. Here, as in 13 other European countries, the bird is protected by law.

▼The female Little eagle incubates her one or two eggs by herself, but her mate usually brings food to her on the nest.

of an undeserved reputation for killing lambs. Lamb carcasses are occasionally found in eagle nests, but although some may be the result of eagle kills, most of the lambs have probably been found already dead. Golden eagles do take some carrion as well as live prey. Their main diet, though, is made up of rabbits and hares, and in North America ground squirrels are often taken. In places where mammals are hard to find, game birds such as grouse and ptarmigan are the main source of food. They are usually caught on the ground, but the Golden eagle can also catch a grouse in flight.

Golden eagle pairs usually have two or three nests on their territory. The nests are called eyries, and are huge affairs made of sticks, placed on rocky ledges high on mountain cliffs. The female usually hatches two chicks, but the first one to hatch often kills the other within the first 2 weeks.

FISH- AND FRUIT-EATERS
Among the most spectacular large eagles are the fishing eagles (11 species) from the Old World and North America. As their name suggests, these birds inhabit coastal regions and the shores of lakes, where they feed on fish, waterbirds and carrion. The only North American species is the Bald eagle – America's national bird. This makes the biggest nest of any eagle. One nest, known to be 36 years old, was 2.6m across and 4m high.

Unlike the osprey, which plunges into the water to catch its prey, the fishing eagles normally snatch their prey close to the surface in a graceful low-level swoop. The one exception in the group is the Vulturine fish eagle or Palm-nut vulture of Africa. The bird does catch fish, but its main food is the fruit of the oil palm tree, and it is never found far from these trees.

SNAKE- AND SERPENT-KILLERS
The snake eagles are a specialized group of 12 species of hunters found in southern Europe, Africa, central and South-east Asia. They have large, owl-like heads, huge yellow eyes, and short toes for grasping their thin-bodied prey. They hunt mainly from perches and drop swiftly on to snakes, frogs and lizards on the ground.

This group also has its odd-bird-out. The magnificent bateleur has black, white and chestnut plumage and such a short tail that it appears in flight like an enormous flying wing. It hunts by gliding across the African plains at speeds of up to 80kph in search of small mammals, birds, carrion and snakes.

►Until recently the southern race of the American Bald eagle was an endangered species. Now its future is safe, due to strict conservation laws.

▲▶Talons outstretched, a White-bellied sea eagle closes in on its target (top). Moments after the strike (centre) its legs are dragged backwards by the weight of the fish, but even a one-footed grip (bottom) is enough to secure the catch.

◀In their spectacular courtship display a pair of African fish eagles grasp each other's talons as they tumble downward through the air like falling leaves.

HAWKS AND BUZZARDS

HAWKS AND BUZZARDS Accipitridae
(part of family) (150 species)

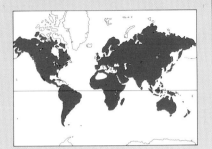

● ◪ ⚹

◪ Habitat: all land habitats.

■ Diet: mammals, birds, snakes, frogs, insects.

◎ Breeding: small species lay 5-7 eggs, large species 1 or 2; incubation period 32 and 120 days respectively.

Size: most species: length 30-70cm, weight 0.5-4kg; largest (Harpy eagle): length 100cm, weight 6kg.

Plumage: very variable, but most species grey or brown, darker above than below.

Species mentioned in text:
Augur buzzard (*Buteo rufofuscus*)
Bat hawk (*Machieramphus alcinus*)
Black kite (*Milvus migrans*)
Common buzzard (*Buteo buteo*)
Cooper's hawk (*Accipiter cooperii*)
Crane hawk (*Geranospiza caerulescens*)
Everglade kite (*Rostrhamus sociabilis*)
Harpy eagle (*Harpia harpyia*)
Hen harrier or Marsh hawk (*Circus cyaneus*)
Northern goshawk (*Accipiter gentilis*)
Philippine monkey-eating eagle (*Pithecophaga jefferyi*)
Red-shouldered hawk (*Buteo lineatus*)
Red-tailed hawk (*B. jamaicensis*)
Sharp-shinned hawk (*Accipiter striatus*)

As darkness falls over a small island in South-east Asia, millions of bats stream out of caves hidden in the depths of the rain forest. Most of them will spend the night feeding, but for some there is danger. Lying in ambush is a Bat hawk, one of Asia's most specialized hawks. Picking its target the hunter dashes in. One strike is enough. The hawk swerves away, transferring its catch from its claws to its bill as it heads back to its nest.

The Bat hawk is found in the rain forests of Malaysia, Sumatra, Borneo and New Guinea, and also in tropical Africa. It is the only known specialist bat-hunter among the birds of prey, and it is also unusual in carrying its catch in its bill. That is something much more typical of owls than of hawks.

UNUSUAL DIETS
The Bat hawk belongs to the group of 31 species of bird called the kites and honey buzzards. Among them are a great many unusual and specialized birds. The Everglade kite, for example, lives in the swamp forests and marshlands of the Florida Everglades, and its main food consists of the large freshwater snails that abound in that habitat. The bird's bill is finely hooked and pointed – the perfect tool for extracting the snails from their shells.

Like all specialists, though, the Everglade kite is at risk. Vast areas of the Florida wetlands have been drained for housing and other types of development. As the swamps are destroyed the snails too disappear, and along with them go the birds that depend on them for food.

The honey buzzards of Europe, Africa and Asia have found another rich source of food – the ground nests and tree nests of various kinds of bee and wasp. The birds tear open the insects' nests with their claws and feed on the honey and larvae inside. However, the adult insects pack a powerful sting and have to be "disarmed" before they can be eaten. The birds do this by snipping off the back end of each insect's body before it is swallowed. Honey buzzards also prey on worms, frogs, small mammals and birds, and some species eat berries.

A TOWN DWELLER

The Black kite of Europe, Africa and Asia is a complete contrast to its specialized relatives. It is a true all-rounder, preying on insects, fish and worms, but often making its living mainly as a scavenger. In the warmer parts of its range, especially across southern Asia, thousands of Black kites inhabit towns and cities. They are often seen on rubbish tips and in the streets. The birds perch on roofs, telegraph poles and dockside cranes then swoop down to pounce on rats and mice or to snatch food from market stalls. There are even cases of them snatching food from astonished shoppers' hands!

THE CUNNING HARRIERS

It is tempting to imagine that all birds of prey catch their food by means of a fast diving attack or a chase. But that is not so. The 10 species of harrier, for example, are birds of open grasslands

▼ **Medium-sized birds of prey** A Grey chanting goshawk (*Melierax poliopterus*) (1) calls from the top of a termite mound. A Black-mantled sparrowhawk (*Accipiter melanochlamys*) (2) and Red kite (*Milvus milvus*) (3) with prey. A Pied harrier (*Circus melanoleucus*) (4) hunting.

and marshes which specialize in slow, low-level flight as their main hunting technique.

Harriers are medium-sized hawks with slim bodies and with long wings and tails that provide the lift and control necessary for low-speed flight. They often fly at speeds as low as 30kph, and if a harrier is flying into a light head-wind it may be moving over the ground at only 15kph. (A falcon can fly at over 160kph.) With brief periods of hovering, this gives the bird plenty of time to search the ground below for prey. The harriers have rather owl-like faces, and like the owls they rely on accurate hearing to pin-point their prey. They can locate their quarry even when it is hidden from sight among dense vegetation.

The Hen harrier, known as the Marsh hawk in North America, is a typical member of the group. It inhabits marshlands and heathlands, and sometimes cornfields too. From the air it silently patrols an area with its wings raised to form an instantly recognizable shallow V-shape. Its diet consists of frogs, mice, large insects, snakes and small birds.

Unlike most other birds of prey the harriers nest on the ground, building

▲ In a North American forest, a young Northern goshawk picks at a Grey squirrel carcass with its hooked beak.

3

4

large mounds of reeds and rushes, well hidden from view. The female does most of the building, but the male helps by collecting nest material. He delivers the material in a most unusual way. Instead of landing at the nest site, he swoops low overhead and drops the material close by, for the female to retrieve. Later, when the eggs have hatched, the male uses the same method to deliver food to the nest for the female and young.

DOUBLE-JOINTED

The two species of harrier-hawk of Africa and the Crane hawk of Central and South America form a group of medium-sized woodland hawks with a unique adapatation for catching their prey. Their legs can bend either way at the middle (tarsal) joint, and this enables the birds to reach into the most awkward crevices in rocks or tree bark to pull out the lizards, frogs, birds' eggs and nestlings that are their main prey. These hawks get into the most unusual positions when searching for food, and will often hang upside down to reach inside a particularly inaccessible tree-hole. At other times they hunt by flying back and forth, scanning the ground below for food, much as the true harriers do.

A FAMILY OF HUNTERS

The family Accipitridae is by far the biggest of the five bird of prey families, and it includes a huge variety of different birds among its 217 species. The eagles (see pages 96-99) and the kites, harrier-hawks and harriers we have met so far are all fairly small groups. Together they make up just over half of the total number of species. The two biggest groups are the sparrowhawks and goshawks, and the buzzards and harpies, each of which contains 53 species.

WOODLAND PREDATORS

The sparrowhawks and goshawks are small- to medium-sized birds found in

▲ A sparrowhawk broods her young in the rain. Like many northern birds of prey, the sparrowhawk is very slowly recovering from the damage to wildlife inflicted by pesticides.

forest, woodland and scrub habitats all over the world. Their wings are short and rounded and their tails are long. These adaptations enable the birds to dash through dense woody vegetation at a breakneck pace, using agility, speed and surprise to run down their prey.

Cooper's hawk is typical of the whole group. It inhabits woodlands of North America from Canada south to Mexico, often roosting perched on one leg in a coniferous tree, but nearly always choosing deciduous woods at nesting time. Its hunting methods are a mixture of skill, speed and trickery. Often the hawk will fly to a partly concealed perch and wait there until a bird or squirrel wanders out into the open, unaware of danger. Then it

dashes out, using its long legs to reach out and snatch the victim on the ground or as it tries to flee.

SWOOPING AND POUNCING

As in most species of sparrowhawk, the female Cooper's hawk is much larger than the male, and while male birds prey on starlings, blackbirds and flickers, the females will take prey as big as grouse.

Both males and females are skilled at using natural cover to get close to their prey. Even a group of birds feeding on the ground in a clearing can be taken by surprise. The hawk swoops in low, using every tree stump, bush and dip in the ground to conceal its approach.

Birds are sometimes deliberately flushed out of cover. The hawk will fly straight towards a bush, then dodge sideways at the last minute, dashing round to the far side to pounce on any birds frightened into coming into the open.

RETURN JOURNEYS

As the abundance of food begins to wane in the autumn, the most northerly Cooper's hawks migrate southwards. Some travel as far as Colombia. As they head south they often join with other hawks – Sharp-shinned, Red-tailed and other unrelated species. The southward mass migration of birds of prey down the "flyway" of the Appalachian Mountains is one of the greatest birdwatching sights in the USA.

The birds return in February and March, usually to the same patch of woodland, although a new nest is made each year. Males and females perform courtship display flights, and the nest-building and mating is accompanied by much displaying and the singing of duets.

BUZZARDS AND HAWKS

The buzzards and their relatives are a very varied group, both in size and in habitat. They range from tiny woodland hawks to the world's biggest, most powerful, and probably rarest birds of prey.

The Common buzzard breeds in woodland, but often hunts over open moorland, plains and mountains. It is found right across Europe and Asia, as far east as Siberia and Japan, but like many birds of prey the buzzard is a migrant. Each year the northern populations move from their summer breeding areas to winter quarters in Africa, India and South-east Asia.

The buzzard is much less striking in colour than its hawk relatives, and spends a lot of time either perched on a fence-post or tree, or slowly soaring back and forth along a rocky hillside as it searches for rodents and small rabbits.

▶Proudly perched on a rocky ledge, a Common buzzard, the most common European bird of prey, surveys its habitat.

In North America, the buzzard's relatives include the handsome Red-shouldered hawk and the Red-tailed hawk. The Red-shouldered hawk inhabits damp lowland forests and marshland in the eastern half of the country. It feeds mainly on mice, frogs and small snakes. The Red-tailed hawk prefers upland regions. Its diet consists primarily of small mammals.

Like several other American species of hawk, these birds have suffered in recent years from the harmful effects of pesticides widely used on agricultural land.

◄The spiky head plume of the Philippine monkey-eating eagle gives the bird an oddly human face.

KINGS OF THE FOREST

Pride of place in the entire bird of prey family must go to the Harpy eagle. This formidable aerial hunter inhabits the lowland tropical forests of South America from southern Mexico to northern Argentina. Despite its great size it is an agile hunter. When hunting it threads its way through the canopy of the Amazon jungle at up to 70kph, pursuing the monkeys that make up a large part of its diet. The Harpy eagle also preys on sloths, opossums and tree porcupines. It will also take snakes and large birds when the opportunity comes along.

Details of the Harpy eagle's breeding behaviour are not well known, but the Harpy's nest is a huge structure of sticks, lined with green leaves. This is

▲Tail fanned like the flaps of an airplane, an Augur buzzard swoops low. This aerial hunter is the most common buzzard of East and southern Africa.

placed in a tree fork 40 to 45m above the ground.

In the rain forests of the Philippines lives another magnificent predator, the Philippine monkey-eating eagle. In every way it is the Asian counterpart of its South American relative – huge, magnificent and, sadly, now listed as an endangered species. Nobody knows how many Harpies survive in Amazonia. In the Philippines there are probably no more than 200 monkey-eating eagles left. In the past, hunting for zoo specimens and trophies was the main threat. Today it is the destruction of the birds' native forests.

FALCONS

A Peregrine falcon shows off its speed and agility in flight as it homes in on a wood-pigeon. Its hunting dive or "stoop" is a breath-taking power dive that reaches speeds of over 200kph.

▲ **Three of the world's falcons** The Barred forest falcon (*Micrastur ruficollis*) (**1**) of tropical South America, an Aplomado falcon (*Falco femoralis*) (**2**) of Mexico and South America, and a Common kestrel (**3**) of Eurasia.

FALCONS Falconidae (*60 species*)

● ◪ ⚐

■ Habitat: very varied, from sea coasts to grassland, woodland, tropical forest and deserts.

■ Diet: mammals, birds, reptiles, insects; also carrion.

○ Breeding: caracaras 2 or 3 eggs, laid in a nest. True falcons up to 9 eggs, (usually 4 or 5), laid on bare rock, in a rough scrape, or in an abandoned nest. Incubation period up to 30 days.

Size: smallest (Asian falconets): length 15cm, weight 40g; largest (caracaras): length 35-60cm, weight 280-1,600g.

Plumage: varied; usually brown or grey, and dark above, pale below. Many species with strong colours and bold markings.

Species mentioned in text:
American kestrel (*Falco sparverius*)
Common kestrel (*F. tinnunculus*)
Gyrfalcon (*F. rusticolus*)
Lanner falcon (*F. biarmicus*)
Mauritius kestrel (*F. punctatus*)
Peregrine falcon (*F. peregrinus*)
Red-throated caracara (*Daptrius americanus*)

The Peregrine falcon is the most widespread and successful of all the birds of prey. It is found in every continent except Antarctica, and on many of the world's island groups too. It is one of the biggest members of the falcon family, measuring up to 48cm long. With its grey-blue back, beautifully banded pale buff undersides, yellow eye-rings and black "moustache", it is also one of the most handsome.

SPEED AND PRECISION

The superb hunting skills of the Peregrine falcon have made it the favourite bird of falconers in many countries. The birds are caught in flight using nets and then trained. They can be used to hunt gamebirds the size of bustards. The Peregrine's hunting method is unique. Unlike the hawks, which usually attack in fast level flight and strike with their front toes, the Peregrine plummets down on to its prey in a dive that has been estimated at speeds ranging from 170kph to a staggering 400kph.

Just before reaching its target the Peregrine slows and levels out, striking the lethal blow with the needle-sharp talons of its rear "toes". The victim is often allowed to tumble to the ground, but the attacker closely follows it. The Peregrine's main prey varies according to where it lives, but its favourite quarry includes pigeons, grouse and small sea-birds. Young Peregrines take smaller prey such as finches.

The Peregrine falcon is found in many different habitats. It seems to prefer rocky crags, and is most common on rocky sea coasts. But it is a versatile bird, and is also found in moorland, open grassland, scrub and desert areas, and even in forests.

A YEAR IN THE LIFE

There are 18 separate races of Peregrine falcon, living in regions as varied as Alaskan river valleys and the tropical grasslands of Africa. The tropical species are year-round residents, but most northern birds migrate in winter to areas with better food supplies. European birds migrate to southern Africa, and North American birds fly far into South America.

▼ A Common kestrel returns to its young with a large rodent. Like most falcons it does not build a proper nest.

At the start of the breeding season the male Peregrine chooses a good breeding ledge on a cliff. When he sees a female he flies out, calling to her, then returns to the ledge. The performance is repeated until a female accepts the male's invitation. After that the two birds swoop and dive and chase each other in a spectacular series of display flights. The birds make no nest and the eggs are

simply laid on the bare rock. The male usually shares the task of incubating the eggs, and also brings food to the nest for himself and the female.

THE PESTICIDE THREAT
During the 1960s the Peregrine populations of North America and Europe began to fall alarmingly. Scientists then discovered that the shells of the birds' eggs were so thin and fragile

▼ ◀A Peregrine falcon with young at a typical mountain nest-site. The Peregrine was one of 20 species of falcon badly affected by DDT in the 1960s. The photograph on the left shows the weakening effect the chemical had on the shells of the bird's eggs.

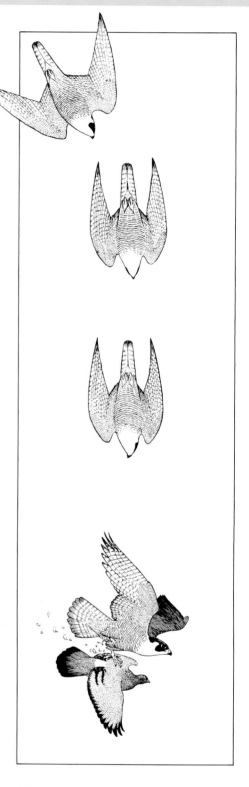

▲Folding back its wings to reduce air resistance, a Peregrine falcon plunges in a near-vertical dive. If it misses its quarry, or is simply "playing", it swoops up again and repeats the attack.

that they were breaking when the incubating birds sat on them. The cause was DDT, a common farm pesticide. The chemical was building up in the bodies of seed- and insect-eating birds, and it passed on to the falcons when they ate these birds.

Many countries have now banned the use of DDT, and in these the Peregrine is making a recovery. (In the developing countries of the tropics and subtropics especially, the use of DDT is on the increase.) It was a sharp lesson in the dangers of using chemicals that remain in the environment long after their job has been done.

THE SMALLER FALCONS

The Peregrine, and the magnificent grey and white gyrfalcon of the Arctic wastelands, are two of the bigger falcons. But there are many smaller species too. One of the most familiar in Europe is the kestrel. This is often seen hovering over the verges of motorways.

The kestrel holds its position in the air with rapid beats of its long pointed wings and with constant adjustments to the angle of its unusually long fan-shaped tail. It is the only falcon to hunt in this way, scanning the ground below for the mice, frogs and small

▲ The Lanner falcon of Africa and the Mediterranean often attacks its prey head-on, instead of approaching from above or behind as most falcons do.

birds like larks, pipits and buntings that make up its diet.

The European kestrel is mainly a bird of grasslands, heaths and open farmland. The American kestrel inhabits much drier country and is even found in the desolate desert around Lima in Peru. There the bird preys on lizards, scorpions and large insects. In the gentler climate of North America it feeds mainly on grasshoppers and other large insects in summer and on

mice and small birds like sparrows during the winter months.

LIZARD- AND MOTH-EATERS

The Mauritius kestrel is now one of the rarest birds in the world. It is a forest-dwelling species, with short rounded wings that are perfectly adapted for twisting and turning among tree trunks and branches. The bird hunts for tree-lizards, beetles and flying insects. Sadly, most of the forest has been cut down for its valuable timber, and for farmland. In 1985 there were only 16 breeding pairs left in the wild. Fortunately this kestrel

breeds well in captivity, and several captive-bred birds have already been reintroduced to the few remaining patches of forest. The species may just survive, but only with total protection for the bird and its habitat – and a good deal of luck.

Smaller still are the pygmy falcons and falconets. One species inhabits the desert areas and grasslands of northern Argentina. There are two pygmy species, one inhabiting woodlands in southern Asia, the other living in the desert and thornbush country of Africa. But smallest of all – barely 15cm from bill to tail tip – are the falconets of tropical Asia. These sparrow-sized hunters are boldly coloured, with black above and white or chestnut-brown below. Their main prey are the large forest dragonflies and moths, usually caught on the wing in a darting attack from a perch.

SOUTH AMERICAN COUSINS

The caracaras are large (buzzard-sized) birds with long legs and broad wings. At first glance it is hard to think of them as falcons. Unlike their dashing relatives they are rather slow, sluggish birds that spend much of their time either perched in the trees or walking about on the ground.

The caracaras are found only in South America, where they inhabit open country, woodland, forest and grassland. They feed mainly on large insects, but they are also carrion-eaters and are often seen in the company of New World vultures, squabbling over the remains of an animal carcass.

The Red-throated caracara is rather vulture-like in appearance. Its plumage is glossy black, shot with green and blue. Its cheeks and throat are bright red and bare of feathers, and it has a habit of perching on a branch screaming and cackling loudly. Its feeding habits are just as strange as it specializes in tearing open wasps' nests to feed on the larvae.

VULTURES

In 1987, in the foothills of the Sierra Nevada, California, a group of scientists watched a huge black-and-white vulture circling slowly in the sky. It was a sad day. Their job was to catch the last California condor in the wild. Years of shooting, trapping and poisoning had almost wiped out this magnificent species, and the only hope for its survival was to take the remaining birds into the safety of California's zoos.

All the 27 surviving California condors are now in captivity. Their close relative the Andean condor is more fortunate. It is still widespread in the mountains of western South America.

These two species, and five others, make up the group called the New World vultures. The group ranges from southern Canada to the tip of South America. They are not closely

VULTURES Cathartidae (7 species), Accipitridae (14 species)

● ◨ ☠

■ **Habitat:** grassland, desert, mountain and other open areas; some species in forest.

■ **Diet:** mainly carrion; small mammals, birds' eggs and fruit. Some species frequent rubbish dumps.

◎ **Breeding:** condors: 1 egg every 2 years; most species 1-3 eggs, laid on ground or rock ledge;

incubated for up to 50 days and nestling period up to 120 days depending on species. Only Old World vultures build nests.

Size: length 60-140cm; weight 0.9-14kg. Wingspan up to 3m.

Plumage: mainly dark brown to black, often with paler patches on the underside of the wings; some species partly white.

Species mentioned in text:
Andean condor (*Vultur gryphus*)
Bearded vulture or lammergeier (*Gypaetus barbatus*)
California condor (*Vultur californianus*)
Egyptian vulture (*Neophron percnopterus*)
European black vulture (*Aegypius monarchus*)
Griffon vulture (*Gyps fulvus*)
King vulture (*Sarcoramphus papa*)
Rüppell's griffon (*Gyps rueppelli*)
Secretary bird (*Sagittarius serpentarius*)

▲The Bearded vulture feeds on the marrow of animal bones, which it breaks open by dropping them on to rocks from a great height. This species is sometimes called the lammergeier.

▲The King vulture inhabits dense tropical rain forests in Central and South America. It finds food in the forest by following other scavenging animals to it.

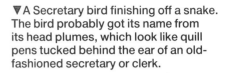

▼A Secretary bird finishing off a snake. The bird probably got its name from its head plumes, which look like quill pens tucked behind the ear of an old-fashioned secretary or clerk.

related to the vultures of Africa and Asia, but they look similar, with bald heads and necks, massive bills, and long broad wings. They also have a similar life-style, soaring high on currents of air, scanning the ground with sharp eyes as they search for carrion (dead animals), which is their main food.

The condors nest on cliff ledges and in caves high in the mountains. Their smaller relatives nest on the ground among the grassland and scrub vegetation of the foothills.

THE OLD WORLD VULTURES

The vultures of Asia and Africa are also mainly scavengers, feeding on the carcasses of animals that have died or been killed by predators. They are usually most active during the hottest part of the day, when they can "ride" the warm air currents (thermals) that rise over desert lands, or the swirling winds in mountain regions. When a vulture spots a carcass, it begins to

◄Rüppell's griffons in Kenyan grassland feeding on a wildebeest carcass. In half an hour nothing will remain but bones. The birds normally eat only very fresh meat.

circle lower. Its neighbours notice this, and fly towards the scene. Within minutes, vultures are converging from all directions.

These vultures vary in their social behaviour. Some, like the Griffon vulture of Europe and Asia, often breed in colonies of several hundred pairs, with nests only a few metres apart. The birds may fly up to 150km from a colony in search of food. Others, like the European black vulture, live in pairs, nesting in trees or on cliffs in widely separated territories. They feed much closer to home, and often take live prey as well as carrion.

The Egyptian vulture is a relatively small bird with mainly white plumage, found in desert and farmland in North Africa and the Middle East. It is not big enough to compete with larger vultures over carcasses so instead it uses speed and agility to dash in and snatch a morsel when it can. It

is also known to smash open ostrich eggs by throwing stones at them.

SNAKE-KILLER

The Secretary bird is so unusual that scientists have placed it in a family all of its own. With its long legs and long tail it looks rather like a heron or stork when it is flying. But it is a true bird of prey, with a very unusual life-style.

Secretary birds are found only on the grasslands of Africa, where they stride through the long grass in search of their favourite prey – snakes. They also eat locusts and grasshoppers, small mammals and birds' eggs, but snake-killing is their speciality. The reptile is often killed by a single kick to the head, but sometimes a long fight takes place, with the Secretary bird battering the snake with its wings as it tries to bite. A stunned snake may be carried into the air and dropped on to the ground to finally kill it.

OWLS

Hunting across open farmland on a moonlit night, the Barn owl looks like a ghostly giant moth. Its softly feathered wings make no sound as it scans the ground listening for the slightest rustling of a mouse in the grass. When the owl makes its attack, it is a silent swooping glide. At the last moment the owl swings its talons forwards to kill its prey.

OWLS Tytonidae (*10 species*), Strigidae (*123 species*)

○ ◧ ⚘

■ Habitat: woodland, forest, grassland, desert, farmland.

■ Diet: small rodents, birds, lizards, insects, frogs, fish.

◎ Breeding: 1-14 eggs depending on food supply (usually 2-6). Eggs hatch after 15-35 days according to species. Nestling period up to 56 days.

Size: typical owls: length 12-72cm, weight 40g-4,000g; barn owls: length 23-53cm, weight 180g-1,300g. Females usually bigger than males.

Plumage: mainly mottled brown or grey. One species white; several black and white.

Species mentioned in text:
Barn owl (*Tyto alba*)
Burrowing owl (*Athene cunicularia*)
Eagle owl (*Bubo bubo*)
Elf owl (*Micrathene whitneyi*)
Little owl (*Athene noctua*)

The Barn owl is the most widespread of the world's owls. It is found on every continent except Antarctica, and many small islands have their own local race of the bird, found there and nowhere else.

In many ways the Barn owl is representative of all owls. It has a short rounded body and a large head, with big forward-pointing eyes located on the front of its face. Its body and wings are covered with soft feathers that make barely a sound as the bird flies.

The bird usually sets out to hunt as night falls, and it flies low along hedgerows, through woodland and over fields. Occasionally it perches for a while, listening intently for the tiny high-pitched noises of mice, voles, shrews and other small mammals scurrying about in the undergrowth. Its ears are its main sensors. The ear openings are hidden beneath the soft plumage on the sides of the owl's head, and they are unusually large for a bird. At the slightest sound, the owl swivels its head from side to side, "homing in" on the source of the noise. When the sound is equally loud in both ears, the owl knows that it is facing directly towards the source. In this way the bird can target its prey with pin-point accuracy.

Unlike most other birds of prey, the owl carries off its prey in its beak, rarely in its claws. Large prey are torn into pieces to eat, but small animals are swallowed whole, head first. The sorting of edible flesh from the hair, teeth, feathers and bones occurs within the owl's stomach. Some time after feeding, the owl coughs up a dry rounded pellet containing all the undigested bits of prey. These pellets are often found littering the ground beneath an owl's favourite feeding perch or nest site.

FAMILY LIFE
Barn owls breed in the spring, and the number of young they raise in a year depends mainly on food supply. The 2 to 6 eggs are always laid one at a time, spread over several days. They hatch

▶ The heart-shaped face, black eyes and unusually long bill are characteristic of the Barn owl. Most typical owls have yellow or orange eyes.

▼ Burrowing owls live on the grassland plains of America. They nest in the abandoned burrows of rabbits.

in the same order, and the first chicks to be born have a big advantage because the oldest and strongest chicks always get the biggest share of the food. If food is scarce, only the first few chicks may survive. If food is plentiful, all will survive and the parents may even produce a second family later in the year. Breeding owls do not build a proper nest. The females simply lay their eggs on a bed of dirt and old feathers in a hollow tree, a small cave in a rock cliff, or the corner of a barn roof.

PYGMIES AND GIANTS

The Barn owl and its relatives form a rather small family. Most of the world's 133 owl species belong to a much larger family known as the typical owls. They too are spread all over the world, and they include the biggest, the smallest and the most specialized owls.

Smallest of all are the 12 pygmy owls of Europe, Asia, Africa and the Americas. They include the Elf owl of North

America, which stands only 14cm tall. It lives in abandoned woodpecker holes in the giant "organ pipe" cacti of the south-western United States and Mexico. It feeds mainly on insects, caught in the air and on the ground, but will also take desert scorpions and spiders.

Not very much bigger, at 22cm tall, is the well-named Little owl. This lives in wooded country, farmland, grassland and semi-desert areas all across Europe from Spain to Russia and in parts of North Africa. It hunts mainly at dusk, but is also often seen in daytime, perched on a fence-post or tree, or flying along with its distinctive bobbing flight. It will take mice and small birds, but nearly half its food consists of insects – especially beetles – which it often catches in a curious bounding run across open ground.

At the other end of the scale are giants like the Eagle owl – a powerful night-time hunter standing 70cm tall. This preys on mammals as large as Roe deer fawns and on birds as big as buzzards. Like most big predators the Eagle owl requires a large territory during the breeding season, and so neighbouring pairs of birds usually nest at least 5km apart. The male and female birds of breeding pairs usually hunt separately. While away from the nest, however, they keep in touch with loud hooting calls that can be heard up to 4km away.

ISLAND RARITIES

Because most owls prey on rats, mice, large insects and other pests, they are popular with people everywhere. They are seldom persecuted, yet the world check-list of endangered birds, published in 1988, lists 21 species of owl as being threatened with extinction. Many of these are island dwellers, and nearly all live in tropical forest of some kind. As the forests are cut down for their valuable timber and to make farmland, the native birds are left with nowhere to go.

►**Typical owls and barn owls.** The Elf owl **(1)** in typical roosting position. A Barking owl (*Ninox connivens*) **(2)** from Australia, with nestlings in a tree hole. A White-faced Scops owl (*Otus leucotis*) **(3)** listening for prey. Tengmalm's owl (*Aegolius funereus*) **(4)** catching a vole. The Common bay owl (*Phodilus badius*) **(5)** of South-east Asia. The Spectacled owl (*Pulsatrix perspicillata*) **(6)** of Central and South America. The Malaysian Eagle owl (*Bubo sumatranus*) **(7)**. A Spotted wood owl (*Strix seloputo*) **(8)** of South-east Asia being mobbed by smaller birds. Pel's fishing owl (*Scotopelia peli*) **(9)** from Africa – one of the seven large fish-catching specialists found in Africa and Asia.

2

3

4

8

9

WOODPECKERS

In the mixed woodlands of the eastern USA, a small black-and-white bird with a red forehead and throat is flitting busily from tree to tree. It drills neat rows of small holes in the bark of each one. The bird is a sapsucker, one of North America's highly specialized woodpeckers. Soon it will return to feed on the sugar-rich sap oozing from the holes, and on the insects that will have gathered there.

The sapsuckers are just one small group in a large and successful family of birds. Woodpecker species are found in most parts of the world. The majority of the birds live in woodlands and forests of various kinds, but some are also found in open grasslands and even in the hottest deserts. A North American species, for example, makes its home in holes in the giant "organ-pipe" cacti that dot the desert landscape of the south-western states.

ENGINEERING MARVELS
Woodpeckers are small- to medium-sized birds with powerful stocky

bodies. They have bills designed for hacking and chiselling into dead or decaying wood so they can get at the grubs inside. The design of the neck and skull is a marvel of natural engineering. Somehow it protects the woodpecker's brain from damage despite the jolting and jarring caused by the bird's feeding method. In the case of the Black woodpecker, this can

WOODPECKERS Picidae
(*200 species*)

Habitat: tropical, deciduous and coniferous forest; also orchards, parkland, grassland and desert.

Diet: insects, spiders, berries, seeds and tree sap.

Breeding: true woodpeckers: 3-11 eggs, incubated 9-20 days, nestling period 18-35 days. Wrynecks: 5-14 eggs, incubated 12-13 days. Piculets: 2-4 eggs, incubated 11-14 days.

Size: smallest (Scaled piculet): length 8cm, weight 8g; largest (Imperial woodpecker): length 55cm, weight 560g.

Plumage: main colours black and white, brown and green, to match habitat. Often with red patches on head.

Species mentioned in text:
Acorn woodpecker (*Melanerpes formicivorus*)
Black woodpecker (*Dryocopus martius*)
European green woodpecker (*Picus viridis*)
Imperial woodpecker (*Campephilus imperialis*)
Sapsuckers (genus *Sphyrapicus*)
Scaled piculet (*Picumnus squamulatus*)
Three-toed woodpecker (*Picoides tridactylus*)

▼ ► A group of woodpeckers Three-toed woodpecker (1). Common flicker (*Colaptes auratus*) (2). Green woodpecker (3). Olive-backed three-toed woodpecker (*Dinopium rafflesi*) (4). Northern wryneck (*Jynx torquilla*) (5). Great spotted woodpecker (*Picoides major*) (6). Red-headed woodpecker (*Melanerpes erythrocephalus*) (7). Pileated woodpecker (*Dryocopus pileatus*) (8). Yellow-bellied sapsucker (*Sphyrapicus varius*) (9).

mean cushioning the shock of up to 12,000 hammer blows each day.

The woodpecker's feet have two toes facing forward and two facing back. Each toe ends in a sharp claw, and the fourth toe on each foot can be turned out sideways so that the bird can vary its grip to cope with any shape or angle of branch.

Even the tail of a woodpecker is special. The feathers have extra strong, stiff shafts, and when the tail is pressed against the tree trunk it both supports the bird and acts like a spring to absorb the shock of the hammering.

FEEDING VARIATIONS

Most woodpeckers feed mainly on insects such as beetles and ants and their grubs, and on spiders. Some of this food is simply picked off the surface of the bark, or pecked out of the cracks. Some is found by prising up large flakes of loose bark.

The Three-toed woodpecker drills small round holes in the tree bark then pokes its long pointed tongue inside to "harpoon" the tasty grubs. Other species have sticky tips to their tongues.

Even average-sized species like the Black woodpecker of Europe can do a surprising amount of damage to a tree. Holes 50cm high, 15cm wide and up to 12cm deep are often hacked in soft-wooded trees such as larch as the bird searches for its favourite food – Hercules ants.

Most woodpeckers vary their diet with seeds, fruits, nuts and berries, and some species even specialize on plant food. The Acorn woodpecker of North and South America feeds almost entirely on acorns, which it stores for the winter in holes specially excavated in a "larder tree". One tree, used by a small party of six Acorn woodpeckers, was found to contain more than 50,000 storage holes! In Europe, the Great spotted woodpecker often carries pine cones to a favourite feeding tree and wedges them into cracks in the bark while it pecks out the fatty seeds.

The majority of woodpeckers can extend their tongue far beyond the end of the bill (up to 10cm beyond in

▲Woodpecker feeding methods The simplest technique (1), gleaning ants and other insects from the bark surface. Using the long tongue (2) to extract grubs from holes drilled in the wood.

◄A male Great spotted woodpecker launches itself from the nest-hole at the start of a hunting trip. Once the chicks are able to fly, each parent will look after half the brood until they are able to fend for themselves.

the case of the European green woodpecker), but the sapsuckers cannot do this. So, instead of excavating deep holes and fishing out grubs and adult insects with their tongues, the sapsuckers drill their shallow holes in the bark and wait for their food to come to them! They lick up the sticky droplets of tree sap with the tip of the tongue, which is fringed with fine bristles rather like a brush.

FAMILY LIFE

Most woodpeckers remain in the same area throughout the year, living in territories "owned" by single birds or by pairs or family groups. By claiming a territory, and defending it against intruders, the birds make sure

they have a good supply of food, plenty of sheltered roosting places, and at least a few old trees that will provide holes for nesting. Acorn woodpeckers have large family territories occupied by up to 15 related birds. With so many helpers on call, the family has no difficulty protecting its acorn stores against raiders.

Woodpeckers have a complicated "language" of signs and sounds. The birds communicate with one another by ruffling the feathers on their head and by fanning their wings. They also use bobbing and dancing movements and they drum on tree trunks and branches with their bill. Courtship begins with drumming and display flights by both sexes. Each bird uses

these signals to announce that it is ready to mate, or that it has a good nest site available. Other displays are used to warn rivals to stay away.

Newly paired males and females share the work of excavating a nest-hole, and this can take 10 to 28 days according to the species. It is quite a task. More than 10,000 wood chips have been found littering the ground beneath a new Black woodpecker nest-hole. Once they have made a hole, a pair will use it for many years and will not usually create another unless they are pushed out of their original home by jackdaws or starlings. Both the male and female share the work of incubating the eggs, and later of feeding the nestlings.

WHAT IS A MAMMAL?

The mammals are one of the most successful groups of animals. They are found in almost every habitat, from the Arctic tundra to the Sahara Desert, from the oceans to the mountaintops. One group of mammals, the bats, has even taken to the air.

Mammals are vertebrates: they have an internal bony skeleton for support. The backbone is made up of a series of bony units called vertebrae. A bony shoulder girdle and pelvic girdle are attached to the backbone. A pair of forelegs is attached to the shoulder girdle and a pair of hind legs to the pelvic girdle (see illustration below).

Unlike fish, reptiles and amphibians (other vertebrate groups), mammals are able to keep their inside temperature fairly constant by producing the heat they need from their own body processes. Scientists now use the term endotherm to describe this type of animal rather than the more familiar term warm-blooded, which can be misleading. The blood of so-called cold-blooded animals, such as frogs

▲ A Cape fox vixen suckles her cubs. The supply of milk helps to give the young a good start in life by providing the necessary food for growth.

and snakes, is cold if their surroundings are cold, but after sunbathing their blood may actually be hotter than the blood of warm-blooded mammals. Being able to control their body temperature regardless of the temperature of their surroundings has allowed the mammals to colonize most parts of the globe. Birds are also endotherms.

MAMMALS' SPECIAL FEATURES
The two main features that distinguish mammals from other vertebrates are hair and milk. Hairs trap a layer of air next to the skin. Air does not easily allow heat to pass through it, so this helps the mammal to stay warm.

When mammals reproduce, the female produces milk from special mammary glands and releases it through nipples on her belly. The milk forms a complete food for the baby mammal until it is strong enough to find food for itself. Milk production has allowed some mammals to give birth to young which may be small and helpless. These mammals can produce more young at a time than if the young had to be independent at birth. Because the young spend a long time with their parents while they grow up, this provides an opportunity to learn from experience and improves their chances of survival.

The mammal skull contains a large brain. The cerebral hemispheres of the brain (the parts dealing with consciousness, mental ability and intelligence) are very large.

The lower jaw is formed from a single bone, which makes it very strong. Mammal teeth are usually of various shapes and sizes, specialized for particular diets. A bony plate, the secondary palate, separates the nose passages from the mouth cavity, allowing a mammal to breathe when its mouth is full. This means that a mammal can spend as much time as it likes chewing its food before swallowing it. Most other vertebrates have to

The skeleton of a Grey wolf

Pelvic girdle

Backbone

Shoulder girdle

Skull housing large brain

Single bone of lower jaw

Rib-cage

5-digit feet

swallow their food whole, or they would run out of breath.

The mammal body is divided by a sheet of muscle, the diaphragm, at the base of the rib cage. Movements of the diaphragm help the animal breathe efficiently. Contraction of the diaphragm, along with moving of the ribs, sucks air into the lungs. The reverse process pushes air out of the lungs.

TYPES OF MAMMALS
There are three classes of mammals, distinguished by the way in which they breed (as shown below).

The Monotremes
These are the egg-laying mammals. They are the most primitive mammals. There are only three species: the duck-billed platypus and two kinds of echidna or spiny anteater. Monotremes are found only in Australia and New Guinea. They lay eggs with leathery shells, rather like those of reptiles. These hatch into tiny, little-developed young. Monotremes have no nipples. The young cling to the fur on their mother's belly and suck at the milk oozing out of the skin where the milk glands open to the surface.

The Marsupials
In this class, which includes the kangaroos, the koala and the opossums, the young develop inside the mother's womb, but are born at a very early stage of development. At birth, they look rather like tiny grubs. They climb up their mother's fur into a pouch on her belly. Inside the pouch are nipples which produce milk.

The Placental Mammals
This is the largest and most "advanced" group of mammals. The young develop inside their mother's womb attached to a placenta. This is a special structure which supplies them with food and oxygen from the mother's blood and carries away their waste products. This food supply allows the young to reach a more advanced stage before being born. Placental mammal mothers produce milk from nipples on their bellies.

▼Some young mammals, like this new-born gazelle, can stand soon after birth.

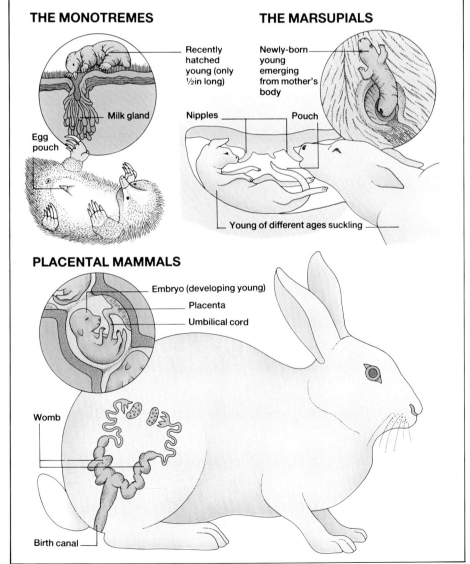

THE MONOTREMES

Recently hatched young (only ½in long)

Milk gland

Egg pouch

THE MARSUPIALS

Newly-born young emerging from mother's body

Nipples

Pouch

Young of different ages suckling

PLACENTAL MAMMALS

Embryo (developing young)

Placenta

Umbilical cord

Womb

Birth canal

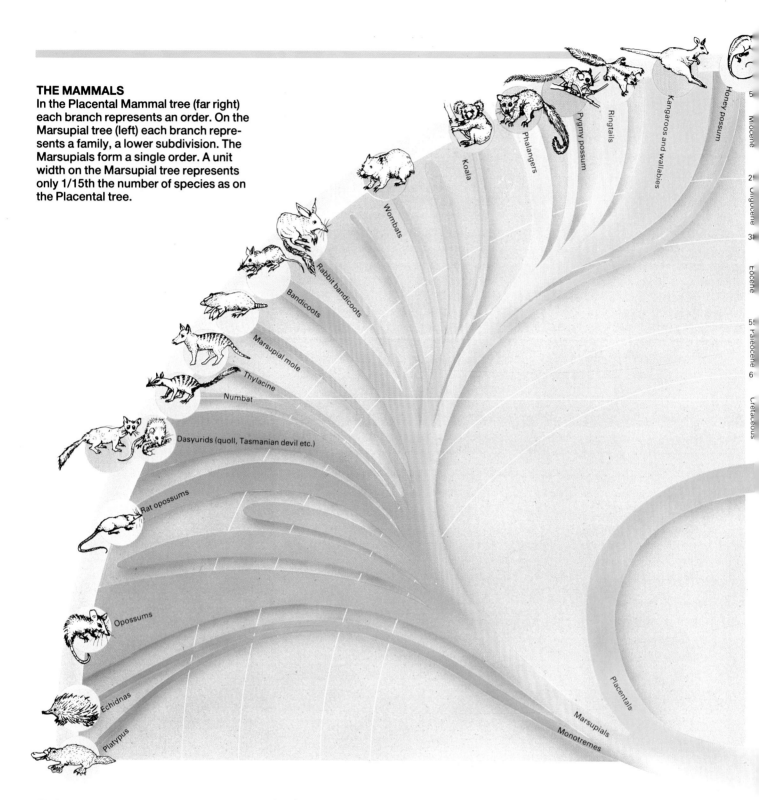

THE MAMMALS

In the Placental Mammal tree (far right) each branch represents an order. On the Marsupial tree (left) each branch represents a family, a lower subdivision. The Marsupials form a single order. A unit width on the Marsupial tree represents only 1/15th the number of species as on the Placental tree.

Honey possum
Kangaroos and wallabies
Ringtails
Pygmy possum
Phalangers
Koala
Wombats
Rabbit bandicoots
Bandicoots
Marsupial mole
Thylacine
Numbat
Dasyurids (quoll, Tasmanian devil etc.)
Rat opossums
Opossums
Echidnas
Platypus

Placentals
Marsupials
Monotremes

Miocene
Oligocene
Eocene
Paleocene
Cretaceous

CLASSIFYING THE MAMMALS

There are over 4,000 different species of mammal, around 1,000 genera and 135 families. Mammals are grouped into Monotremes (3 species), Marsupials (266) and Placental mammals (over 3,750, of which a quarter are bats). They can be further sorted according to their body structure, especially the number, shapes and arrangement of the bones and teeth.

Each mammal's body is suited it to its particular way of life. Thus cheetahs have long legs and flexible backbones

▲ This mammal family tree shows how the mammals have increased in variety with time. The ancestors of the mammals first appeared on Earth about 300 million years ago. Since then, mammals have evolved a wide range of feeding habits and life-styles, allowing them to spread to most parts of the globe.

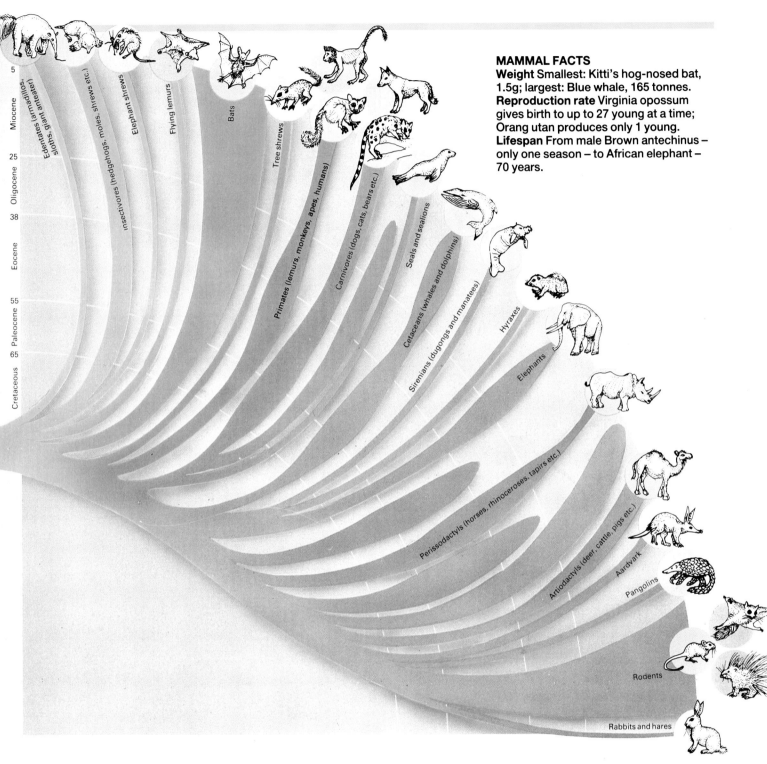

Miocene 5
Oligocene 25
38
Eocene
55
Paleocene 65
Cretaceous

Edentates (armadillos, sloths, giant anteater)

Insectivores (hedgehogs, moles, shrews etc.)

Elephant shrews

Flying lemurs

Bats

Tree shrews

Primates (lemurs, monkeys, apes, humans)

Carnivores (dogs, cats, bears etc.)

Seals and sealions

Cetaceans (whales and dolphins)

Sirenians (dugongs and manatees)

Hyraxes

Elephants

Perissodactyls (horses, rhinoceroses, tapirs etc.)

Artiodactyls (deer, cattle, pigs etc.)

Aardvark

Pangolins

Rodents

Rabbits and hares

During these 300 million years, the continents have moved around the globe, and the climate has changed. Not all the mammals that arose were successful. Some branches of the tree do not reach to the present day. Others, like the rodents and bats, are still expanding and changing today.

for chasing after prey, seals have flippers for swimming, and bats have wings for flying.

A mammal's jaws and teeth reveal how it feeds. Lions have special sharp teeth for seizing prey, tearing flesh and crushing bones. Sheep have large

flat teeth for grinding leaves. Baleen whales have huge plate-like sieves for filtering sea water.

Classifying the mammals according to their body structure naturally arranges them in groups with similar life styles and feeding habits.

123

SQUIRRELS

The Sun rises over the dry plains of central North America. The inhabitants of a small colony are already awake, preparing for the day ahead. Suddenly a male spots a puma and he barks out a warning. His companions dash back into their homes, while he stands erect on a look-out mound, keeping watch as he cleans his whiskers. This is, of course, not a human town. About 2,000 Black-tailed prairie dogs live here, in burrows under the short, dry grass.

All squirrel species grip small items of food firmly in their forepaws, like the Cape ground squirrel (above left). The

European red squirrel leaves many feeding signs (above right) as it opens cones and nuts to extract the seeds.

It may seem odd to think of squirrels living underground rather than in trees. But the burrowing prairie dogs are just some of the members of the very numerous and widespread squirrel family. This family includes the familiar Grey and European red squirrels and other tree-dwelling species, the flying squirrels and the ground-dwelling prairie dogs, chipmunks, ground squirrels and sousliks.

Squirrels, being so variable in their way of life and habits, are found in many different types of country – from mountain meadow to rocky cliff, dry grassland and tropical rain forest. Members of the family are found on every continent except Australia and Antarctica.

THE SQUIRREL'S MENU

A typical squirrel has a long rounded body, large eyes, strong legs and claws and a bushy tail. The long, chisel-shaped front teeth show that they are members of the rodent group. These

teeth are well suited for chopping and opening nuts and seeds, snipping off flowers, fruits and shoots and levering strips of sappy bark from a tree trunk. Plant food is the main diet of most types of squirrel, as well as mushrooms and other fungi.

▶ The European red squirrel is many people's idea of a typical squirrel, with its large eyes, pricked ears and long, bushy tail.

SQUIRRELS Sciuridae (*267 species*)

● ◪

◼ Habitat: tropical forest to woods, grassland and gardens.

▨ Diet: plant parts such as seeds, nuts, bark; some small animals.

◯ Breeding: most species have one spring litter after pregnancy of 3-6 weeks; number of young varies: 1 or 2 (flying squirrels) to 9 or more (Grey squirrel).

Size: smallest (African pygmy squirrel): head-body 7cm, tail 5cm, weight 10g; largest (Alpine marmot): head-body 73cm, tail 16cm, weight 8kg.

Colour: shades of red, brown or grey.

Lifespan: 1-2 years in smaller species, 8-10 years for some marmots.

Species mentioned in text:
African pygmy squirrel (*Myosciurus pumilio*)
Alpine marmot (*Marmota marmota*)
Belding's ground squirrel (*Spermophilus beldingi*)
Black-tailed prairie dog (*Cynomys ludovicianus*)
Cape ground squirrel (*Xerus inaurus*)
European red squirrel (*Sciurus vulgaris*)
Giant flying squirrel (*Petaurista species*)
Grey squirrel (*Sciurus carolinensis*)
Shrew-faced ground squirrel (*Rhino-sciurus laticaudatus*)
Siberian chipmunk (*Tamias sibiricus*)
Woodchuck (*Marmota monax*)

One of the reasons for the squirrels' success is their broad diet. Many species eat beetles or other insects. Some are omnivorous, and their diet includes lizards, small birds, eggs and worms as well as plant food. The Shrew-faced ground squirrel is unusual in that it mostly eats insects, such as termites and caterpillars.

LEAPING AND GLIDING

Tree squirrels are very agile animals. They can run straight up or down a tree trunk and leap several metres through the branches, clinging with their sharp claws. They have keen sight, which helps them judge distances accurately when scampering among the twigs.

Flying squirrels are specialized not for true flying but for gliding. There is a furred flap of skin down each side of the body, stretching between the front and back legs. As the flying squirrel jumps, it extends all four legs to stretch the skin and form a parachute. The tail is free to move from side to side, like a rudder for steering.

Flying squirrels, unlike other species, are active at night. When searching for food or avoiding a predator, they swoop from high in one tree to low on the trunk of another. The larger species, such as the Giant flying squirrel, can glide 100m or more.

◀A female Belding's ground squirrel stands erect and calls to warn her neighbours of an approaching coyote.

A WINTER'S TAIL

The squirrel's tail has many uses, depending on the species. In flying squirrels and tree squirrels it acts as a rudder when leaping, and as a counterweight when balancing on a branch. It may also be used as a signal, informing other squirrels of anger, acceptance or readiness to mate. Species living in hot places fluff out their tails over their backs, to act as a sun-shade. In winter, many tree squirrels sleep in their nests with their tails wrapped around them for warmth.

Grey, red and other tree squirrels do not hibernate. They may stay inside their stick-and-twig nests, called dreys, for several days during bad weather. But they emerge on fine winter days to feed and drink. However, many ground squirrels and marmots hibernate for about 6 months, when their body temperature falls to only a few degrees above freezing.

The woodchuck or groundhog, a marmot of North America, is a famous

▼Young ground squirrels (called "pups") leaving their burrow for the first time. These pups are about 27 days old.

▲**Types of tree squirrel** An African
pygmy squirrel **(1)** carries a nut. An Abert
or Tassel-eared squirrel (*Sciurus aberti*)
(2) holds food in its forepaws. An Indian
giant squirrel (*Ratufa indica*) **(3)** leaps
to a nearby branch. An American red
squirrel (*Tamiasciurus hudsonicus*) **(4)**
hangs by its hind claws while cracking
a nut. A Southern flying squirrel
(*Glaucomys volans*) **(5)** glides from its
tree hole. Prevost's squirrel (*Callosciurus
prevosti*) **(6)** keeps watch from a
sawn-off branch.

hibernator. Legend says that it wakes on February 2nd each year – Ground-hog Day. If it sees its shadow, this means sunny cold weather, and it returns to its burrow for another 6 weeks. (This story is unfounded.) When it emerges in spring, it is very thin and has lost up to half its weight.

MAKING A LARDER

Squirrels are famous storers of nuts, seeds and other food to last them through the winter. The Siberian chipmunk may store up to 6kg of food, perhaps 100 times its body weight, in its burrow. This is its source of food when the chipmunk wakes in spring, before new plant growth becomes abundant.

Tree squirrels bury food or hide it in undergrowth, to dig up in winter. European red squirrels can smell pine cones they have buried 30cm below the surface. Grey squirrels may carry acorns 30m from an oak tree before hiding them in a hole. But many squirrels forget where they have buried food, so their activities help to spread seeds and to plant them for future growth.

BREEDING AND SOCIAL LIFE

Most squirrels, like other rodents, are able to breed within a year of being born. There is usually one litter per year. Newborn young are blind and helpless but develop fast, and within 2 months they are ready to leave their nest and fend for themselves.

Most tree squirrels live alone. Each has a territory and chases away intruders. The territory of a male may overlap those of several females. During spring, boundaries break down, and animals come together for a few days to mate.

Ground squirrels tend to be more social and live in groups. Fifty or more Alpine marmots may occupy a large burrow system, with males, females

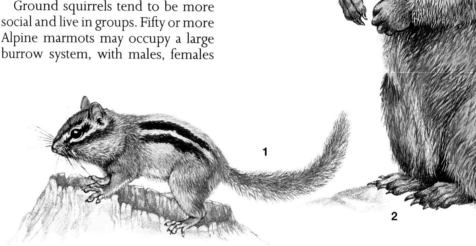

▲ **Types of ground squirrel** A Siberian chipmunk with cheek pouches full of food (**1**). An Alpine marmot stands upright and gives an alarm whistle as it spots a wolf (**2**). A Shrew-faced ground squirrel, also called the Long-nosed squirrel, extracts termites from a hole in a fallen branch (**3**). A Western ground squirrel (*Xerus erythropus*) indicates worry by arching and fluffing its tail (**4**).

◄ The female Belding's ground squirrel carries up to 50 loads of dry grass to line her nest before giving birth.

► Black-tailed prairie dogs relax in the Sun. The mound around their tunnel entrance helps to prevent the tunnel flooding.

and young living as one large family. Prairie dogs form even bigger colonies, called "townships", of perhaps 5,000 animals. Each township consists of several family burrows called "coteries". In summer, prairie dogs from different coteries are friendly to each other. In winter, when food is scarcer, coterie members defend their burrows and territories.

SQUIRREL DAMAGE

Two species of squirrel are officially listed as being endangered. But squirrels in general are common, and some species are regarded as pests in certain areas. Prairie dogs used to cause great damage to crops and destroy grassland grazed by farm animals. Poisoning has now made some of them scarce except in remote areas and national parks. The Grey squirrel, in particular, is unloved by foresters, because it strips bark from young trees, probably to eat the sweet-tasting sapwood – but also killing the tree in the process. Guns and traps may reduce its numbers for a time, but there seems to be no permanent answer.

MICE

A Chocolate Dutch doe mouse has given birth to 12 cubs, but she doesn't have enough milk for them all. Fortunately, the breeder has a Himalayan doe that has lost most of her cubs and has plenty of milk. So he rolls six of the Dutch cubs in the urine of the Himalayan doe and places them in her nest. The smell of the urine masks the cubs' "strange" smell and allows the foster doe to accept them as her own.

All domesticated mice are derived from the wild House mouse, a species that came originally from central Asia. Wild mice began living with people about 10,000 years ago. That is when humans first developed farming and began to store grain in large quantities on which the mice could feed.

Mice were first domesticated in the Far East several centuries ago. By the 1700s, several fancy breeds had become established in Japan, including chocolate-coloured, albino (white) and black mice. There were also so-called Waltzing Mice, which "danced" because of a defect in their balance organs. Since then many more varieties with different coloured coats have been selectively bred.

JUST LIKE ANY OTHER MOUSE

As well as fancy breeds for showing and keeping as pets, large numbers of mice are bred as laboratory animals. By continuous inbreeding, a "standard mouse" has been bred among which all individuals carry the same genes and are virtually identical to one another. This makes it easier for scientists to compare the effects on different mice of different treatments.

▶ Two Albino Mice. Several mice can be kept in the same cage, but only if they are reared together. (All males eventually fight savagely, even littermates.)

MICE (Mus musculus)

◼ Diet: cereals, nuts, bread, dog biscuits; occasionally fruit and vegetables.

◯ Breeding: 8-12 offspring, after pregnancy of about 21 days.

Distribution: worldwide in the wild and as pets.

Size: about 8cm long, with a tail of similar size.

Colour: brown, chocolate, cream, silver, gold, black, white; often patterned.

Lifespan: up to about 2 years as pets.

Tame mice differ from wild ones in that they are docile and easy to handle; they have a larger body and a longer tail; and their ears are bigger and their eyes more prominent.

SELFS AND SATINS

The so-called self-coloured varieties of mouse, or selfs, are the same colour all over. They include black, blue, chocolate, red and cream. These have black eyes. Champagne, fawn, silver and white varieties have pink eyes. Tans are varieties that have one of the recognized colours for the main coat, but with a golden-tan belly.

Some of the most distinctive mice have a marked, or patterned coat. The Dutch has similar markings to the Dutch rabbit – a white nose, coloured

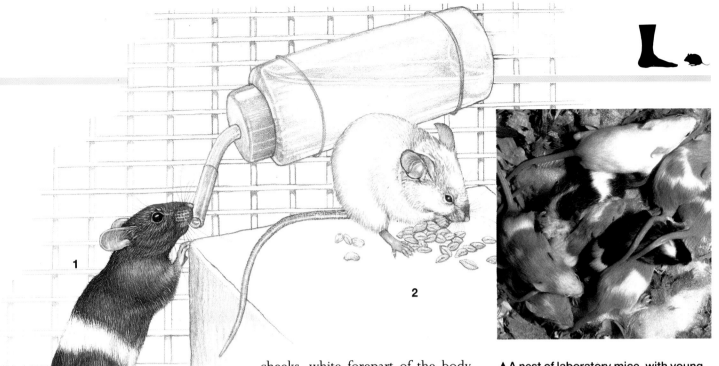

▲A nest of laboratory mice, with young of various colours.

▲▼Colour difference among varieties of mice (The mice shown are all females.) Chocolate Belted Mouse (1) drinking from a water bottle. Chocolate has been a favourite coat colour for centuries. Himalayan Mouse (2) feeding on grain. This variety has red eyes, but some have black eyes. Lilac Mouse (3). Black and Tan Mouse (4) sniffing the ground. Yellow Mouse (5) eating.

cheeks, white forepart of the body, but coloured hindpart. The beige-coated Siamese has similar markings ("points") to the Siamese Cat, with brown-tipped hairs on the nose, ears, feet and tail.

Various types of coat are found in domestic mice. In the rex the coat is tightly curled, and in the astrex it is loosely waved. Longhairs have a silky coat nearly twice the normal length. Satins have a coat with a sheen to it.

QUICK-BREEDERS

Mice breed as readily in captivity as they do in the wild. The females start to come on heat at the age of about 6 to 7 weeks, and every 4 or 5 days thereafter. The buck (male) mouse should be allowed in with the doe (female) for a while to allow mating to take place, but then removed. The doe gives birth 3 weeks later to about 10 young, called cubs. They are born blind, deaf and naked. Their eyes do not open until about a week later.

At this stage, the buck should not be allowed back with the doe because she can become pregnant again immediately after she has given birth. If breeding were allowed to continue freely, the doe could produce as many as 100 cubs in a year!

PORCUPINES

Grunting quietly to itself, an African porcupine is digging up roots for its evening feed. It is so busy that it does not hear the soft padding footsteps of the young leopard closing in behind it. The cat pounces, but instead of an easy meal it gets the shock of its life. With a snort of rage the porcupine raises its quills and charges backwards. Almost too late the leopard sees the danger. As it throws itself to one side, the needle-sharp quills miss its face by less than a metre.

All 22 species of porcupine have quills and spines. They are more obvious in some species than in others, and they come in many shapes and sizes. These quills and spines are highly modified hairs, providing their owners with a very effective defence.

SPECTACULAR QUILLS
The most spectacular of these specialized hairs are the 50cm black-and-white quills of the crested porcupines of Africa and Asia. They cover the animal's back from the shoulders to the tail, and they can be raised by muscles under the skin. They cannot be "shot" at attackers but they often stick in the face, neck or paws of an attacker and break off. They are not poisonous, but can become infected and so can cause serious injury.

The crested and brush-tailed porcupines of Africa and Asia also have clusters of tail quills modified into rattles. When the animal is frightened or cornered it shakes the tail to give a warning rattle. If that does not work, the African porcupine stamps its hind feet and grunts, and as a last resort charges its attacker.

The protective quills of the North American porcupine are different. They are only about 3cm long and are

PORCUPINES Hystricidae
and Erethizontidae (*22 species*)

● ◨ ⚑

◼ Habitat: forest, open grassland, desert, rocky areas.

◼ Diet: leaves, roots, fruits.

○ Breeding: 1 or 2 young after pregnancy of about 210 days (North American porcupine), 93 days (Cape), 112 days (African).

Size: smallest (Prehensile-tailed porcupine): head-body 30cm, weight 900g; largest (crested porcupines): head-body 85cm, weight 27kg.

Colour: from black, white and grey, through yellow-brown to grey-brown.

Lifespan: up to 17 years.

Species mentioned in text:
African porcupine (*Hystrix cristata*)
Brush-tailed porcupines (*Atherurus* species)
Cape porcupine (*Hystrix africaeaustralis*)
Crested porcupines (*Hystrix* species)
Indonesian porcupines (*Thecarus* species)
North American porcupine (*Erethizon dorsatum*)
Prehensile-tailed porcupine (*Coendon prehensilis*)
South American tree porcupine (*C. bicolor*)

hidden in the animal's long coarse hair. They are very loosely fixed in the porcupine's skin, and an attacker is likely to find itself with nothing but a mouthful of hair and spines. To make things even more painful, the tips of the quills are covered in tiny barbs.

▼A Cape porcupine feeding on desert gourds. Most porcupines feed in this way, holding the food with their front paws and nibbling at it.

►A South American tree porcupine caught on the ground as it crosses from one tree to another. Just visible in the grass is the bare patch on the upper surface of the end of the tail. This patch of hard skin (the callus) helps to improve the grip of the prehensile tail.

▼Distant cousins Three members of the porcupine family from widely separated parts of the world. The North American porcupine (1) spends most of its time on the ground. The Indonesian porcupine (2) has a dense coat of flat, flexible spines. There are three species – in Borneo, Sumatra and the Philippines. The African porcupine (3) is one of five crested species. It is very adaptable and is found in desert, grassland and forest.

WORLDS APART

The porcupines are grouped in two large families. The Old World porcupines live in a wide range of habitats in Africa and Asia. New World porcupines are found in forest and grassland areas from northern Canada down to northern Argentina. The two groups have similar quills, teeth and jaw muscles. But scientists have still not worked out whether they are descendants of the same ancestors or whether evolution has come up with the same design in two separate families.

"OLD WORLD" SPECIES

All the Old World porcupines are ground-dwelling animals. They feed on roots, bulbs, fruits and berries, usually at night, either alone or in pairs. During the day they rest in caves, in holes among rocks or in burrows. Sometimes they take over old aardvark holes.

In many parts of Africa, porcupines are hunted for their arguably tasty meat. They are also killed by farmers because of their habit of raiding crops of maize, groundnuts, melons and potatoes. In spite of this, the porcupine is still common in Africa, probably because its natural enemies – lions, leopards and hyenas – are themselves becoming rare.

The sharp quills of the crested porcupines make mating rather dangerous, but somehow the animals manage. The young are born in a grass-lined chamber in a burrow or rock shelter, usually in summer. The babies are born with their eyes open. They are covered with fur and even have tiny soft quills which harden within a few hours.

The Cape porcupine of South Africa lives in family groups of up to eight. The older animals help to look after the babies, keeping close to young porcupines when they first start to feed outside the burrow at about 6 to 7 months.

IN THE AMERICAS

Unlike their Old World relatives, the porcupines of North and South America are mainly tree-dwellers. Their feet are equipped with large claws and hairless pads that provide a good grip. Most specialized of all are the Prehensile-tailed porcupine and the tree porcupines that live in the Central and South American forests. They have long muscular tails, which they can coil round branches to give extra support when climbing.

These animals too are nocturnal. They feed mainly on leaves, but also take fruits and seeds and sometimes come down to the ground to feed on roots and tubers. In winter, the North American porcupine feeds on pine needles, leaves and tree bark. It is especially fond of Red spruce and Sugar maple. In summer it often feeds on grasses and on roots, berries and flowers on the forest floor.

Destruction of South America's forests has placed several species in danger. The Prehensile-tailed porcupine is threatened in parts of Brazil. And the South American tree porcupine is listed as endangered by the Brazilian Academy of Science.

◀ The Prehensile-tailed porcupine spends most of its time high in the trees. It is near-sighted, relying heavily on touch and smell.

▶ Despite its slowness, a hungry North American porcupine will sometimes climb 18-20m to reach young leaves.

RABBITS AND HARES

In the late afternoon of a spring day, a male and female hare face each other at the edge of a field. For several minutes they glare at each other without moving. Suddenly the female hare leaps right over the male, giving him a vicious two-footed drop-kick as she goes by. The male hare spins round and kicks back. Then the two animals drop back on their haunches and sit upright, face to face, cuffing and boxing furiously with their forepaws. Eventually the male decides he has had enough. He turns to run. But even as he dives for the safety of the nearby hedge, the female victor gets in one last kick.

The "mad March hares" that perform such crazy antics during the mating season belong to one of the world's most successful animal groups. The common European rabbit is the most familiar rabbit of open fields and grasslands, but it has cousins that live in the snow-covered Arctic wilderness, and others that live in deserts and tropical forests and even on the tops of mountains.

ACROSS THE GLOBE
World wide there are 44 species of rabbit and hare. There are native species in North America and parts of South America, all over Africa and right across Europe and Asia. Some parts of South America, and all of Australia and New Zealand, originally had no native rabbits and hares, but European animals were taken there by settlers and very quickly made themselves at home. In Australia the European rabbit is still a pest. Only Antarctica and the huge island of Madagascar are completely without rabbits and hares.

RABBITS AND HARES Leporidae (*44 species*)

○ ◨ ☠

■ Habitat: virtually everywhere, from coast fields, grassland and forest to desert and high mountains.

▣ Diet: grass, leaves, bark; also crops and tree seedlings.

◎ Breeding: rabbits: litters of 3-12, up to 5 times a year, after pregnancy of 30-40 days; hares: litters of 1-9, up to 4 times a year, after pregnancy of up to 50 days; northern species mainly spring/summer; others breed throughout year.

Size: smallest (Pygmy rabbit): head-body 25-30cm, weight 0.3kg; largest (European hare): head-body 50-76cm, weight 5kg.

Colour: reddish-brown through brown, buff and grey to white; Arctic species change from brown to white in winter.

Lifespan: usually less than 1 year; domestic (pet) rabbits up to 18 years.

Species mentioned in text:
Arctic hare (*Lepus timidus*)
Black-tailed jackrabbit
  (*L. californicus*)
Bushman hare (*Bunolagus monticularis*)
Cottontails (*Sylvilagus* species)
European hare (*Lepus europaeus*)
European rabbit (*Oryctolagus cuniculus*)
Hispid hare (*Caprolagus hispidus*)
Pygmy rabbit (*Sylvilagus idahoensis*)
Snowshoe hare (*Lepus americanus*)
Sumatran hare (*Nesolagus netscheri*)
Volcano rabbit (*Romerolagus diazi*)

▶ **Rabbits and hares of the world** The Hispid hare **(1)** is an endangered species from India. It seldom leaves the shelter of the forest. Volcano rabbit of Mexico **(2)** shown sitting in the long grass recycling its droppings. The European hare in its "boxing" position **(3)**. Greater red rock-hare (*Pronolagus crassicaudatus*) **(4)** of Southern Africa in alert posture. Male Eastern cottontail (*Sylvilagus floridanus*) **(5)** in alert posture.

10

9

◄The very rare Sumatran hare (6) grooming its muzzle and spreading scent from scent glands. Bunyoro rabbit (*Poelagus marjorita*)(7) hopping along. The species is common in parts of Central and Eastern Africa. Adult male European rabbbit (8) scratching his chin. Bushman hare (9) of the Southern African river banks, now an endangered species. The Amami rabbit (*Pentalagus furnessi*) (10) is found on just two small Japanese islands. The total population is about 5,000, and the species has protected status.

FLEET OF FOOT

Rabbits and hares are very similar in shape, though they vary in size. They have long, soft fur, which covers the whole body including the feet, and a small furry tail which is usually white, or at least white underneath. The tail is always turned upwards, so that as the animal runs, the white fur may act as a target for predators, keeping them away from vital areas of its body. The animal's alarm signal is to thump its back feet on the ground.

The front legs are quite short but strong, and the five toes on each forefoot have sharp claws for digging. The back legs are very much longer

▼ Two-week-old European rabbits in the burrow where they were born. These kittens have opened their eyes for the first time, but have not yet seen the outside world.

and are clearly designed for running and bounding over open ground. Some of the largest hares can reach speeds of up to 80 kph when fleeing from danger.

Both rabbits and hares have large eyes, placed high on the sides of the head. They give clear vision in twilight and at night, which is when many species are most active. The position of the eyes also gives the animals very good vision to the sides, and even above and behind them. This is very important to an animal that makes such a tasty and tempting target for eagles, wild cats, polecats and a host of other predators.

FOOD PROCESSING

Rabbits and hares live entirely on plant food, mainly grasses, leaves, bark and roots. Like the rodents, they have two large front teeth which grow continuously. But they differ from rats and mice by having a second, much

smaller pair of front teeth tucked behind the main pair.

Their internal organs too are especially developed to cope with large amounts of low-quality vegetable food. The ground-up food passes into the stomach, and then into the gut. But instead of passing straight out through the last section of the gut it is held for a while in another stomach-like bag where bacteria help to break down the coarse food more thoroughly.

Rabbits and hares produce two kinds of dropping. When the animal is most active, normal firm dry droppings are left, often in special "latrine" areas. But when the animal is resting, much softer droppings are produced. These are eaten again and recycled through the digestive system for a second time so that useful chemicals such as vitamin B can be absorbed into the animal's body.

Because rabbits breed very quickly,

and can eat a great variety of food, they can easily become a nuisance. In some areas they are "public enemy number one" for farmers and foresters. In the United States, for example, Black-tailed jackrabbits cause widespread damage to crops in California, while the cottontails and the Snowshoe hare can ruin new forestry plantations by nipping the growing shoots off the tender young tree seedlings.

BURROWS AND HOLLOWS
The biggest differences between rabbits and hares can be seen in their choice of where to live and in the way they bring up their young.

Most rabbits live in underground burrow systems called warrens. The young rabbits (kittens) are born in a warm nest, snugly lined with hair and soft grass, either in the main warren or in a nursery burrow near by. They are hairless, and their eyes do not open for several days (10 days for European

rabbits). The female (doe) feeds her young for only a few minutes in each 24 hours. She then seals them in by covering the burrow entrance with earth, and goes off to feed.

The young rabbits do not venture outside for about 3 weeks.

Hares are very different. Only a few of them make burrows of any kind. Usually they rest in a shallow hollow, called a form, in soft earth or in long grass. The young hares (leverets) are well developed at birth. They are covered with warm fur, and their eyes are open. When they are just 2–3 days old the mother places each one in a seperate form, well hidden among rocks or tall grass. There they remain until the family meets up, usually around sunset, for the one feed of the day. Because they live out in the open, young hares can run almost from birth. Their main protection, however, is to remain absolutely still.

With so many different species, living in so many different habitats it is not surprising to find that not every one follows these "rules." A number of hares do make burrows. Black-tailed jackrabbits, for example, sometimes dig short burrows to escape from the fierce summer heat in the American deserts. Arctic hares in Scotland may dig burrows for their young to use in times of danger. Not all rabbits dig burrows either. Many of the cottontails either use holes made by other animals or simply hide themselves among thick vegetation.

THE NUMBERS EXPLOSION
European rabbits are famous for the speed at which they can reproduce. Females often produce five litters in a year, each of 5 or 6 young (occasionally up to 12). Each young female, in turn, will be ready to produce her own first family by the time she is 3 months old. At that rate it is no surprise that rabbits can quickly become a major pest.

Hares do not multiply quite so

quickly, but they too are fast breeders.

The European hare was taken to Argentina in 1888. In just 100 years it has spread throughout the whole country. It is now found spread over 5 million sq kilometres. In the central pampas region, 5–10 million hares are caught each year for their light meat.

RARE RABBIT RELATIVES
The family that contains one of the most common animals on Earth also includes a number of surprisingly rare species. Some are on the international list of endangered species.

One of the rarest is the Sumatran hare, which is found in the remote mountain forests of the South-east Asian island of Sumatra. Only 20 have ever been seen, and only one has been seen in the last 10 years. If the forests are cut for their valuable timber, this unusual striped hare will disappear for ever.

In the sal forests of northern India and Bangladesh, the Hispid hare is also becoming more and more rare. Its woodland habitat is being destroyed to make way for cattle grazing. The Bushman hare of Southern Africa faces a similar threat. Its natural habitat is the dense vegetation along river banks, but these are also the most fertile areas and so they are being taken over by farmers, leaving the hares with nowhere to go.

Strangest of all is the case of the Volcano rabbit, which lives at 3–4 kilometres on the flanks of two volcanic mountain ranges near Mexico City. It is one of the world's smallest rabbits, and lives in groups of up to five animals in burrows among open pine woods and grassy slopes. It is active mainly durng the day, using a variety of calls to keep in touch with one another. Unfortunately the 17 million people of Mexico City are barely half an hour's drive away, so the rabbits are threatened now by hunters and noisy tourists as well as by the destruction of their habitat.

LION

It is dawn on the East African plains. A herd of wildebeest and zebras graze in the pale sunlight. Suddenly, the early morning quiet is shattered by the roar of a lion. But the zebras and wildebeest carry on feeding peacefully. They have nothing to fear. The lion is a male and his fearsome roars are not directed at them. Instead, they are a signal to other males: "This is my home area and these are my females. Keep away!" For the grazing animals, danger will come later in the day. Then, a group of lionesses begin their prowl in search of animals to kill and eat.

LION *Panthera leo*

● ■

◯ **Habitat:** grasslands of E. Africa, desert areas. Some in India.

■ **Diet:** antelope, gazelle, warthogs, wildebeest, zebra, smaller animals.

◓ **Breeding:** litters of 1-5 after pregnancy of 100-119 days.

Size: head-body 2.4-3.3m; weight 122-240kg; males larger.

Colour: light tawny, belly and inside legs white, backs of ears black, mane of male tawny to reddish or black.

Lifespan: 15-24 years.

The lion's strength and haughty expression have led people to call it the "King of Beasts". Like all the cats, the lion has a sleek, muscular body with a deep chest. The short powerful jaws are well-armed with a fine set of sharp teeth, designed for chewing and tearing meat and even for cracking open bones. The feet have a set of powerful claws and, together with keen hearing and sight, a lion is superbly equipped for the hunting life.

Male lions are heavier than females (lionesses) – sometimes half as big again. Being larger enables the male to push his way between females at a kill and get at the best meat. Males sometimes steal carcasses killed by other animals, but mostly they feed on animals killed by the females.

Only the male lion has a mane of long hair on the head and shoulders. This makes him look larger and fiercer than he really is, and is useful in arguments with other males – a smaller male will retreat before starting a fight. If there is fighting, the thick mane protects its owner against the teeth and claws of a rival. The main role of male lions is to defend the home area of the family group and to protect females from other groups of male lions.

THE MIGHTY HUNTER

Male lions rarely hunt. Most hunting is carried out by lionesses. The prey consists of large animals such as gazelles, antelopes, warthogs, zebras and wildebeest. Lions also kill and eat lizards, birds and smaller mammals such as rats. An adult male lion needs about 7kg of meat a day, while the smaller female requires 5kg each day.

Lionesses usually hunt together. Several females stalk and spread out to surround a prey animal. They try to get as close as possible, using long grass or bushes as cover. A lioness can run as fast as 58kph, but some of its prey can run much faster than this, so a slow, quiet approach is just as important as speed.

Only one in four charges by lionesses ends with a kill. After being knocked to the ground, the animal is

▼This male lion has killed a horse which strayed from a farm. Now, using all his might, he drags it to cover.

◀Two males from the same pride groom each other. They are probably brothers or half-brothers, and grooming maintains the bond between them.

▼Family life in a resting pride of lions. A lioness (1) suckles three cubs, only one of which (2) is hers. The others belong to females (3) and (4). Two dozing males (5) seem not to mind the playing cubs (6).

killed by a bite to its throat, which breaks the windpipe, or by having its jaws clamped shut by the lioness. Either way, it chokes to death.

Although lions are good hunters, up to three-quarters of the animals they eat are killed by hyenas and stolen by the lions. People usually think of hyenas as being scavengers, but in fact lions are more so.

A PRIDE OF LIONS

Lions are the most social of all cats. They live in groups called prides. A pride usually has 4 to 12 adult females and their young, with 1 to 6 adult males. The females are usually related to each other, most often as cousins. The males are also related to each other – mostly as half-brothers – but not to the females.

A pride has its own home area or territory. The size of this area depends on how many prey animals it contains. A pride of lions lets other prides know where its territory ends by patrolling the boundary, roaring, and marking it with urine at regular places. Although both sexes will defend territories against intruding males, it is the males of a pride that do most of this.

Lions first breed when they are between 36 and 46 months old, and females can breed several times a year. Within a pride, there is little fighting between males over females. Instead, the first male to meet a willing female mates with her.

At between 109 and 119 days after mating, a lioness gives birth to a litter of 1 to 10 cubs. The cubs stop suckling milk from their mother at about 6 months old, although they start eating meat earlier than this. As many as three-quarters of all lion cubs die of starvation before they reach 2 years of age.

LIONS AND PEOPLE

For thousands of years, people have respected lions for their strength and bravery. Many royal families in Europe had lions on their flags and coats-of-arms.

Because lions are thought to be so fierce and strong, people could show how brave they were by killing a lion. Many hunters went to Africa from Europe and North America to kill lions and bring back their heads or skins as trophies.

Nowadays, the hunting of lions in Africa is strictly controlled and most visitors go to photograph animals instead.

Although there are still many lions in Africa, they are under some threat. When scrub is cleared for farming, prey becomes scarce and lions may then disappear from the area, or may be shot if they begin to hunt farm animals.

Lions and their prey animals are both threatened when the vegetation in the areas they inhabit changes. Lions used to be found all over northern India, the Middle East and Africa north of the Sahara Desert. As the deserts increased in size and encroached on scrubland, the lions disappeared.

Up to 2,300 years ago, lions lived in Greece, and cave paintings show that in much earlier times the lion was widespread in most of Europe. The last lions in the Middle East were wiped out by hunting about 100 years ago. Today, lions live only in Africa south of the Sahara and in one forest nature reserve in north-west India.

MAN-EATERS

The Romans imported lions from North Africa and used them to kill prisoners as a kind of public entertainment. Many early Christians were killed in this way. Lions, though, are not normally man-eaters. Stories of man-eating lions in Africa usually result from old or sick lions attacking humans because they are easier to catch than normal prey.

Sometimes, though, healthy lions will eat people if their supply of game has been reduced by farming or other human activities. A famous example took place in the late 1800s, when the railway between Kenya and Uganda was being built. So many workmen were killed by a pair of lions that work on the railway had to be stopped until the lions were shot.

If lions are to survive, we must ensure that they and their game animals have plenty of space. This is provided by the great game parks and nature reserves of Africa, but even here lions are under threat as human numbers increase and the need for farmland becomes greater.

◄A group of resting lionesses on a rocky outcrop. Lions spend much of their time sleeping, especially during the heat of the day and after a heavy meal. But these seven lionesses have woken suddenly after being disturbed and are very alert.

TIGER

A lone tiger pads softly through the dappled sunlight of an Indian forest. Silently, he picks his way through the undergrowth, stopping at frequent intervals to sniff the air. Perhaps he is searching for a female on heat or for a suitable animal to prey on. Soon he will take to a stream to cool down in the heat of the day. There, he drinks and may rest, or simply wait for an unwary deer to come for a drink.

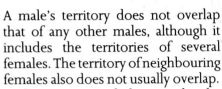

1

2

TIGER *Panthera tigris*

○ ▢ ☠

△ Habitat: tropical rain forest, northern coniferous and broad-leaved forest, mangrove swamp.

■ Diet: wild pig, deer, sometimes rhinoceros and elephant calves.

◎ Breeding: litters of 3 or 4 after pregnancy of 103 days.

Size: male Javan and Sumatran: head-tail 2.2-2.7m, weight 100-150kg; male Indian head-tail 2.7-3.1m, weight 180-260kg.

Colour: black stripes on a tawny, brownish or yellowish background.

Lifespan: up to 15 years, 20 in captivity.

Tigers are found only in Asia, where they live in forests with plenty of cover. They are the largest living cats and, unlike lions, are solitary hunters. There are eight races or subspecies of the tiger, some of which are now extinct. All surviving races are endangered, despite the setting up of tiger reserves in India.

The tiger is well armed for its life as a stalk-and-ambush hunter. The hind legs are longer than the forelegs, for powerful leaping, and long sharp claws on the front feet enable it to grasp and keep hold of struggling prey. The tiger eats whatever it can catch, but most of its prey are medium to large-sized animals, including wild pigs and deer.

HOME RANGES

Each tiger has its own home range or territory. Those of females (tigresses) are about 20sq km in area, while male territories range from 60 to 100sq km.

A male's territory does not overlap that of any other males, although it includes the territories of several females. The territory of neighbouring females also does not usually overlap.

The tiger regularly patrols the borders of its home range. It marks the borders with urine mixed with a scent from the anal gland, which it sprays on to trees, bushes and rocks. It also deposits droppings throughout its area.

For a female tiger, owning a territory has advantages. She gets to know the area well and discovers the best places to find prey. Having control over the prey in her area is important

▼ Camouflage – dark stripes on a pale background break up the body outline of a tigress lying in ambush.

▶▼This tiger may have walked 20km in search of prey. **(1)** It stalks a deer to within 20m, before **(2)** leaping on it with a few bounds, **(3)**, seizing it with powerful claws and **(4)**, bringing it to the ground. With a long-held bite to the throat, the tiger suffocates the deer, before dragging it off into cover to feed on until only skin and bones remain.

3

4

▼A zoo-bred "white tiger", whose ancestors came from north and central India.

if she has cubs to look after. For a male, with his much bigger territory, access to prey is probably not so important. His advantage lies in being able to monopolize the females living within his borders.

SOLITARY MOTHERS
Tigers begin to breed when they are 3 to 4 years old. They mate at any time of the year in the tropics, but only in winter further north. A female has a litter of three or four cubs, each weighing about 1kg. The cubs live in a den until they are 8 weeks old, after which they follow their mother around.

The female looks after the cubs until they are 18 months, and they may remain in her territory for 2½ years before leaving to find their own home ranges.

CHEETAH

A female cheetah sits on top of a termite mound in Africa, while her three cubs frolic below. For the moment, she is content to let them play. But she will soon carry on teaching the cubs how to hunt and kill prey. They will follow her white-tipped tail through the long grass, stopping at her command before she chases down a gazelle. Then she will call them to the prey. While she holds it down, they will practise the killing bite.

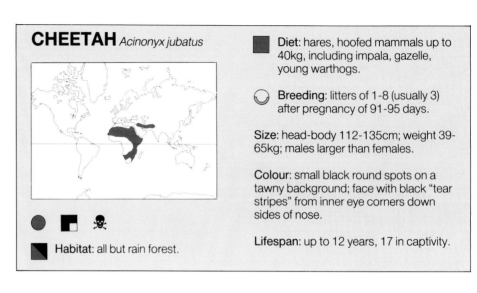

CHEETAH *Acinonyx jubatus*

Diet: hares, hoofed mammals up to 40kg, including impala, gazelle, young warthogs.

Breeding: litters of 1-8 (usually 3) after pregnancy of 91-95 days.

Size: head-body 112-135cm; weight 39-65kg; males larger than females.

Colour: small black round spots on a tawny background; face with black "tear stripes" from inner eye corners down sides of nose.

Habitat: all but rain forest.

Lifespan: up to 12 years, 17 in captivity.

▲Powered by long, muscular hind legs, a cheetah sprints at 96kph. A flexible spine allows it to make very long strides. The claws, even when held back, are not covered by a sheath but exposed, giving it a better grip on the ground.

▼With the acceleration of a high-powered sports car, a cheetah breaks cover to chase a Thomson's gazelle. An average chase covers 170m and lasts less than a minute. About half of these chases end with a successful kill.

With its small head and slim, loose-limbed build, the cheetah is the most distinctive of the big, spotted cats. Once common over much of Africa and the Middle East, only about 25,000 now survive in Africa.

FASTEST ON EARTH
The cheetah is best known as the fastest animal on Earth, capable of speeds up to 96kph. This skill is put to good use when it pursues hares and its more normal range of prey species, which include impala and gazelles.

Every year in Africa, the female cheetah follows the migration of its

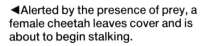

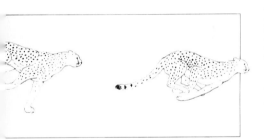

prey animals, moving through a home range of up to 800 sq km. The female is not territorial, so the home ranges of two or more females may overlap.

The male cheetah is aggressive. He will fight other males, sometimes to the death, in defence of his territory. Males usually live in groups, remaining together for life and marking their territories by spraying urine at regular intervals on landmarks such as tree stumps. Males also hunt together.

The cheetah breeds all the year round. The male does not help with rearing the young. At birth the cubs weigh 250 to 300g, and their eyes open at 2 to 11 days. When a few weeks old,

◄Alerted by the presence of prey, a female cheetah leaves cover and is about to begin stalking.

they leave their hiding-place and follow the mother around, eating some of the prey she catches. She weans them at about 3 months, but they remain with her until they are 17 to 23 months old, when female offspring leave one by one. The young males leave as a group – they are usually chased away from the area by older, more experienced males.

SECRETS OF SUCCESS
The cheetah shares the same areas as lions, leopards and hyenas. Its legendary speed helps it survive in this fierce competition. The cheetah also tends to hunt around the middle of the day, when the other large animals are usually asleep.

Daytime hunting, though, has its disadvantages. Vultures may drive a cheetah away from its kill and, at the same time, attract the attention of other hunters, which may then steal the prey. The cheetah avoids this by taking the kill to a hiding-place.

▼A strangling bite to the throat has killed this Thomson's gazelle. The cheetah now drags it to cover.

WOLVES

A long, piercing howl shatters the quiet of a northern forest. The howl grows into a chorus of many voices, and the forest valley soon echoes to the chilling sound. The leader of a wolf pack started this noise and other members joined in. The howling warns other wolf packs to keep away. There may be young cubs to protect or a kill to be guarded. For nearby farmers, the howling may mean that livestock become anxious and need to be calmed.

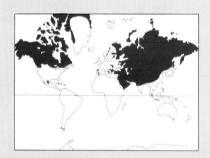

▶ **Wolves of the world** Red wolf **(1)**. Arabian Grey wolf **(2)**. Mexican Grey wolf **(3)**. European Grey wolf **(4)**. Tibetan Grey wolf **(5)**. Grey wolf/husky cross **(6)**.

Only two species of wolf survive today. The Grey wolf lives in the northern half of North America, Northern Europe and much of Asia. It is extinct in Britain and remains in Western Europe only in a few isolated areas. The decline of the Grey wolf is the result of the expansion of the human population, which led to the destruction of habitats. People have for centuries killed wolves, seeing them as a threat to farm animals. Our pet dogs are descended from wolves. The Red wolf once lived throughout south-east North America. It is now extinct in the wild except for a small group recently released in North Carolina.

LIFE IN THE PACK

Wolves are social animals and live in packs. A pack has 7 to 20 members, its size depending on the abundance of local prey. Wolves mate for life, so each pack consists of several pairs and their young.

Wolf packs have very large home ranges. The smallest is about 100sq km, while the largest may extend over 1,000sq km – the size depends on the amount of food available. Within each home range, a pack has its own territory which it guards against other

▲ With lowered tail and flattened ears, a wolf greets the pack leader (1), while two cubs play (2).

▼ A wolf pack sets off in single file in search of prey. Their travels may cover an area up to 1,000sq km.

packs. Wolves mark the boundaries of these areas by frequent scent-marking with urine and, less often, by howling. Wolf packs avoid each other as much as possible. When they do meet, there may be fights that result in deaths.

A strong, aggressive male leads each pack. His mate is the dominant female, and this leading pair breeds more often than the other pairs. A wolf signals its dominance by snarling and displaying its teeth, while other individuals show their acceptance of their lower position by holding their ears back and their tails between their legs. While an individual may be

lower in rank than the pack leader, it can also be dominant over other members of the pack.

BREEDING AND HUNTING

Wolves breed late in the winter. A female gives birth to a litter of between 4 and 7 blind, helpless cubs in a den. After about 4 weeks the cubs leave the den. They are looked after not only by their parents, but also by "helpers" among the other members of the pack.

By hunting together, a wolf pack can run down and kill animals which would be too big for a solitary wolf. They prey on deer, caribou and antelope, as well as smaller animals. Wolves also eat berries and scavenge at rubbish tips.

FOXES

It is a warm, moist evening. The Red fox is quietly padding across the grassy meadow, ears pricked for the slightest sound. Then he hears it, the rasping of an earthworm's bristles on the grass. Finding the exact source of the sound, he poises, before plunging his muzzle into the grass to grab the worm. The worm, though, still has its tail in its burrow. So the fox pulls it taut and tugs until the worm comes free.

FOXES Canidae (21 species)

● ■ ☠

■ **Habitat:** general, including urban.

◩ **Diet:** small mammals, birds, insects, eggs, fish, fruits, berries, carrion.

◎ **Breeding:** up to 8 offspring after pregnancy of 3 months (Red fox).

Size: smallest (Fennec fox): from head-body 24cm, tail 18cm, weight 1.5kg; largest (Small-eared dog): up to head-body 100cm, tail 35cm, weight 9kg.

Colour: grey to reddish-brown coat, sometimes white, silver, cream or black.

Lifespan: up to 6 years.

Species mentioned in text:
Arctic fox (*Alopex lagopus*)
Argentine grey fox (*Dusicyon griseus*)
Azara's fox (*D. gymnocercus*)
Bat-eared fox (*Otocyon megalotis*)
Colpeo fox (*Dusicyon culpaeus*)
Crab-eating fox (*D. thous*)
Fennec fox (*Vulpes zerda*)
Grey or Tree fox (*V. cinereoargenteus*)
Indian fox (*V. bengalensis*)
Kit or Swift fox (*V. velox*)
Red fox (*V. vulpes*)
Small-eared dog (*Dusicyon microtis*)

◀A Grey fox keeps watch from its vantage point up in a tree. It has the white throat typical of many species of fox.

▼Eight vulpine species Foxes of the genus *Vulpes* shown dashing after and swiping at a bird. Grey fox (**1**). Swift fox (*Vulpes velox*) (**2**). Cape fox (*V. chama*) (**3**). Fennec fox (**4**). Rüppell's fox (*V. rüppelli*) (**5**). Blanford's fox (*V. cana*) (**6**). Indian fox (**7**). Corsac fox (*V. corsac*) (**8**).

Foxes, like dogs, belong to the family of canids. Compared with dogs, they have a flattened skull, a pointed muzzle and a long bushy tail. Their triangular ears are fairly big and stand erect. The tip of the tail is often a different colour from the rest of the coat, usually black or white. Several species, including the Red fox, have a white chin.

THE TYPICAL FOX

The Red fox is often thought of as the "typical" fox because it is found so widely. But, with a head-to-tail length of over 110cm and weight up to 6kg, it

1   2   3   4

is bigger than its relatives in the genus *Vulpes*. More typical is the slighter-built Indian fox, which inhabits the open forest, scrub and steppe land of India, Pakistan and Nepal. This fox has a sandy-brown coat, with darker legs and tail.

The Grey fox of North and South America can grow nearly as big as the Red fox. It is also known as the Tree fox because it has the habit of climbing trees. It often sleeps in trees.

MOST ADAPTABLE
The Red fox is the most widespread and most successful of all the fox species. It is found from the far north of North America, Europe and Asia, south to the deserts of Central America and North Africa. It can adapt to a variety of climates from the frigid cold of the Arctic to the searing heat of the desert. It can also adapt to life in the city.

The Red fox is also very adaptable when it comes to food. It will eat almost any food that is available, not only small mammals, birds, eggs, worms, rabbits, but also in season fruits such as blackberries and apples and even rose hips. Fruits can form as much as 90 per cent of its diet.

▲ Two male North American Red foxes battling in the woods on an autumn day. It is a test of strength to see which one will be dominant.

5

6

7

8

POLAR BEAR

A hole appears in a smooth bank of deep snow, high in the Arctic. Out of the hole peeps a black nose. The hole gets larger and the black nose is followed by a broad, massive white head. Eventually the huge bulk of a female Polar bear looms out of the hole and moves slowly down the bank. She stops and waits as two smaller heads appear at the hole. Her cubs blink at their first sight of the Sun as they leave the den where they were born.

Polar bears are the largest living four-legged carnivores. They survive in one of the harshest areas of the world, braving the freezing cold of the high Arctic. Much of their time is spent on the pack-ice, far from land.

Everything about Polar bears is geared for survival in extreme cold. They are well insulated by a thick fur coat and a layer of fat – only the nose and pads of the feet are without fur. Small ears and a very short tail also prevent the loss of body heat.

PATIENT HUNTERS

Polar bears are excellent swimmers and can swim for hours through icy-cold water. Their feet are slightly webbed, and each foot has five long, curved claws. The claws help them to grip not only the slippery ice but also their prey. And the white coat camouflages a Polar bear against the snow, allowing it to sneak up unnoticed on basking seals.

Polar bears mostly hunt seals, especially the Ringed seal. For most of the year they hunt by waiting patiently for seals to appear at their breathing-holes in the ice. In April and May they break into the dens of Ringed seals, killing the mothers and the pups.

Polar bears may even attack and kill small whales and walruses. They also

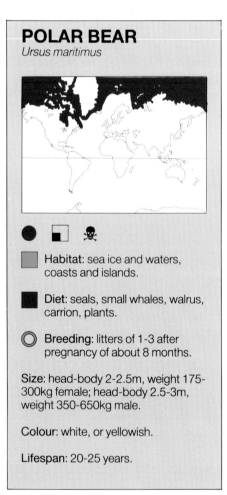

POLAR BEAR
Ursus maritimus

● ◻ ☠

Habitat: sea ice and waters, coasts and islands.

Diet: seals, small whales, walrus, carrion, plants.

Breeding: litters of 1-3 after pregnancy of about 8 months.

Size: head-body 2-2.5m, weight 175-300kg female; head-body 2.5-3m, weight 350-650kg male.

Colour: white, or yellowish.

Lifespan: 20-25 years.

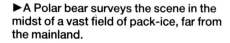

►A Polar bear surveys the scene in the midst of a vast field of pack-ice, far from the mainland.

eat carrion and, in summer, some plant material. Polar bears are mostly solitary animals, though up to 30 may gather at a good food source such as a dead whale.

A male Polar bear finds a female on heat by following her smell. A single male may have a large home area which includes the home areas of several females. Breeding begins when Polar bears are 5 years old. They mate in April, May and June.

WINTER IN THE DEN

In November and December pregnant females dig dens in the snow. Each female remains in her den until March, and it is here that she gives birth to a litter of up to three cubs, each weighing 600 to 700g.

Polar-bear milk is about one-third fat, which helps the cubs to keep their body temperature up through the permanent night of the Arctic winter. Although the female Polar bear does not feed while she is in the den, she is not in true hibernation.

The cubs leave the den with their mother when they are about 3 months old and weigh 8 to 12kg.

▲A cub follows its mother across the ice. It will remain with her until it is about 28 months old.

▼Polar bears scavenge at a rubbish tip in Alaska. This happens when towns are built on bear migration routes.

GRIZZLY (BROWN) BEAR

It is spawning time for the Pacific salmon. As the large fish labour upstream along a Canadian river, a Grizzly bear and her cubs come tumbling down the bank into the shallows, where the salmon are leaping. With her claws and teeth, the female Grizzly catches fish after fish and neatly strips the flesh from both sides.

Grizzly bears are famous for their strength and speed. A Grizzly can bite through a steel bolt 12mm thick. Despite its lumbering weight of nearly half a tonne, it can charge at 50kph.

Grizzly bears are forest animals and today are found in north-west North America and Europe and northern Asia. They are often called Brown bears and are rare, with only a few small isolated populations remaining.

Grizzlies eat mainly plants, especially young leaves and berries – they use their strong claws to dig up tubers and roots. They also eat insect grubs, rats and mice, salmon, trout and young deer. Sometimes Grizzlies will attack farm animals.

SPRING COURTSHIP
Male Grizzlies are solitary animals. Each adult male has a home range of up to 1,000sq km, which he defends fiercely against other males. They often fight to the death. Females also have territories, which they may share with a few young daughters. Their territories are smaller than those of males, up to 190sq km. Females, too, defend their territories against other females, so that they can enjoy exclusive access to food.

In spring, male Grizzlies seek out females. After a short courtship of 2 to 15 days they mate in May and June. As with all bears, the fertilized egg does not implant in the womb until October or November. At this time, the

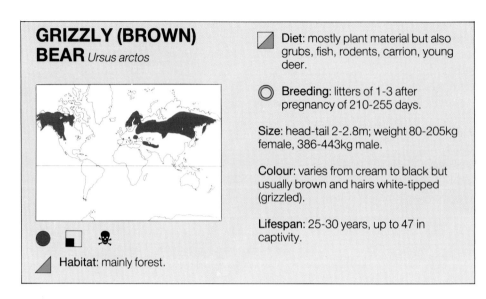

GRIZZLY (BROWN) BEAR *Ursus arctos*

Diet: mostly plant material but also grubs, fish, rodents, carrion, young deer.

Breeding: litters of 1-3 after pregnancy of 210-255 days.

Size: head-tail 2-2.8m; weight 80-205kg female, 386-443kg male.

Colour: varies from cream to black but usually brown and hairs white-tipped (grizzled).

Lifespan: 25-30 years, up to 47 in captivity.

Habitat: mainly forest.

female either digs out her own den or finds a natural cave or a hollow tree. She remains there throughout the winter, not feeding, but relying on her store of body fat.

She gives birth to two or three naked, helpless cubs, each weighing only 350 to 400g. They remain in the den until April, May or June and stay with their mother for up to about 4½ years.

▼Grizzlies love water and spend much time in and around salmon rivers bathing, frolicking and feeding.

FEW SAFE AREAS
Grizzlies are now endangered in many parts of North America. They are sometimes shot when they feed at rubbish tips and have been wiped out in many areas.

Despite their fierce reputation, Grizzlies rarely attack people. When a bear does attack, it is sometimes because with its poor eyesight it mistakes a person for another bear.

▶A bear hug: two young male Grizzlies in a play fight, which is good practice for adult fighting.

AMERICAN BLACK BEAR

A black bear forages among the bushes. Her two cubs clamber up a nearby tree and slither down the trunk. They jump on one another and wrestle, rolling over on the ground. They bump into their mother, and she cuffs them with her paw. But they carry on playing. The mother bear puts up with their games. She is too busy eating to join in. She is thin after having the cubs, and she is making good use of the late summer to feed on berries.

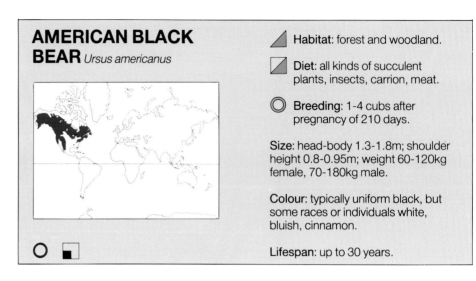

AMERICAN BLACK BEAR *Ursus americanus*

Habitat: forest and woodland.

Diet: all kinds of succulent plants, insects, carrion, meat.

Breeding: 1-4 cubs after pregnancy of 210 days.

Size: head-body 1.3-1.8m; shoulder height 0.8-0.95m; weight 60-120kg female, 70-180kg male.

Colour: typically uniform black, but some races or individuals white, bluish, cinnamon.

Lifespan: up to 30 years.

▼Apart from an occasional dash to catch prey, the pace of life for an American black bear is slow. For many, in the northern parts of their range, food is scarce and slow-growing. Bears are often seen scratching the ground for food, like the one shown here. A female black bear may wander over an area of 100sq km in a year to find enough food.

The American black bear once roamed over most of the woods of North America from central Mexico to Canada. Where people have built towns or cleared the woods, the bears have vanished with their habitat. But where there are forests, American black bears can still be found. They do not often go into open country.

In spite of their name and usual colour, there are several varieties of black bear. Near the west coast in British Columbia there are even pure white "black bears", as well as brown and bluish forms. In the east pure black bears are usual. This is also where the largest bears come from, the biggest on record being a male that reached 272kg and almost 2m from nose to the tip of its stubby tail.

▼Black bears like meat if they can catch it, or will feed on carrion. This one has found a cow killed in a storm.

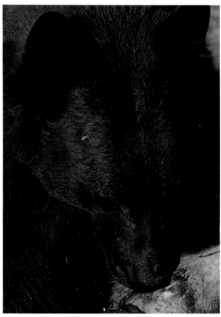

SWEET TOOTH

An American black bear needs up to 8kg of food a day. It feeds on bulbs, tubers, young shoots, and nuts and berries in season. It also kills animals from the size of mice to young deer if it has the chance. It digs up insect grubs and is fond of honey and sweet things. The black bear is a good climber and sometimes goes up trees in search of food.

Black bears mate in the summer. In the winter most den up, sometimes for as long as 7 months, so they spend more than half their lives asleep. While asleep during the winter the heartbeat slows down, and the body's temperature drops a little. This cuts down the bear's use of energy.

It is in the den, in January or February, that the cubs are born. Each cub is naked and weighs only 250g. They stay denned with the mother through the cold weather until the spring and suckle until the late summer. They may stay with the mother as long as 2½ years.

When the cubs first emerge from the den they weigh about 2kg. The mother is very protective. Her alarm grunt may send the youngsters scrambling up a tree out of reach of enemies. Accompanying their mother, the cubs learn how to dig out all kinds of delicacies.

Bears do not begin to breed until they are from 3 to 5 years old. Even in good conditions a female has cubs only once every 2 years.

BEGGING BEARS

Black bear numbers have declined as people have settled across North America, but there are more left than there are Brown (Grizzly) bears. They usually avoid people, but when hungry they may scavenge for scraps. In National Parks, where they are not molested, some bears get into the habit of begging for food beside roads. They can become dangerous if not given what they want.

◀Black bears scavenge at waste dumps or dustbins. This habit brings them into conflict with people.

▼An American black bear kills an unwary beaver and pulls it ashore to eat. Such meals supplement a mainly vegetable diet.

PANDAS

A Giant panda pushes its way through the bamboo forest with a rolling walk. It is seeking the spot it found yesterday where tender new bamboo shoots were sprouting. It comes to the clearing it remembers, but the place is already occupied. Another panda is sitting there, chewing on the bamboo. The new arrival mutters a few growls, then sits in the clearing far from the other panda. It turns its back and starts to feed.

►The Giant panda looks very human as it sits with its body upright and puts food to its mouth with its front paws.

▼As well as five toes, the Giant and the Red panda have an enlarged wrist bone that can be folded over to work as a "thumb". In this way pandas can grasp the bamboo shoots that they love to eat.

▼Giant pandas look like bears, which genetic evidence shows are their closest relatives.

PANDAS Procyonidae
(2 species)

◢ Habitat: mountain forest.

◢ Diet: bamboo shoots, grasses, bulbs, fruits, some insects, rodents and carrion.

◎ Breeding: 1 or 2 cubs after pregnancy of 125-150 days (Giant panda); 1-4 young after pregnancy of 90-145 days (Red panda).

Size: Red panda: head-body 0.5-0.6m plus 40cm tail, weight 3-5kg; Giant panda: head-body 1.2-1.5m plus 12cm tail, weight 100-150kg.

Colour: black and white (Giant panda); reddish chestnut, black below, light markings on face (Red panda).

Lifespan: 14-20 years.

Species mentioned in text:
Giant panda (*Ailuropoda melanoleuca*)
Red panda (*Ailurus fulgens*)

There are two species of panda. The Giant panda is black and white and bear-like. It lives in central and western China. The Lesser or Red panda has a beautiful reddish-chestnut back, darker below and on the legs, and lighter face markings. It is shaped like a chubby cat and has a long tail. It is found from Nepal to western China in mountain forests.

The Red panda was known to Western scientists a long time before the Giant panda was discovered in 1869. The Red panda finds most of its food in trees. It eats bamboo, fruit, acorns, lichens, roots and some small animals. Like the Giant panda it has an extra wrist bone that can be used as a thumb, though not so well. It is nocturnal and lives a solitary life.

BAMBOO DIET
The Giant panda, like the Red panda, belongs to the group of mammals called the Carnivores. Most of its relations, such as lions and wolves, eat meat most of the time, but the Giant panda has adapted to a life of feeding mainly on bamboo. It feeds on both the shoots and the roots but, whenever available, it prefers the leaves and slender stems. The Giant panda's cheek teeth are specialized for slicing and crushing food, and it can cope with stems up to about 40mm in diameter. It also eats some bulbs and tubers of other plants, grasses and some small animals.

Although bamboo forms the main part of its diet, the Giant panda's gut is not especially efficient at digesting it, and much of the bamboo passes straight through the body. To get enough nourishment the Giant panda may spend as much as 12 hours a day feeding.

MATING AND RAISING YOUNG
The Giant panda is largely solitary in the wild. There are scent glands beneath its tail, and it rubs these against large objects in the surround-

▲ The Red panda has big whiskers. With its long tail, short legs and sharp claws it is well built for climbing.

ings. This probably marks the territory and keeps away other pandas of the same sex. Even males and females are little interested in one another except in the brief mating season in the spring. Male and female find one another by scent and sound. After a brief mating they separate again.

A pair of cubs, sometimes three, are born in a sheltered den. Normally only one survives. Cubs are small, blind and helpless, weighing only about 100g. Their eyes do not open for 6 or 7 weeks, and the cub cannot follow its mother until it is about 3 months old. It is weaned at 6 months. At a year old it may move off to live independently. Female Giant pandas are able to reproduce when about 4 or 5 years old, but the males are probably

not fully mature until about 6 or 7 years old. Full-grown males are about 10 per cent larger and 20 per cent heavier than females.

PANDA PROBLEMS
The Giant panda is a rare animal. Fewer than 1,000 survive in the wild. It has probably always been a rare animal, because its way of life confines it to a limited area – bamboo forests at heights of 2,600 to 3,500m. Although it is protected and lives in remote areas, its populations are so small that it is likely to die out.

One of the panda's chief foods is a bamboo which flowers only about every 100 years and then dies back. This has happened recently in some parts of the panda's range, and some pandas may have starved as a result. Yet as a species the Giant panda must have survived these flowerings many times before and can do so again.

RACCOONS

Late in the evening, at the edge of a marsh sits a raccoon. It reaches down with its hands to feel and grope in the water among the mud and plant roots. The raccoon does not seem to watch what its hands are doing. Suddenly it pulls out a hand, grasping a small frog. Dunking its catch back in the water, it washes the frog backwards and forwards, before finally eating it.

Raccoons are American relatives of the pandas of south-east Asia. Four species are each found on a single island. Two species are widespread.

The Common raccoon lives as far north as southern Canada and as far south as Central America. The Crab-eating raccoon is found in Central America and northern South America. Raccoons eat a wide range of foods, foraging in trees, on the ground and also in water.

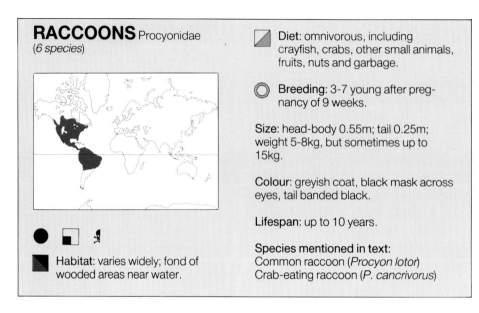

RACCOONS Procyonidae
(6 species)

● ■ ♗

■ Habitat: varies widely; fond of wooded areas near water.

⬚ Diet: omnivorous, including crayfish, crabs, other small animals, fruits, nuts and garbage.

◯ Breeding: 3-7 young after pregnancy of 9 weeks.

Size: head-body 0.55m; tail 0.25m; weight 5-8kg, but sometimes up to 15kg.

Colour: greyish coat, black mask across eyes, tail banded black.

Lifespan: up to 10 years.

Species mentioned in text:
Common raccoon (*Procyon lotor*)
Crab-eating raccoon (*P. cancrivorus*)

MOBILE HANDS
A raccoon's hands are very mobile and have a good sense of touch. It uses them to explore food, especially in water. This behaviour is so ingrained that a raccoon in captivity may take food, place it in water, and then retrieve it. This has led to the myth that raccoons "wash" their food.

LIVING WITH PEOPLE
Raccoons are fond of crayfish, but they will eat foods ranging from mice and worms to birds and their eggs. They also eat fruit and corn and sometimes raid crops, which makes them unpopular with farmers. They are curious and will investigate all kinds of places and sources of food.

▲ The Crab-eating raccoon is a good climber and has a long tail. It also spends time in and near water.

▶ A Common raccoon rests at the entrance to its den. Raccoons are active mostly during the night.

Raccoons sometimes make dens in barns and sheds, living close to people and making a living on their left-overs. This is probably one reason why the Common raccoon has been able to spread northwards in recent years. Unfortunately, it is an important carrier of the disease rabies, so its presence is not always welcome.

▲Raccoons live alone, but many may gather where food is plentiful. These are begging for scraps at a roadside.

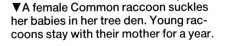
▼A female Common raccoon suckles her babies in her tree den. Young raccoons stay with their mother for a year.

▲A Common raccoon raids a dustbin. Raccoons have learned to live even in areas where there are many humans.

WINTER DENS

In the northern part of its range the Common raccoon puts on fat in autumn. It stays in a den for much of the winter, although it does not truly hibernate. Dens may be in hollow trees or below ground. A family of raccoons may den together, even though the young go their own way to find food. As many as 23 raccoons have been found squeezed together in a winter den.

Common raccoons are born in the spring. A mother produces her litter in the security of a tree den. The young are tiny and undeveloped, only about 70g in weight. It is 7 weeks or more before they are able to leave the den unaided, and not till 10 weeks old do they follow their mother.

Raccoons begin to breed when they are 1 or 2 years old. Males grow rather bigger than females.

SKUNKS

A female Striped skunk is out on a night's foraging. She has dug some beetles from the soft earth. Now she is at the edge of a wood, listening and waiting for the chance to catch a young rabbit. Another animal, a fox, steals along the edge of the wood. The skunk does not run away from it. She stamps in annoyance and walks stiff-legged in the moonlight. She is easy to see, holding her bushy tail straight up. The fox hesitates, then quickly goes past, keeping well clear of the skunk.

SKUNKS Mustelidae; sub-family Mephitinae (*13 species*)

Diet: insects, small mammals, eggs, some fruit.

Breeding: 2-9 young after pregnancy of 42-66 days.

Size: head-tail 40-70cm; weight 0.5-3kg.

Colour: mainly black, with white stripes or spots.

Lifespan: up to 10 years.

Species mentioned in text:
Hooded skunk (*Mephitis macroura*)
Pygmy spotted skunk (*Spilogale pygmaea*)
Striped skunk (*Mephitis mephitis*)

Habitat: woods, open country, desert.

All species of skunk live in North, Central or South America. There are three main types. Seven species of hog-nosed skunk live in the southern USA, Central and South America. They have a long bare muzzle and large claws, which are both adaptations to digging.

The four spotted skunks live in the USA and Central America. They are light in build and are good climbers. Spotted skunks are striped, but these stripes may be broken into spots. The Striped skunk is a common species in North America and northern Mexico. The Hooded skunk is found in the south-west USA.

MAKING A STINK
The weasel family all have anal scent glands, but these are best developed in the skunks. Skunks are able to spray the contents of the two glands in the direction of an enemy. The spray is aimed at the face and causes intense irritation of the skin – sometimes even temporary blindness.

The spray is accurate over 2m or more. It contains sulphur compounds with an unbearable and very clinging smell. Although this is a good deterrent against most enemies, Great horned owls still attack skunks. Other animals may also attack if desperate with hunger. But usually a skunk is safe and not afraid of these predators. Skunks and their dens do not smell of the powerful spray.

THREAT DISPLAYS
Skunks do not hide from enemies. Instead they put on a warning display.

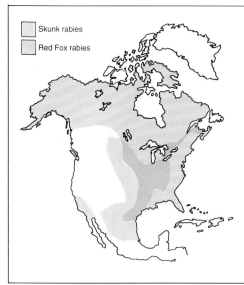

Skunk rabies
Red Fox rabies

◄Skunks are common carriers of the disease rabies in the USA. Infected skunks have the rabies virus in their saliva and tend to bite almost anything that moves. The map shows where rabies occurs in skunks and Red foxes in North America.

►Most animals avoid a skunk that gives a threat display or sprays. Rabid foxes, though, may still attack it, so infecting the skunk and spreading the disease.

Together with their obvious black and white colour this is usually enough to put off an enemy. Only as a last resort does the skunk shoot its stinking spray.

The ability to spray scent develops at only a month old. When a skunk is born it is blind and hairless, but even then the skin shows signs of the pattern that will develop in the fur. The Striped skunk's eyes open at about 3 weeks, by which time the fur has grown. At 5 weeks the young begin to move around with the mother, finishing suckling at about 2 months. By the autumn after their birth (usually in May) the young are looking after themselves.

▲The Pygmy spotted skunk is a rare species found only on the Pacific coast of Mexico. Spotted skunks have silky fur.

Skunks are found in many habitats, including towns. They are basically meat-eaters, but consume almost any food. They rest up in dens in bad weather. Skunks suffer from fleas, ticks and flatworms and from diseases such as rabies and distemper.

▼**Species of skunk** A Western spotted skunk (*Spilogale gracilis*) (1) does a handstand, a threat made before spraying its scent. The Hooded skunk (2) of the south-west USA. The Hog-nosed skunk (*Conepatus mesoleucus*) (3) has a long bare snout. In the very common Striped skunk(4, 5) the white stripes vary in number and thickness.

OTTERS

Off the Californian coast a Sea otter dives to the sea bed. It digs out a clam and a stone, then returns to the surface. The otter lies on its back at the surface balancing the stone on its chest. Taking the clam in one hand, it bangs it down repeatedly on the stone. The clam shell cracks, and the otter feeds on the flesh inside. Then it washes off the remains by rolling over. The stone stays in the otter's hands, to be used again.

As well as the Sea otter of the North Pacific there are another 11 species of otter found across most continents except Australasia and Antarctica. Several species venture into the sea, but most prefer the rivers, lakes and marshes. Otters can move across country, but like to be near water, where they find food.

HUNTING SESSIONS
Otters have tight-packed underfur with long guard hairs. The coat repels water and soon dries. An otter's body

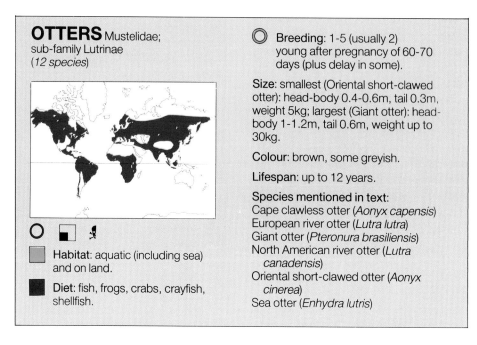

OTTERS Mustelidae; sub-family Lutrinae (*12 species*)

○ Breeding: 1-5 (usually 2) young after pregnancy of 60-70 days (plus delay in some).

Size: smallest (Oriental short-clawed otter): head-body 0.4-0.6m, tail 0.3m, weight 5kg; largest (Giant otter): head-body 1-1.2m, tail 0.6m, weight up to 30kg.

Colour: brown, some greyish.

Lifespan: up to 12 years.

Species mentioned in text:
Cape clawless otter (*Aonyx capensis*)
European river otter (*Lutra lutra*)
Giant otter (*Pteronura brasiliensis*)
North American river otter (*Lutra canadensis*)
Oriental short-clawed otter (*Aonyx cinerea*)
Sea otter (*Enhydra lutris*)

○ ◧ 🦦
Habitat: aquatic (including sea) and on land.

Diet: fish, frogs, crabs, crayfish, shellfish.

is very supple. The tail is thick and muscular at the base, flattened below and in some species flattened above too. It helps in swimming. Most kinds of otter have webbed paws.

Otters are active and energetic. Many species have several hunting sessions in a day. An otter may eat daily 1kg of food spread over several meals. The teeth are very strong, helping otters crush the bones of their

prey. They digest their food quickly, giving them boundless energy.

MANY VOICES
Most otters, such as the European and North American river otters, live singly except when breeding. Then a

▼An Oriental short-clawed otter shows its streamlined shape under water, when its ears and nostrils are closed.

▲The Cape clawless otter uses its hands to catch and eat prey. Its long whiskers help it sense moving prey.

pair may stay together for just a few months. Other otters, such as the Cape clawless otter, live in pairs all the time. The most social otters include the Giant otter and the Oriental short-clawed otter. These move around in larger groups based on families.

Otters make many sounds. They chirp or bark to keep in touch and make a chattering sound when close. They also growl. Another way otters communicate is by scent. They may deposit droppings, urine or scent from the anal glands. These scents mark out territories and give information to other otters about the animal that left them. Groups of Giant otters in Brazil make communal scent areas on river banks, clearing all the plants in a wide semicircle.

▶Clever hands The Oriental short-clawed otter (1, forepaw a) catches prey with its hands and is good at feeling and grasping, as is the Cape clawless otter (b). The Spot-necked otter (*Hydrictis maculicollis*) (2) has webbed fingers (e) and catches food with its mouth. So does the Giant otter (c). The Indian smooth- coated otter (*Lutrogale perspicillata*) (3), has webbed fingers (d) but can hold a shell to its mouth. North American river otter (4,f) has a bare nose. Species can be told apart (i-viii) by the nose's shape.

TRUE SEALS

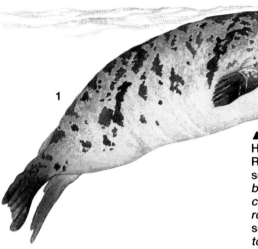

Smooth sleek bodies bask on the shore in the golden sunlight of late afternoon, their mottled fur blending with the rocks. They are Grey seals. Sometimes one of them rolls over and lazily strokes its belly with a flipper. In the swirling sea near by a round grey head with large dark eyes scans the scene before diving out of sight. Below the waves the supple bodies of more Grey seals twist and turn as they chase fish for supper. Exhausted, other Grey seals haul themselves out of the spray to join their sunbathing companions.

Seals are sleek, plump mammals that live in polar and temperate seas and oceans. They are graceful swimmers with short stubby flippers. Their bodies glide easily through the water as they swim. Seals' foreflippers are modified wrists and hands, their hind flippers ankles and feet.

EARLESS SEALS

True seals have no external ear-flaps, and this marks them out from sea lions and fur seals, their close rel-

▲▶ **Northern and southern true seals**
Hooded seal (*Cystophora cristata*) **(1)**. Ringed seal **(2)**. Grey seal **(3)**. Harp seal **(4)**. Bearded seal (*Erignathus barbatus*) **(5)**. Ribbon seal (*Phoca fasciata*) **(6)**. Ross seal (*Ommatophoca rossi*) **(7)**. Weddell seal **(8)**. Crabeater seal **(9)**. Leopard seal (*Hydrurga leptonyx*) **(10)**. Southern elephant seal **(11)**. Hawaiian monk seal (*Monachus schauinslandi*) **(12)**.

▼Harp seals look out for danger in the Canadian pack ice.

TRUE SEALS Phocidae
(*19 species*)

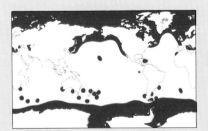

Habitat: offshore rocks and islands, pack-ice, land-fast ice, some large lakes.

Diet: prawns, squid, fish and (larger species of seals) sea-birds and smaller seals.

Breeding: usually 1 young after pregnancy of 10-11 months.

Size: smallest (Ringed seal): head-tail 117cm, weight 45kg; largest (Southern elephant seal): head-tail 490cm, weight 2,400kg; sexes usually the same size, but males of some species and females of others are much larger.

Colour: shades of grey or brown, often with dark spots or patches; young of some species white or tan at birth.

Lifespan: up to 56 years.

Species mentioned in text:
Crabeater seal (*Lobodon carcinophagus*)
Grey seal (*Halichoerus grypus*)
Harbour seal (*Phoca vitulina*)
Harp seal (*P. groenlandica*)
Northern elephant seal (*Mirounga angustirostris*)
Ringed seal (*Phoca hispida*)
Southern elephant seal (*Mirounga leonina*)
Weddell seal (*Leptonychotes weddelli*)

atives. True seals' flippers are weak and they cannot raise their bodies off the ground when on land. A true seal moves on land by using first its chest and then its belly to take its weight.

True seals are more powerful swimmers than sea lions. They use their hind flippers to propel themselves through the water, swinging the back end of their body from side to side.

UNDERWATER HUNTERS

Seals are underwater hunters. They feed on fish, shrimps, squid and sea-birds, which they catch with their pointed teeth. Their large eyes help them see in the dim underwater world.

Sea water is cool, especially at depth, and seals have a thick layer of fat (called blubber) under the skin which prevents them losing heat too quickly. It also helps to give them their smooth shape. The Weddell seal, like other seals, is a good diver, able to go 600m below the surface. It can close its nostrils and hold its breath for more than an hour.

THE SEAL YEAR

Seals breed slowly. The females are not usually ready to breed until they are at least 3 or 4 years old, and they produce only one pup at a time. Seals have to come on to land to give birth, usually in spring or early summer. New-born seals have soft and warm fur, which is not very waterproof.

Female seals (cows) produce some of the richest milk known. In just a few weeks a baby Crabeater seal can grow from 25kg to 120kg feeding only on its mother's milk. Suckling may last from 10 days to 12 weeks. Then the cow is ready to mate again.

Male true seals (bulls) often mate with more than one cow. Elephant seals and the Grey seal gather in large numbers on beaches to breed. Each bull defends his own patch of beach and his cows. The bulls roar and slash at each other with their teeth. Weddell seals, Ringed seals and Harbour seals defend underwater territories instead.

After mating, the seals return to the sea to feed. The females are now pregnant, but the babies inside them will not start to develop for 2½ to 3½ months.

▶A pregnant Ringed seal digs out a snow cave above a crack in the pack-ice (inset). Here she will give birth. In this cave, the mother and her pup will be hidden from enemies like the Polar bear and Arctic fox. The snow above will help to keep out the cold.

▶The huge nose of the male Northern elephant seal can be inflated to impress a rival. On his neck are rolls of blubber which may be up to 10cm thick.

STILL IN DANGER

In the past, seals have been killed on a large scale for their fur, skins, meat and blubber. Today, international laws limit the numbers that can be killed, and some species are completely protected. But the monk seals are still in danger of becoming extinct, especially in the Mediterranean. This is mainly because the warm coasts where they live are much disturbed by tourists, fishermen and divers.

▼This may look like a family group, but the male Crabeater seal is not the pup's father. He is waiting to mate with its mother.

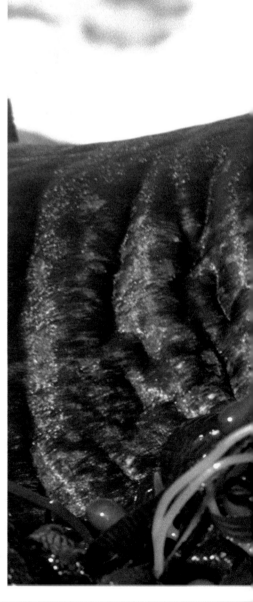

SEA LIONS AND FUR SEALS

Brown shadows weave in and out of the pounding surf, riding the waves and diving back underneath them. California sea lions are playing where the foamy sea meets the land. Beyond the breakers, more sea lions are exploring the sea bed for lobsters and octopus, trailing streams of bubbles behind them. Bull sea lions bark as they argue over ownership of their watery domains.

Sea lions and fur seals are sometimes called eared seals because, unlike the true seals, they have external ear-flaps. The males have thick manes of fur around their necks – the reason for the name sea lions. Fur seals have much thicker fur than sea lions.

SEA LIONS AND FUR SEALS Otariidae (*14 species*)

● ■

░ **Habitat:** offshore rocks and islands.

■ **Diet:** fish, shrimps, lobsters, octopus and other sea creatures, sometimes sea-birds and young seals.

◎ **Breeding:** 1 young after pregnancy of 12 months.

Size: smallest (Galapagos fur seal): head-tail 120cm male, weight 27kg; largest (Steller sea lion) head-tail 287cm male, weight 1,000kg (males larger than females).

Colour: shades of brown, grey and tan, males often darker than females, juvenile coat often paler.

Lifespan: up to 25 years.

Species mentioned in text:
Antarctic fur seal (*Arctocephalus gazella*)
Australian sea lion (*Neophoca cinerea*)
California sea lion (*Zalophus californianus*)
Galapagos fur seal (*Arctocephalus galapagoensis*)
Northern fur seal (*Callorhinus ursinus*)
Steller sea lion (*Eumetopias jubatus*)

ACROBATS OF LAND AND SEA

Sea lions are popular performing animals because they are at home on land and in water. They can chase fish underwater or romp around the rocks, tossing fish in the air and catching them in their mouths.

To walk, a sea lion lifts its body off the ground, using its long foreflippers, and swings its hind flippers forwards under its body. When a sea lion wants to go faster over land, it gallops, putting both foreflippers down together, then the hind flippers, then the foreflippers again, and so on. A large fur seal can run faster than a fully grown man.

In the water, sea lions and fur seals are very agile swimmers, but they cannot hold their breath as well as true seals. They rarely dive for more

◄Bull sea lions paddle with their foreflippers as they patrol their water territories.

▼Species of sea lion and fur seal
Males are larger and usually darker than females. Often males have a large mane of thicker fur. Sea lions (**1-4**) have broader snouts than fur seals (**5, 6**), which have thicker coats. Male California sea lion (**1**). Female Steller sea lion (**2**).

Female South American sea lion (*Otaria avescens*) (**3**). Male New Zealand sea lion (*Phocarctos hookeri*) (**4**). Female South American fur seal (*Arctocephalus australis*) (**5**). Male Northern fur seal (**6**).

171

▲ Male California sea lions use ritual threats to argue over territory boundaries on the beach. By using gestures instead of fighting, they have more energy left for mating. Head-shaking and barking as the males approach the boundary (1). Bulls look sideways at each other and make lunges (2). More head-shaking and barking (3). During the lunges, males try to keep their foreflippers away from each other's mouths. The thick skin on their chests softens the blows.

than 5 minutes. Unlike true seals, they use their foreflippers for swimming, flexing their hindquarters for extra power.

BATTLES ON THE BEACHES

In spring and early summer large numbers of sea lions and fur seals gather on their favourite breeding beaches to give birth and mate. The females are heavily pregnant when they arrive and soon give birth. About a week after giving birth, they are ready to mate.

Each male (bull) tries to mate with several females. To compete with other bulls for the females, he tries to defend a section of beach and the females in it. If every dispute led to a fight, the bulls would soon become too exhausted to mate. Instead, they make threatening displays and gestures, from which they can usually judge which animal is the stronger.

For a bull to defend his territory throughout the breeding season, he must stay on his patch. So most bulls do not feed at all during this time. Sometimes they may fast for 70 days. They can do this because they live off their fat (blubber). The biggest bulls have the most fat, so they are usually the most successful in holding a territory. The weather is usually warm at this time, and the seals get very hot on the beach. So the most prized territories are those nearest the water.

◀ This Australian sea lion pup will soon shed his two-colour coat for a dark-brown adult one.

WELL-FED PUPS

Mother sea lions and fur seals stay with their pups for the first week of their lives, suckling them frequently. The pups need to be protected from the bulls, which can easily trample them during a fight.

As each pup grows bigger, its mother spends longer at sea feeding, returning from time to time to suckle her young. She finds her pup by calling to it and listening for its answering call. Many pups do not leave their mother until the next pup arrives 1 to 3 years later.

The Northern fur seal migrates hundreds of kilometres to different feeding areas in summer and winter. Its pups stop suckling when the migration starts. Female pups reach maturity at about 4 years old and male pups at 5 to 8 years of age.

PROTECTED POPULATIONS

Instead of having mainly long coarse hairs with just a few shorter ones, like the sea lions, the fur seals have a dense layer of woolly underfur. Glands among the hairs keep the animals coated with waterproof oil.

The thick fur causes problems in summer, when fur seals suffer badly from the heat. The only part of their bodies that can lose heat is the flippers. The animals often wave their flippers in the air to cool themselves.

But the fur seals' coats have caused them bigger problems than this. They have been much sought by hunters. By the end of the nineteenth century so many fur seals had been killed that some species were almost extinct. Laws were later passed to prevent the slaughter. Exploitation continues, but under strict international controls.

During the twentieth century fur seals have made a strong recovery. The Antarctic fur seal, whose population was reduced to probably fewer than 50 animals, now numbers around a million, and the population is increasing. Scientists think that this is partly because so many whales have been killed. The whales used to compete with the seals for one of their favourite foods, the tiny shrimp-like krill.

The Australian sea lion is the best example of the improved relationship between seals and people. In places, it is so accustomed to human visitors that tourists can mingle with the seals on the beach.

▼An Antarctic fur seal with a plastic packing band cutting into its neck. Harmful waste kills many seals.

WALRUS

With a grunt and a splash the large bristly snout of a walrus comes out of the water. It is followed by 1,000kg of brownish-pink flesh. Using his long pointed tusks as levers, the walrus hauls himself out of the sea on to an ice-floe. He shuffles towards a group of dozing walruses and flops down on the ice to snooze, using the belly of another walrus as a pillow.

The walrus is rather like a giant pink sea lion. It has flippers instead of legs, and a fat spindle-shaped body. It is a powerful swimmer and can stay at sea for up to 2 days at a time. When on land, the walrus props up its body on its foreflippers, tucking its hind flippers underneath. It walks awkwardly, shuffling along on its flippers.

The females (cows) and young males have short velvety coats. Adult males (bulls) have little hair and look naked. Their skin is up to 5cm thick, wrinkled like an old leather bag.

The walrus has such a short thick neck that its head seems to be joined directly to its shoulders. Its squarish snout is covered in stiff bristles. One pair of teeth in the upper jaws of both sexes form tusks up to 55cm long.

WHY HAVE TUSKS?

The walrus does not use its tusks for feeding. It feeds on the sea bed, using the bristles on its snout to feel for clams, mussels and other sea creatures. It digs in the mud with its snout, which is covered in extra tough skin. Sometimes it shoots a jet of water from its mouth to blast prey animals out of their burrows.

The walrus uses its tusks like ice-axes to haul itself on to ice-floes, or to smash breathing-holes in the ice.

A walrus also uses its tusks to establish its place in the group. Walruses usually live in very large groups, sometimes of several thousand animals, and there are often arguments. The male walruses with the largest tusks get the best places on the ice or beach and the best chance of mating with the females. Walruses display to each other, showing off their tusks. If a display does not settle a dispute, the walruses may stab at each other with their tusks.

For thousands of years, Eskimos have hunted walruses for their skins and meat. Where stocks allow, this continues today.

▶Sunbathing walruses look pink as their blood flows to the surface to absorb the Sun's warmth. The walrus just leaving the water is much paler, its blood flowing deeper to avoid losing heat to the cold water.

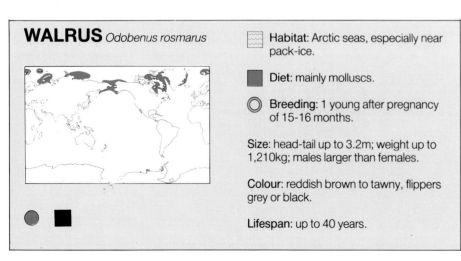

WALRUS *Odobenus rosmarus*

Habitat: Arctic seas, especially near pack-ice.

Diet: mainly molluscs.

Breeding: 1 young after pregnancy of 15-16 months.

Size: head-tail up to 3.2m; weight up to 1,210kg; males larger than females.

Colour: reddish brown to tawny, flippers grey or black.

Lifespan: up to 40 years.

DOLPHINS

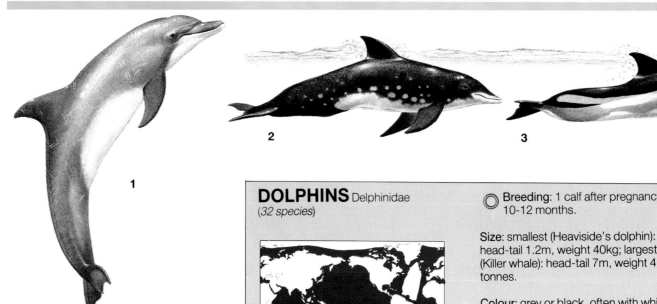

1

2

3

A group of dolphins have found a shoal of fish. They spread out round the edge of the shoal, leaping out of the water and diving back. They herd the fish into a tighter bunch. Now the dolphins feed well. They snap up fish one after the other. At last they are full. They begin to play, chasing, leaping and spinning.

DOLPHINS Delphinidae
(*32 species*)

Habitat: mostly coastal shallows, some open ocean.

Diet: fish, squid, other animals.

◎ Breeding: 1 calf after pregnancy of 10-12 months.

Size: smallest (Heaviside's dolphin): head-tail 1.2m, weight 40kg; largest (Killer whale): head-tail 7m, weight 4.5 tonnes.

Colour: grey or black, often with white patches, sometimes with other patches of colour.

Lifespan: 20-50 years.

Species mentioned in text:
Bottle-nosed dolphin (*Tursiops truncatus*)
Dusky dolphin (*Lagenorhynchus obscurus*)
Heaviside's dolphin (*Cephalorhynchus heavisidii*)
Killer whale (*Orcinus orca*)

▲▶Species of dolphin in common poses Bottle-nosed dolphin (1). Rough-toothed dolphin (*Steno bredanensis*) (2). Atlantic white-sided dolphin (*Lagenorhynchus acutus*) (3). Spotted dolphin (*Stenella plagiodon*) (4). Common dolphin (*Delphinus delphis*) (5). Northern right whale dolphin (*Lissodelphis borealis*) (6). Dusky dolphin (7). Atlantic humpbacked dolphin (*Sousa teuszii*) (8). Melon-headed whale (*Peponocephala electra*) (9). Commerson's dolphin (*Cephalorhynchus commersoni*) (10). False killer whale (*Pseudorca crassidens*) (11). Killer whale (12). Risso's dolphin (*Grampus griseus*) (13).

13

Dolphins are small whales. They are found in all the world's oceans. In most dolphins the jaws form a well-developed beak. Above this there is usually a "melon", a protruding rounded forehead. The nose is not on the beak. A dolphin breathes through a blowhole up on top of the head above the melon. Dolphins have a single dorsal fin which curves backwards.

Dolphins belong to the side of the whale family tree known as toothed whales. The description fits, because most have between 100 and 200 teeth in their jaws. Some have as many as 224. The teeth are all similar and sharply pointed. They are ideal for holding slippery prey.

Most dolphins feed on fish. Some prefer squid, and others will even eat shrimps. Many kinds of dolphin make use of shoals of fish swimming near the surface, but others will also dive deep for prey, or even pick fish from the sea bottom.

SOUND SENSE
Dolphins have good hearing and make many sounds themselves. Hearing is very important to them, both for keeping in touch with one another and for catching prey. Dolphins make some clicking sounds and whistles we can hear, and also other sounds which are much too high for the human ear. Some of the whistles are made when they are in particular moods or doing particular things. These can give information to other dolphins.

The very high sounds are used to beam out in front of the dolphin and produce echoes from objects. The dolphin hears the echoes and from them can tell what is around. Dolphins especially use this system to find prey. The melon on a dolphin's forehead helps to focus the sound. Although we cannot hear them, some high-pitched sounds produced by dolphins are very loud. They may frighten and confuse prey, and perhaps even stun them.

MERCILESS HUNTER
The biggest of all the dolphins is the Killer whale. It is long-lived and intelligent. It is also one of the fastest swimmers, able to travel at 38kph. The Killer whale is widespread but is commonest in cool seas where there is plenty of prey. It lives in groups called pods of up to 40 individuals which know one another and are able to co-operate in hunting.

The Killer whale eats squid and fish, including sharks. It also kills seals, walruses and porpoises and may even attack larger whales. One Killer whale is recorded as having the remains of 15 seals and 13 porpoises inside it. Killer whales have been seen tipping ice-floes to catch seals as they fell off. Although it is so strong, there is no

▲ Dolphins can be inquisitive and playful. Here Bottle-nosed dolphins investigate two odd creatures at the edge of the sea.

record of a Killer whale making an unprovoked attack on a human.

GATHERING IN GROUPS

Killer whales stay together in their groups for life. In a group there is likely to be an adult male, three or four adult females and some younger whales of both sexes.

Other dolphins live in groups too, but they are often less fixed than those of Killer whales. The pair and calf, or mother and calf, keep together, but may join or leave bigger groups. Species that live inshore may form herds of 12 or so, and sometimes larger numbers come together where feeding is good. Some ocean dolphins form herds of 1,000 or even 2,000 at feeding areas. Dolphins are able to co-operate in hunting, driving the shoals of fish together.

Some dolphins live in small individual areas, such as the Bottle-nosed dolphin, which may keep within about 85sq km. The Dusky dolphin is very different – it may roam over 1,500sq km.

BORN BACKWARDS

Mating and birth can take place at any time of year, but in many species most births take place in summer. A baby dolphin is born underwater, tail first. As soon as the head is out, the baby must be got to the surface to take a breath and fill its lungs. The mother, and often other female dolphins, help the baby do this.

Once it is breathing, the youngster can swim, but the mother and "aunts" are very protective. Dolphin babies suckle underwater between breaths. The mother's milk is very fatty. She pumps it quickly into the baby.

BIG BRAINS

Dolphins have large brains compared to their body size. In animals this is usually a sign of intelligence. Dolphins can learn tricks readily, can remember complicated routines and can mimic some sounds and actions. It is doubtful, though, whether they are really much more intelligent than some other mammals such as dogs or elephants. Much of the large brain seems to be for dealing with the sounds that are so important to a dolphin.

DOLPHINS AND PEOPLE

Dolphins are curious, and sometimes are interested in humans. There have been several instances of "friendships" being struck up between wild dolphins and people.

People, though, are not always good for dolphins. Many dolphins have been killed by fishing boats using large nets. The animals get tangled and drown. Each year in the 1960s and 1970s about 110,000 dolphins were killed this way in the Eastern Pacific alone.

Now tuna fishermen can use special nets which reduce the threat to dolphins. The nets have a panel of fine mesh furthest from the boat. Fleeing dolphins do not get tangled in this and can escape over the net rim. Some countries, such as the United States, use human divers stationed in the nets to help trapped dolphins.

▶ Killer whales have large dorsal fins. As well as eating fish, they feed on warm-blooded prey, including other dolphins.

PORPOISES

▲A Dall's porpoise ploughs through the sea. This species is the one most often attracted to boats.

6

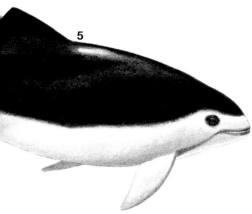

5

◀The six types of porpoise The Gulf of California porpoise (1), endangered by competition with fishermen. The little-known Burmeister's porpoise (*Phocoena spinipinnmis*) (2). The Finless porpoise (3) lacks a triangular back fin. The strikingly-colored Dall's porpoise (4). The black eye-rings give the Spectacled porpoise (*Phocoena dioptrica*) (5) its name. The Harbour porpoise (6) is the most frequently seen species, but its numbers are in decline.

Drifting out on the north Pacific Ocean, some fishermen on a small boat are startled by the sudden appearance of a Dall's porpoise, which swims boisterously around them. They glimpse at the blunt "smiling" face, and hear a loud snorting. Then, with a flick of its tail, the porpoise speeds away through the waves.

Porpoises are streamlined, fish-shaped mammals related to whales and dolphins. Unlike dolphins, they do not have a long snout, but, like all whales, they breathe through a blow-hole behind the blunt head. They swim at great speed, using the flat tail for power and flippers for steering.

Porpoises usually live alone, mainly in warmer coastal waters and estu-aries. During the breeding season, though, porpoises form small groups called schools. After mating, the male and female pairs split up and each female rears her young (calves) with-out the help of the male. The com-mon Harbour porpoise begins breed-ing at the age of 5 or 6 years. Dall's porpoise matures later, at around 7 years. A female Harbour porpoise suckles her calf for about 8 months, while Dall's porpoise may produce milk for up to 2 years. The calf may stay with its mother for a year or two after weaning, until the mother be-comes pregnant again. Young Finless porpoises often hitch a ride on their mothers' backs by holding on to a series of small ridges.

Females and calves may form small groups of four to six, sometimes with additional young males. The young males may eventually form their own small, all-male groups.

USING SOUNDS
Porpoises communicate with each other using a wide range of sounds, including clicks, squeaks and grunts.

They hunt fish using keen eyesight and echolocation. They make high-pitched sounds which bounce back off squid or small shoals of fish and which the porpoises hear. An adult Harbour porpoise needs 3 to 5kg of food per day, while the larger Dall's porpoise eats 10 to 12kg daily. The Finless porpoise probably finds much of its food by digging about with its snout in the sandy or muddy bottoms of estuaries.

Harbour porpoises eat mostly herr-ing, sardine and mackerel, while Gulf of California porpoises eat fish called grunts or croakers. The other species of porpoise probably live on mullet, anchovies and squid. All porpoises usually swallow their prey whole.

PORPOISE PROTECTION
Although porpoises are often seen in coastal waters and estuaries, little is actually known about their way of life. This makes their steady fall in numbers particularly worrying. We do not know how best to protect them. Porpoises, like whales, often "beach" themselves on shallow coast-lines. It is possible then to examine the stomach contents of animals which die in this way to see precisely what they eat.

Fishermen also depend on the prey caught by porpoises, and many feel themselves to be in competition with these animals. Many porpoises be-come trapped in fishing nets because they cannot detect the fine mesh with their echolocation. They just follow the shoal of fish into the trap. They can be released unharmed if they are handled with care, but many are deliberately killed.

Some scientists would like to see all nets "labelled" with a device which makes a sound to warn off porpoises, but this would be very expensive. Chemical pollution of the seas also kills porpoises, and here the solution is simple and obvious. Only the will to do something about it seems lacking.

SPERM WHALES

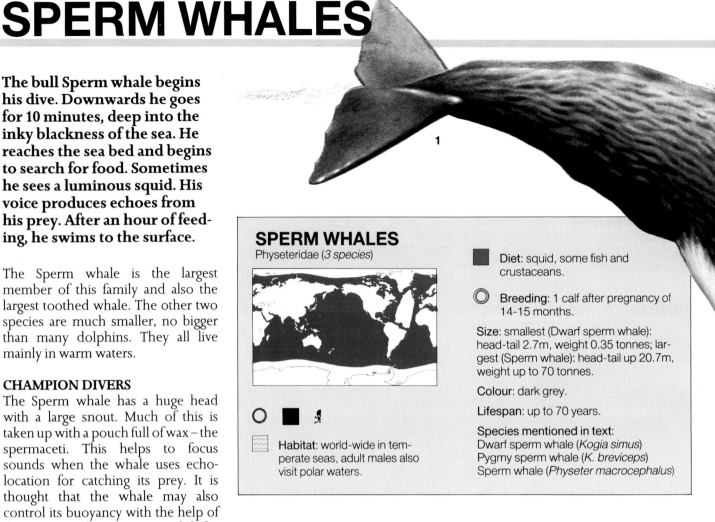

1

The bull Sperm whale begins his dive. Downwards he goes for 10 minutes, deep into the inky blackness of the sea. He reaches the sea bed and begins to search for food. Sometimes he sees a luminous squid. His voice produces echoes from his prey. After an hour of feeding, he swims to the surface.

The Sperm whale is the largest member of this family and also the largest toothed whale. The other two species are much smaller, no bigger than many dolphins. They all live mainly in warm waters.

CHAMPION DIVERS

The Sperm whale has a huge head with a large snout. Much of this is taken up with a pouch full of wax – the spermaceti. This helps to focus sounds when the whale uses echo-location for catching its prey. It is thought that the whale may also control its buoyancy with the help of the wax, cooling it to a solid for sinking, and warming it to liquid for rising.

Sperm whales make the deepest dives of all mammals. They have been picked up on sonar at 1,200m depth. They have been found to have eaten bottom-living sharks in an area where the sea bed was 3,200m down. Females can dive for an hour. The bulls, which are on average 4m longer and twice as heavy, can dive for longer.

HUNGRY FOR SQUID

Sperm whales eat many things, but much of their food is squid. Most of their prey are about 1m long, although some are smaller. One Sperm whale was found with 28,000 small squid inside it. Sperm whales sometimes also catch Giant squid, which are over 10m long, although then they may be scarred by bites or sucker marks.

SPERM WHALES
Physeteridae (*3 species*)

Habitat: world-wide in temperate seas, adult males also visit polar waters.

Diet: squid, some fish and crustaceans.

Breeding: 1 calf after pregnancy of 14-15 months.

Size: smallest (Dwarf sperm whale): head-tail 2.7m, weight 0.35 tonnes; largest (Sperm whale): head-tail up 20.7m, weight up to 70 tonnes.

Colour: dark grey.

Lifespan: up to 70 years.

Species mentioned in text:
Dwarf sperm whale (*Kogia simus*)
Pygmy sperm whale (*K. breviceps*)
Sperm whale (*Physeter macrocephalus*)

▼A pod (small herd) of Sperm whales rise to the surface to breathe. The blow-holes are on the left of the heads.

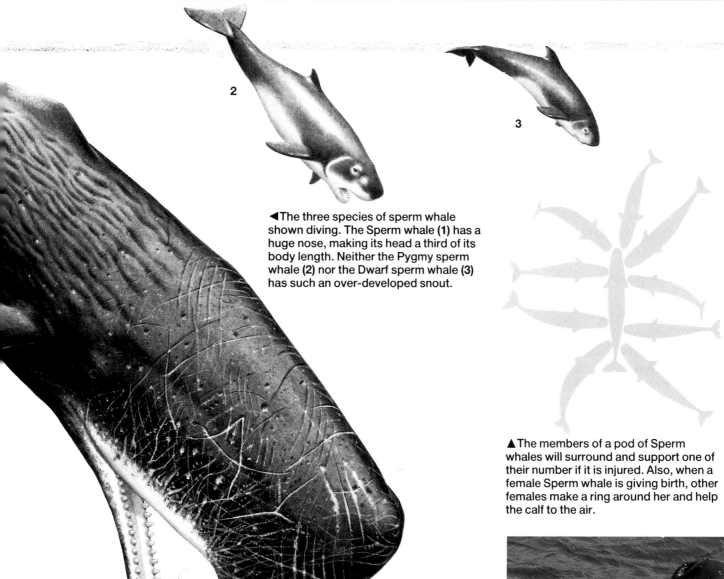

◀The three species of sperm whale shown diving. The Sperm whale **(1)** has a huge nose, making its head a third of its body length. Neither the Pygmy sperm whale **(2)** nor the Dwarf sperm whale **(3)** has such an over-developed snout.

▲The members of a pod of Sperm whales will surround and support one of their number if it is injured. Also, when a female Sperm whale is giving birth, other females make a ring around her and help the calf to the air.

TRAVELLING THE OCEANS

Sperm whales are commonest where ocean currents meet or water rises from the deep. Here there is plenty of food. The female Sperm whale lives in groups, and so do young males. Big bulls live alone except during the breeding season. Then they may fight for a harem.

Mating and birth take place near the equator. Afterwards the Sperm whale herds move to cooler water. The big males go much farther than others, as much as 8,000km to the cold waters near the North and South poles. Then all move back for the next breeding season.

About one-third of the weight of a Sperm whale is blubber that helps it keep warm in water. Blubber is a unique source of some lubricating oils, as is spermaceti. For these products, and for its meat to eat, the animal has been hunted relentlessly.

▶A Sperm whale calf breaks the surface, showing the dark wrinkled skin of this species.

WHITE WHALES

From high above, the scene looks peaceful as a herd of white whales go gliding through the clear water. But underwater there is a barrage of sound. The whales are belugas, and as they swim they call to one another. Squeals, clangs and whistles echo through the water. Sometimes there are chirps and mooing sounds. Their noises long ago earned them the sailors' name "sea canaries".

There are two species of white whale, the beluga and the narwhal. The beluga is always white as an adult. The narwhal has an unusual coloration, with a back covered in little patches of grey-green, black and cream, but this animal too whitens with age, from the belly upwards.

FLEXIBLE NECK

The beluga has a far more flexible neck than most whales and can turn it sideways to almost a right angle. It swims slowly on the surface, staying in shallow water. It dives to the bottom to find shoaling fish and crustaceans.

Groups of beluga sometimes work together to herd fish into shallow water or to a sloping beach, where they are more easily caught. A beluga can also hunt individual prey on the bottom. It can purse its lips and suck or blow water to move sand or dislodge prey. The beluga has up to 40 teeth, but they are not important in feeding. They may serve in visual threat displays and jaw-clap noise-making, used as communication.

▼A group of male narwhal show their iridescent grey-green-and-black backs as they swim in a dark blue icy sea.

WHITE WHALES
Monodontidae (*2 species*)

○ ■

≈ Habitat: coastal Arctic seas.

■ Diet: fish, shellfish, crabs, squid.

◎ Breeding: 1 calf after pregnancy of 14-15 months.

Size: head-tail 3-5m; weight 0.5-1.6 tonnes.

Colour: white, grey, black or mottled.

Lifespan: up to 40 years.

Species mentioned in text:
Beluga (*Delphinapterus leucas*)
Narwhal (*Monodon monoceros*)

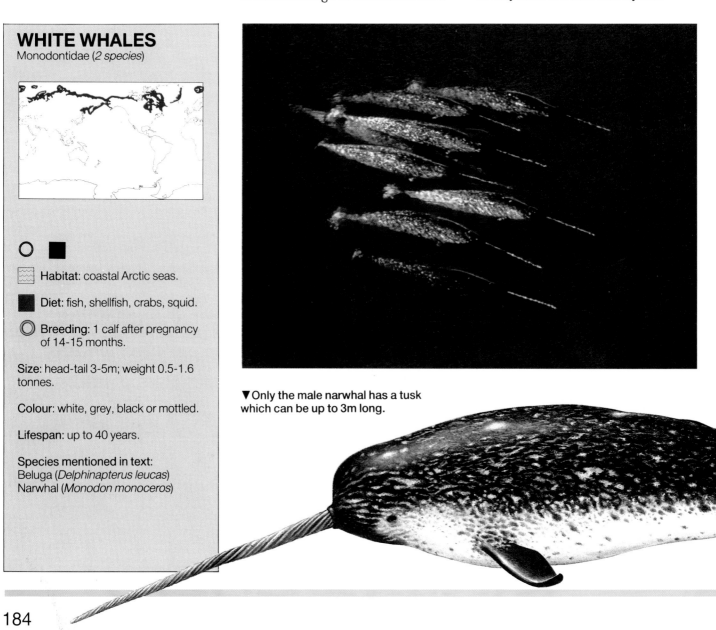

▼Only the male narwhal has a tusk which can be up to 3m long.

UNICORN OF THE OCEANS
The teeth of the narwhal also seem useless for feeding, although they can be enormous. Females have just two small teeth. Males also have two teeth, but the left one grows into a long pointed tusk. Sometimes both teeth grow. The tusk seems to have no purpose, other than showing that its owner is a male, and occasionally being used in a kind of jousting between males.

HERDS OF HUNDREDS
Throughout the year beluga are in groups, but in mid- to late summer they gather into larger herds and migrate to shallow estuaries. Here the young from the previous year's mating are born. These herds are hundreds or even thousands strong. By virtue of its colour, and as most join these big groups, the beluga is relatively easy to count from the air. The world population is about 30,000.

Beluga mothers separate from the herd for a short while to give birth, but soon rejoin a herd. The calf swims so close to the mother that the two are touching. The mother is protective of the calf, which suckles for 2 years.

A MUSEUM PIECE
Commercial hunting of the beluga has greatly reduced its numbers. It is also threatened by shipping activities. The narwhal is often killed for its tusk, which is valued by museums.

▲ A newborn beluga is brown. By one year old, like this baby with its mother, it is grey. An adult beluga is white.

▼ The forehead "melon" of the beluga is small in babies (1), but has begun to grow at 1 year old (2), and is large by maturity (3) at 5-8 years. Belugas use many sounds and facial expressions to "talk" to one another. At rest the beluga seems to smile (4). A beluga can produce a loud bang by clapping its jaws together (5). A pursed mouth (6) is used in feeding on the sea bottom.

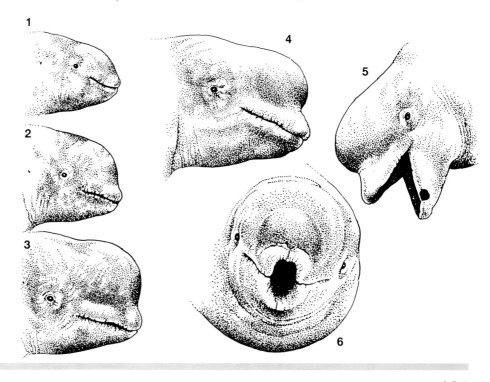

GREY WHALE

With a flick of its huge tail, the Grey whale power-dives its way down to the sea bed. There it swims along the bottom, its head ploughing through the thick layer of sediment. It scoops up a mouthful of crustaceans, worms and muddy water and returns to the surface. On the surface it expels the muddy water through its plates of baleen and swallows the food filtered out. Then it dives again.

▼Grey whale mother and calf. The calf is especially sleek and smooth-skinned.

GREY WHALE *Eschrichtius robustus*

○ ◨ 🦐

〜 Habitat: mainly coastal waters.

■ Diet: bottom-dwelling marine animals, such as crustaceans and worms.

◎ Breeding: 1 offspring after pregnancy of about 13 months.

Size: head-tail 11.9-14.3m, weight 16 tonnes male; head-tail 12.8-15.2m, weight (pregnant) up to 34 tonnes female.

Colour: mottled grey.

Lifespan: up to 77 years.

◄Large clusters of barnacles cover much of the Grey whale's skin as it gets older. Pale spidery whale lice live in the barnacle clusters.

▲The Grey whale blows as it comes up to the surface for air (1). Soon it dives again (2). Sometimes it "spy-hops" to get its bearings (3).

The Grey whale is one of the baleen whales. These whales feed on small sea creatures, which they catch by straining mouthfuls of sea water through horny plates called baleen (whalebone). The Grey whale's baleen is much shorter and stiffer than that of the other baleen whales, such as the Blue and Right whales. Like all the whales, it is a mammal whose young are, from birth, raised on the mother's milk.

There are two main populations of Grey whales, which migrate between Arctic and Southern Pacific ocean waters. The western or Korean population migrates between Siberia and South Korea. This population is probably almost extinct.

The eastern or Californian population migrates between the Bering Sea and the southern coast of California. It has recovered well from a devastating century of whaling, which ended in the 1940s. Today the population numbers are estimated to be more than 15,000.

CALIFORNIAN MIGRATION
The Californian Grey whales make an annual migration of up to 20,000km. They keep quite close to the North American coast in waters less than 100m deep.

In the summer the whales feed in the nutrient-rich waters of the Bering Sea. They put on weight fast, building up a thick blubber layer beneath the skin. They need this blubber as an energy store, because when they migrate they eat very little.

They start moving south in the autumn, reaching southern California by December. There they mate. By March they are heading north again for their summer feeding grounds.

The pattern is repeated each year. In December, in the seas around California, the females that became pregnant the previous year give birth.

▲ With most of its gigantic body submerged, a Grey whale blows, expelling stale air from its lungs. It may do this up to five times after surfacing.

NURSING MOTHERS
The whale young, or calf, measures nearly 5m at birth. It has difficulty in breathing and swimming at first, and often the mother has to support it on the surface with her back or tail fins. The mother's teats are hidden, but they spurt milk into the calf's mouth when it nuzzles the right spot.

The calves stay close to their mothers on the long migration north in the spring. By the time they reach the northern feeding grounds they have become skilful swimmers and have built up a thick insulating layer of blubber.

RORQUALS

The 60-tonne bulk of a Humpback whale surges upwards through the water, driven by thrusts of its powerful tail. It breaks the surface and arches into the air, then falls back with a loud smack that makes the sea boil. No other whale performs this action, called breaching, so acrobatically.

RORQUALS
Balaenopteridae (*6 species*)

Habitat: all main oceans.

Diet: plankton, krill, fish.

Breeding: 1 offspring after pregnancy of 10-12 months.

Size: smallest (Minke whale): head-body 11m, weight 10 tonnes; largest (Blue whale): head-body 27m, weight 150 tonnes.

Colour: black or blue-grey, often white underneath.

Lifespan: 45 years (Minke whale) to 95 years (Humpback whale).

Species mentioned in text:
Blue whale (*Balaenoptera musculus*)
Fin whale (*B. physalus*)
Humpback whale (*Megaptera novaeangliae*)
Minke whale (*Balaenoptera acutorostrata*)
Sei whale (*B. borealis*)

▲The head of a Blue whale breaks the surface. It is sucking in air through the blowholes, ready for its next dive into the deeps.

The family of whales known as the rorquals includes the largest animal that has ever lived on this planet, the Blue whale. When fully grown, the Blue whale weighs more than 30 African bull elephants and is as long as eight cars placed bumper to bumper. The Fin whale grows almost as long, although it is slimmer and only about half the weight. Then in order of bulk come the Sei, Humpback, Bryde's and Minke whales.

The great stocks of these whales that once lived in the oceans have been devastated by whaling. Thousands were killed each year. Now they are protected, but they are still vulnerable to other hazards, such as pollution.

FILTER-FEEDERS
Like all whales, the rorquals are mammals. They are filter-feeders,

▼Species of rorqual Five of the six rorquals. Humpback whale "breaching" **(1)**. Smallest of the rorquals, the Minke whale **(2)**. Bryde's whale (*Balaenoptera edeni*) **(3)**. Blue whale **(4)** – the slightly smaller Pygmy blue whale (*B. musculus brevicauda*) is found in southern waters. Fin whale **(5)**, which may have most baleen plates and throat-grooves.

3

4

5

straining their food from the water using comb-like plates of baleen (whalebone) in their upper jaws. First they take a mouthful of water containing food and then force the water out through the baleen. The food gets trapped by bristles on the plates and is then swallowed.

All the rorquals have folds or grooves in the throat extending back along the belly. They allow the whales to increase enormously the volume of their mouths when gulping water to feed.

The favourite food of the rorquals is krill, a shrimp-like creature a few centimetres long. An adult Blue whale can eat as much as 2½ tonnes of krill every day.

Smaller plankton called copepods and fish such as herring, mackerel and cod are also part of the rorquals' diet. The water-thumping behaviour of breaching may be one way in which whales help scare and concentrate the fish before they feed.

GRACE AND PACE

Despite their huge bulk, the rorquals are graceful swimmers. Their bodies are beautifully streamlined, and they propel themselves by up and down movements of their large tail fins. The Sei whale is probably the fastest swimmer, able to reach speeds of 35kph for short periods.

Rorquals use the flippers on the sides of the body to steer. The flippers of the Humpback are especially large and have a jagged leading edge. All the whales have a small dorsal (back) fin to the rear of the body.

Other body features include a ridge between the snout and the blowholes (the whale's nostrils). The whale breathes out of the blowholes after surfacing, sending a spout of spray into the air.

BREEDING CYCLE

Rorquals are found in all major oceans of the world, the Atlantic, Pacific and Indian, in both Northern and Southern hemispheres. Most species spend the summer feeding in polar waters, where plankton and fish abound. They migrate south from the Northern hemisphere or north from the Southern hemisphere to winter in warmer waters. There they mate.

Males and pregnant females return to their feeding grounds for the summer, and the cycle begins again. When next they return to the warm water breeding grounds, the pregnant females give birth to their calves (young). They usually suckle their calves for 6 or 7 months, by which time they are back feeding again.

HAUNTING MELODY

As well as being a skilful acrobat, the Humpback whale is a fine singer. Most whales communicate with each other by sound – but while the others squeak and grunt, the Humpback sings a haunting melody.

The Humpback's song is made up of six basic themes, repeated over and over again. Each song can last for up to 35 minutes and may form part of a much longer recital. The variety of notes the animal uses have been described as resembling snores, whos, yups, chirps, ees and oos.

The whales' songs are studied using hydrophones (underwater microphones). Scientists have found that all the whales within a certain region of ocean sing much the same song. But the song changes according to the region and the season. The animals sing mainly when in shallow coastal waters and can keep in touch with one another over distances of more than 185km.

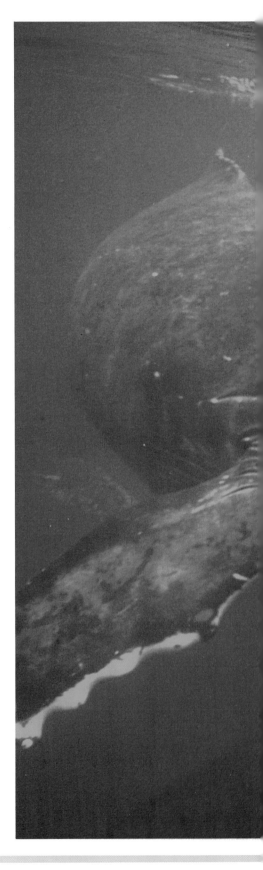

▶Underwater photographs of rorquals, such as these Humpback whales, show that the body is sleek and pointed towards the snout and not baggy as previously thought from dead animals seen floating at the surface or pulled out of the water.

BABOONS

A group of about 30 Hamadryas baboons are picking their way through the stony desert landscape. A male near the front of the ragged line looks round to see if the rest of the group is keeping up. He sees one of the females lagging behind and dashes down the line towards her. Seeing him coming, she hurries to catch up. But it is too late. He sinks his teeth into the back of her neck and shakes her angrily. Squealing, she follows him closely back into line.

The Hamadryas baboon lives in very large troops, sometimes of more than 200 animals. A small group of 30 may form a clan of perhaps three families. A number of clans group into a band of 80 or 90 animals, and several bands join together to form the troop.

The smallest group, the family unit, is a harem, led by a male. The leader is followed by his female mate, their daughters and a few male "hangers on". Some of these quietly join the clan to court the young females and in time attract them away to start a

BABOONS Cercopithecidae
(*6 species*)

Habitat: savannah, woodland, rain forest, desert.

Diet: grass, roots, fruit, seeds, insects, other small animals.

Breeding: 1 offspring after pregnancy of about 6 months.

Size: smallest (Savannah baboon): head-body 56-79cm, weight up to 14kg female, 21-25kg male; largest (drill): head-body 70 cm, weight up to 50kg.

Colour: tinged greys and browns, coloured rump.

Lifespan: up to 30 years.

Species mentioned in text:
Hamadryas baboon (*Papio hamadryas*)
Mandrill (*P. sphinx*)
Savannah, Chacma, Olive, Yellow baboon (*P. cynocephalus*)

separate family of their own.

Another species, the Savannah baboon, also lives in huge groups. Savannah baboon families include several adult males rather than just one.

SAVANNAH TO HIGHLANDS
Baboons are the largest of the monkeys. They live almost every-

where in Africa where there is water to drink.

The Savannah or Common baboon is widespread in the grasslands and bush and along forest edges from Ethiopia to South Africa. There are three different forms of the Savannah baboon, each from a different region. They are recognizable by the colour of their coat. The Yellow baboon (its coat is yellowish-grey) lives in lowland East and Central Africa; the Olive baboon (olive green-grey) in the East African highlands, and the Chacma baboon (with a dark grey coat) in southern Africa.

The Hamadryas baboon lives in Ethiopia and neighbouring Somalia and, across the Red Sea, in Saudi Arabia and South Yemen. It is found in rocky desert areas of scattered grass and thorn bush.

COLOURFUL FEATURES
Baboons have a naked face and a muzzle rather like that of a dog. Males and females can often be recognized by their coat. The adult male Hamadryas baboon, for example, has long silvery-grey hair, forming a kind of cape over its shoulders. The female's coat is brown.

One can also identify the sexes by the colour of the face. Females have a black face, males a bright red one. The males also have a distinctive bright red rump.

The mandrill is the most colourful among baboon males. Its face is marked red and blue, and its bare rump is blue to purple. The female has similar but duller colouring and is only half the male's size.

When they are ready to mate, adult female baboons develop swellings on their rump and thighs. Each individual has a characteristic pattern of swellings.

◀Drills and baboons Red-and-blue-faced mandrill (1) Drill (*Papio leucophaeus*) (2) Gelada (*Theropithecus gelada*) (3) showing bare patches on its neck and chest. Hamadryas baboon (4), with red naked skin on its face and rump. Guinea baboon (*Papio papio*) (5). Olive baboon (6), a form of the Savannah or Common baboon, of highland East Africa, shown with its dead prey, a hare. Chacma baboon (7) another form of the Savannah baboon, of southern Africa. Each example is of the adult male.

CHIMPANZEES

Two groups of chimpanzees meet for the first time in days. They know one another, but there is tension in the air. A male from one group suddenly gets up and charges towards the other group. None of the opposing males wants to accept his challenge today.

▼ The face and ears of the adult Common chimpanzee are brownish-black. When it was young, they would have been pink.

The two species of chimpanzee both live in tropical Africa. The Common chimpanzee is found in West and Central Africa, north of the River Zaire. It inhabits thick forest and also more open savannah country.

The Pygmy chimpanzee, or bonobo, is found only in the rain forests of Zaire. Although called "Pygmy" it is not noticeably smaller than the Common species, but it is of slighter build. One main difference between the two species is in face colour. The Common chimpanzee has a pink to brown face, the Pygmy chimpanzee an all-black one.

Both species spend much of the time on the ground. They sometimes walk upright on two feet, but they usually walk on all fours, using the knuckle not the palm of each hand.

STICKS AND STONES
Like the other apes, chimpanzees are mainly vegetarian, and they prefer to eat ripe fruit. But they also kill and eat animals such as monkeys, baboons, pigs and antelopes.

CHIMPANZEES
Pongidae (2 species)

Habitat: tropical rain forest, deciduous forest, mixed savannah.

Diet: fruit, leaves, flowers, seeds, some animals.

Breeding: 1 offspring after a pregnancy of 7½-8 months.

Size: head-body 70-85cm, weight 30kg female; head-body 70-90cm, weight 40kg male.

Colour: coat black, greying with age.

Lifespan: up to 45 years.

Species mentioned in text:
Common chimpanzee (*Pan troglodytes*)
Pygmy chimpanzee or bonobo (*P. paniscus*)

Chimpanzees eat insects as well, such as caterpillars and ants. To reach ants inside a nest, they bring their stick-tools into action. They put the sticks into the nest and wait for the ants to crawl up. Chimpanzees also use sticks and sometimes stones to crack open fruit shells that are too hard to bite.

Once it was thought that only human beings used tools. But this use of sticks and stones shows how intelligent chimpanzees are. In fact, with gorillas, they are the second most intelligent creatures on Earth, after humans. Chimpanzees in captivity have learned to use some of the hand signals of the sign language of hearing impaired people.

GANG WARFARE

Every chimpanzee belongs to a large loose group or community of perhaps as many as 120 animals. Some live alone for much of the time, but most travel in small groups. There are mixed-sex family groups and also all-male groups of up to 12 that are a threat to other groups because they challenge the breeding males.

Displays of charging and stick throwing take place regularly in chimpanzee groups. They are usually performed by the strongest or most aggressive male as a challenge to other males. If they still accept him as boss, they bob up and down, panting and grunting. But if a male takes up the challenge, a noisy fight breaks out until one or the other runs away.

►The chimpanzee has one of the most expressive faces of all primates. (1) The relaxed play face. (2) The pout, used when begging for food. (3) The display face, which shows aggression. (4) The full open grin, showing fear or excitement. (5) The horizontal pout, showing surrender after being attacked. (6) The fear grin, displayed when approaching an animal of higher rank.

▼Chimpanzees are threatened by destruction of their forest homes and by hunting for bushmeat.

GORILLA

Twice as big as the females around him, a mature "silverback" gorilla sits in the forest chewing a mouthful of leaves. Hearing a crashing in the undergrowth, he jumps to his feet. Advancing on him threateningly is a much younger "silverback". When they see each other they roar loudly, beating on their chests with both hands. The younger gorilla knows he's outclassed.

The gorilla is the largest of all the primates. Mature female gorillas are heavier than most human males. Mature males – known as silverbacks because of their silvery-white saddle – are twice as heavy again. Along with chimpanzees, gorillas are the most intelligent animals next to human beings.

Gorillas live in groups, usually of 5 to 10 animals. Each group is made up of one adult male and a number of females and their young.

GENTLE GIANTS

For most of the time, gorillas lead a peaceful life. They spend the greater part of the day feeding, since they need to eat a lot of food, mainly leaves, to maintain their huge bulk. In between they rest to allow plenty of time for digestion. At night they make platform nests of twigs and branches either on the ground or in low trees.

Gorillas spend more time on the ground than up in the trees. They occasionally walk on two feet, but for the most part they walk on all fours. Like chimpanzees, they walk on the soles of their feet and on the knuckles of the hands. Only young gorillas spend much time up in the trees.

Threat displays between rival gorillas can sometimes end in ferocious fights. The worst clashes occur between the silverback with a well-

▲An Eastern lowland gorilla eating a plant stem. Gorillas have large teeth and powerful jaws to crunch the huge amounts of leaves and stems they eat. Their jaws are worked by large muscles attached to a bony crest on the skull.

established "harem" and the lone young silverback. The loner tries to steal some or all of the other's females and set up a harem of his own.

In the wild gorillas do not feel threatened by human beings, and will allow them to approach quite close. But human visitors must stay quiet,

▼A silverback Mountain gorilla, leader of his "harem" of smaller females.

GORILLA *Gorilla gorilla*

 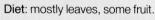

△ Habitat: tropical forest.

▢ Diet: mostly leaves, some fruit.

◡ Breeding: 1 offspring after pregnancy of 8-9 months.

Size: height up to 180cm male, 150cm female; weight up to 180kg male, 90kg female.

Colour: coat black to brownish-grey.

Lifespan: up to 40 years.

Races mentioned in text:
Eastern lowland gorilla (*Gorilla gorilla graueri*)
Mountain gorilla (*G. g. beringei*)
Western lowland gorilla (*G. g. gorilla*)

◄▼A gorilla group rests at midday after a morning's feeding. They gather, with the females and babies closest, around the silverback, the only mature male. One of the females grooms him. Older infants play together. Females with no offspring and maturing males stay on the edge of the group.

must sit or squat and above all must not stare. Staring is considered very rude in gorilla society.

SHRINKING HABITAT

The gorilla is a single species, but there are three separate races or sub-species. All are under threat, like so many other animals, from the destruction of their forest habitat. Hunting and trapping the young for sale to zoos are also reducing their numbers.

Most under threat is the Mountain gorilla, of which only about three or four hundred remain. The Mountain gorilla is found in Zaire, Rwanda and Uganda at altitudes between about 1,500m and 3,800m. A few thousand Eastern lowland gorilla remain, living in eastern Zaire. The Mountain and Eastern lowland gorillas have black coats. The male's silvery-white saddle is only on the back.

The Western lowland gorilla has a brownish tinge to its coat, and the male's saddle extends to the rump and thighs. It is found in Central West Africa from Cameroon to the Congo. About half of the total population (around 9,000) are concentrated in Gabon.

►A Mountain gorilla nursing her baby. She will feed it for up to three years and probably have another baby a year or so later. Gorillas make caring and affectionate mothers, but their babies do not always survive. In her lifetime a female gorilla may successfully raise only three or four offspring.

ANTEATERS

The Giant anteater lumbering across the dried grassland is heading for one of the anthills dotting the landscape. It can't see the mound because of its poor eyesight, but it can smell the ants. When it reaches the earthy mound, it slashes a hole in it and thrusts in its snout. Flicking its long tongue in and out, it begins to feed on the startled insects.

The Giant anteater is the largest of the anteaters of South and Central America. They all feed almost entirely on ants and termites. They have a tube-like snout and a long narrow tongue covered with a sticky saliva. The Giant anteater can flick its tongue a distance of some 60cm up to 150 times a minute.

The ants stick to the saliva on the tongue and are taken into the mouth.

The mouth opening is surprisingly small – not much bigger across than a pencil. Anteaters have no teeth. They lightly chew their prey using little hard lumps on the roof of the mouth and on the cheeks.

▼ The Southern tamandua's gold, brown and white patterned coat gives it good camouflage in the scrubland and forest where it lives.

ANTEATERS
Myrmecophagidae (*4 species*)

● ■ ☠

◢ **Habitat**: savannah, scrub, steppe, forest.

■ **Diet**: ants, termites.

◎ **Breeding**: 1 offspring after pregnancy of 4½-6 months.

Size: smallest (Silky anteater): head-body 16cm, tail 16cm, weight 300g; largest (Giant anteater): head-body 120cm, tail 90cm, weight 39kg.

Colour: grey, brown, with black or pale shoulder or dorsal stripes.

Lifespan: Giant anteater up to 26 years, Northern tamandua 9 years.

Species mentioned in text:
Giant anteater (*Myrmecophaga tridactyla*)
Northern tamandua (*Tamandua mexicana*)
Silky anteater (*Cyclopes didactylus*)
Southern tamandua (*Tamandua tetradactyla*)

"STINKERS OF THE FOREST"

The Giant anteater is usually active during the day, but it spends part of the time asleep. The other species of anteaters are mainly nocturnal and spend much of their time in the trees. Unlike their giant relative, they have a prehensile tail which helps them grip the branches when they climb.

The two species of tamandua, the Northern and Southern, are only about half the size of the Giant anteater. They have a striped coat, which gives them their alternative name: Collared anteater. They have also been given the nickname "stinker of the forest" because of the unpleasant smell they sometimes give off.

The much smaller Silky anteater hardly ever comes down from the trees. Its snout is much shorter than that of the other species. It is often called the two-toed anteater because three of its five fingers do not show. It has short silky fur.

POWERFUL CLAWS

All the anteaters have large sharp and powerful curved claws on their forefeet; tamanduas have three, the Giant and Silky anteaters two. They use these claws to open up anthills and termite mounds and also to defend themselves.

When alarmed or attacked, anteaters rise up on their hind legs, using their tail as a prop to steady themselves. As their attacker gets closer, they slash at it with their claws, which on the Giant anteater are up to 10cm long. Another powerful weapon is a crushing bear-hug, delivered with their strong forelimbs.

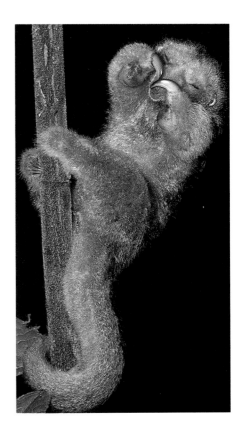

►On the defensive, a Silky anteater covers its face with its claws, while clinging to a branch with feet and tail.

▼A young Giant anteater rides piggyback on its mother. Both are identical in colour, making the young one rather difficult to see.

ARMADILLOS

It is late evening in the heart of Florida's swampland. Coming to a stream, an armadillo stops as if wondering what to do next. Then it steps into the water and disappears beneath the surface. Holding its breath, it walks along the bottom of the stream. More than five minutes pass before it reappears on the other side and continues on its way. Had the stream been any wider, the armadillo would have swum across, swallowing air to make it float better.

▼ Southern three-banded armadillo (1), pichi (2) and Lesser fairy armadillo (3).

There are 20 species of armadillo in the Americas, ranging from Oklahoma in the north to Argentina in the south. Most widespread is the Common long-nosed armadillo, also called the Nine-banded armadillo, found in the United States.

The Spanish word *armadillo* means "little armoured one". This is a very good description of an animal that is covered with a number of hard bony plates, called scutes. Broad shield-like plates usually cover the shoulders and rear of the body. In the middle are a varying number of circular bands, which flex as the animal moves. The head, tail and limbs are also protected by armour. The underside of the body is covered only by hairy skin, but an attacker is rarely able to reach this weak-spot.

GREAT DIGGERS

Armadillos have short but powerful limbs, tipped with strong claws. The animals use their claws when digging for insect prey or making a burrow to sleep in. The Common long-nosed armadillo is an especially efficient digger. When it smells insects or other small prey in the soil, it digs frantically for them, keeping its long nose pressed to the ground. It holds its breath while digging, to stop itself inhaling the dirt.

The burrows armadillos dig can be as much as 2m underground and have two or more entrances. They contain one or two nest chambers lined with grass and other plant material. An armadillo may dig 10 or more such burrows, which it uses on different days in no fixed pattern.

  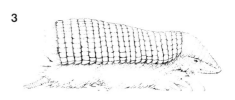

ARMADILLOS
Dasypodidae (*20 species*)

● ◪ ⚊

◪ **Habitat:** wide range, desert, savannah, scrub, forest.

■ **Diet:** insects, especially ants and termites, other small animals.

◎ **Breeding:** number of offspring varies, 1 (fairy and three-banded armadillos), 4 (most long-nosed armadillos), 12 (Southern lesser long-nosed armadillo). Pregnancy usually 60-65 days.

Size: smallest (Lesser fairy armadillo): head-body 12.5cm, tail 2.5cm, weight 80g; largest (Giant armadillo): head-body 100cm, tail 45cm, weight 60kg.

Colour: pinkish or yellowish dark brown armour, pale or dark brown hairs between plates and on underside skin.

Lifespan: up to 15 years.

Species mentioned in text:
Brazilian lesser long-nosed armadillo (*Dasypus septemcinctus*)
Common long-nosed or Nine-banded armadillo (*D. novemcinctus*)
Giant armadillo (*Priodontes maximus*)
Larger hairy armadillo (*Chaetophractus villosus*)
Lesser fairy or Pink fairy armadillo (*Chlamyphorus truncatus*)
Pichi (*Zaedyus pichiy*)
Southern lesser long-nosed armadillo (*Dasypus hybridus*)
Southern three-banded armadillo (*Tolypeutes matacus*)

GIANTS AND FAIRIES

Armadillos spend most of their lives alone. They mark their home territory with their urine and droppings and with a yellowish smelly liquid given off by glands at their rear. When armadillos do cross into each other's territory, they may fight, with much kicking, chasing, and squealing.

When an armadillo is being hunted by a predator it may dig itself out of trouble and disappear beneath the soil. Or it may simply crouch low on the ground so that only its armour shows. Three-banded armadillos can roll themselves completely into a ball, safe even from jaguars.

There is a great difference in size among armadillos. Largest of the family is the increasingly rare Giant armadillo which measures up to 150cm from head to tail. The smallest is only one-tenth this length. This is the almost shrimp-like Lesser fairy armadillo, also called the Pink fairy armadillo, which has a dense coat of white hair on its sides and under-parts. The Lesser fairy spends much of its life tunnelling underground – something its giant relative could never do.

▲ Like all the armadillos, this Larger hairy armadillo has large strong claws for digging. It can take a variety of foods, including maggots from inside the rotting carcasses of other animals. It sometimes burrows deep within a carcass.

▼ The Brazilian lesser long-nosed armadillo digs a shallow burrow to rest in during the day. Like all the other armadillos it is classed as an *Edentate* (without teeth) but has a set of up to 100 primitive teeth.

BATS

It is the darkest time of night. The herd of cattle have settled down to rest. Out of the darkness comes the faint flutter of tiny wings. A vampire bat is swooping in for its night-time feed. It settles lightly on the shoulders of a young calf. With a swift movement of its tiny head, it slits the animal's hide with razor-sharp teeth. The calf doesn't feel a thing. The vampire's tongue then sets to work, flicking in and out of the wound as the blood starts oozing out.

▶The Mexican Long-nosed bat uses its enormous tongue to reach the nectar in desert flowering plants such as cactus.

▶A Greater false vampire bat swoops on a mouse. It may take its catch back to its roost to eat it there.

BATS Megachiroptera and Microchiroptera (*up to 1,000 species*)

● ■ ☠

■ Habitat: general.

◢ Diet: most bats: insects; vampire bats: blood; flying foxes: fruit; also eaten by different species: nectar, spiders, frogs, lizards, fish, rodents.

◯ Breeding: varies, mostly 1 off-spring per year; 2-3 offspring in some species; pregnancy lasts from 40 days, sometimes delayed up to 10 months.

Size: smallest (Kitti's hog-nosed bat): head-body 2.9cm, weight 1.5g; largest (flying foxes): head-body 40cm, weight 1.5kg.

Colour: mainly brown, grey and black, tinged red, yellow, orange, silver.

Lifespan: up to 30 years, average about 5 years.

Species mentioned in text:
Common vampire (*Desmodus rotundus*)
False vampire (*Vampyrum spectrum*)
Greater false vampire bat (*Megaderma lyra*)
Greater spear-nosed bat (*Phyllostomus hastatus*)
Hammer-headed bat (*Hypsignathus monstrosus*)
Kitti's hog-nosed bat (*Craseonycteris thonglongyai*)
Large mouse-eared bat (*Myotis myotis*)
Lesser mouse-tailed bat (*Rhinopoma hardwickei*)
Little brown bat (*Myotis lucifugus*)
Mexican long-nosed bat (*Leptonycteris nivalis*)
Natterer's bat (*Myotis nattereri*)
Samoan flying fox (*Pteropus samoensis*)
Schreiber's bent-winged bat (*Miniopterus schreibersi*)

A bat looks rather like a flying mouse. It is the only flying mammal. (The so-called flying squirrel does not fly but just glides, using flaps of skin between its feet.) The bat truly flies, flapping its wings like a bird.

BAD REPUTATION
The Common vampire bat is one of 1,000 species of bat living all around the globe, except in the polar regions. Almost all of the others are harmless and even useful creatures. They help keep down insect pests and vermin and pollinate plants and fruit trees.

But bats in general have had a bad reputation. People have killed them in huge numbers in the past. Today the biggest danger to bat species is the destruction and disturbance of their habitats by human activities.

WINGS AND FINGERS
A bat's wing is a thin membrane or layer of skin, supported by four long

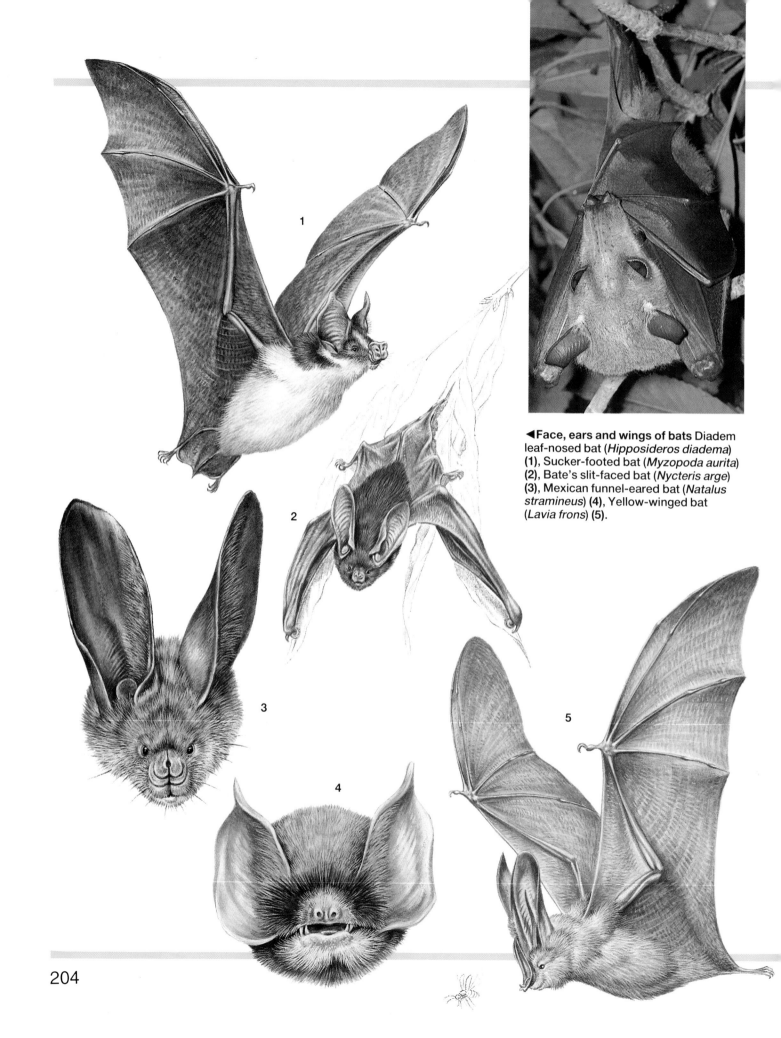

◄Face, ears and wings of bats Diadem
leaf-nosed bat (*Hipposideros diadema*)
(1), Sucker-footed bat (*Myzopoda aurita*)
(2), Bate's slit-faced bat (*Nycteris arge*)
(3), Mexican funnel-eared bat (*Natalus
stramineus*) (4), Yellow-winged bat
(*Lavia frons*) (5).

◄A female Hammer-headed bat roosts in a tree, wings wrapped around its body. Only the male has the hammer-shaped head.

bony fingers. A little clawed thumb protrudes at the front. The thumb is used mainly when the bat is moving around the roost. The wing membrane extends to the bat's legs and, in some species, between the legs to a tail. In other species, such as the Lesser mouse-tailed bat, the tail is free. Some flying foxes have no tail or tail membranes. The bat with the largest wingspan is believed to be the Samoan flying fox. Its wing tips can be as much as 1.5m apart.

In most species the legs are weak. The feet have five toes tipped with claws. Bats hang upside-down by their feet when roosting. The Common vampire bat has unusually strong legs. It can run and leap well.

SEEING BY SOUND
Bats sleep during the day in roosting places such as caves, old buildings and trees. They go foraging for food at dusk. Most bats eat insects, which they take on the wing. They have tiny eyes and rather poor eyesight (hence the expression "blind as a bat"). To "see" in the dark, bats rely mainly on sound. They find their way and detect their prey by echo-location or sonar.

When a bat goes in search of insects, it sends out pulses of ultrasound, sound waves too high-pitched for human ears to hear. Sending out about five pulses a second, the bat listens for any echoes. If it receives an echo reflected back from an insect, it increases the pulse rate up to about 200 pulses a second.

►The wing membranes of Davy's naked-backed bat (*Pteronotus davyi*) (1) reach over the back to meet in the middle. The Honduran disk-winged bat (*Thyroptera discifera*) (2). Both species are insect-eaters of the Americas.

From the echoes it receives back, the bat can pin-point exactly where the insect is and snatch it from the air. Usually this is done with the mouth, but the Natterer's bat and some other species first catch insects in their tail membrane.

Bats make these sounds through the open mouth or through the nostrils. The species that use their nostrils have complicated, often grotesque-looking noses. They include the leaf-nosed, hog-nosed, spear-nosed and horse-shoe bats. The "leaves" or flaps of skin on the nose help change and focus the sounds coming out.

The ears of bats that use sonar are also unusual. They are large, ridged and folded, which makes them receive the echoes clearly.

FRUIT-EATING BATS
Not all bats navigate and find their food by sonar. Most species of flying foxes use their eyes. These are large bats that feed mainly on fruit; they are often called fruit bats. They eat not only fruit, but also flowers and nectar.

This is how they provide a valuable service in pollinating the plants they visit and spreading the seeds.

Flying foxes look different from the small, odd-faced insect-eaters. They have a long face, large eyes and simple ears, spaced well apart. Their head does look rather like that of a fox. Their eyesight is very good, like that of birds, and they have a strong sense of smell.

Flying foxes are widespread in tropical and subtropical regions of Africa, India, South-east Asia and Australia. Only in the Americas are they absent. There, species of spear-nosed bats are the fruit-eaters.

CARNIVORES AND VAMPIRES
Other species of the spear-nosed bat family are carnivores, eating frogs, rodents and other small animals. Among them is the False vampire, the largest American bat, with a wingspan of up to 1m.

The Americas are also the home of the Common vampire. This bat's range extends from Mexico southwards to Argentina. The Common vampire feeds mostly on the blood of domesticated livestock, especially large herds of cattle. Attacks on humans are very rare. It takes only a little of an animal's blood and so does not harm it in that way. But the Common vampire can infect animals with diseases, including the deadly rabies.

BAT COLONIES

Bats feed mostly by night and roost by day. Flying foxes roost in the open, hanging from the branches of trees. Some bats nest in holes in trees, others in buildings, canal tunnels and other human constructions. The largest numbers of all roost in caves. Some colonies of cave-dwelling bats contain a million individuals or more.

Caves are ideal roosting places. They are safe and dark and have a steady temperature. With their skill at echo-location, bats have no problem finding their way around inside.

Among most species males and females roost together for much of the year. But some species roost in single-sex groups. There is not much pattern in the way bats mate, although there are a few exceptions. The Greater spear-nosed bat forms harems of females, with just one male mating with them.

Mating takes place at roost. Sometimes pregnancy is delayed until the climate is more suitable, maybe as long as 7 months after mating. Few other mammals do this. The young are sometimes born with their mother hanging upside-down. Otherwise the mother turns her head upwards and then catches the young in her tail membrane. The young begin suckling their mother almost immediately. In most bat colonies all the mothers and young roost together in a kind of nursery.

BEATING THE CLIMATE

In parts of the world where the climate is always warm, bats usually

▲ Looking like a whirlwind, a huge colony of bats leave a cave in Java to feed at dusk.

▶ Red and naked, hundreds of newly born Schreiber's bent-winged bats on the roof of a nursery cave in Australia. They will remain in the cave for about 3 months.

stay active all the year. In the tropics bats may sleep through the hottest parts of the year. This period of sleep is called aestivation.

In cooler climates, bats have two main problems in winter. Their supply of food (notably insects) decreases; and the temperature falls. To cope with this, some bats migrate, making their way to warmer climates.

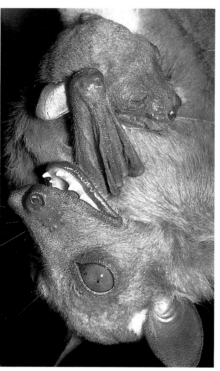

◄A colony of fruit bats roosting during the daytime, their wings wrapped around them. In hot weather, they open out and flap their wings to keep cool.

▼Flying fox mother with newly born young. Three months may pass before it is ready to fly.

Others hibernate, sleeping through the winter cold.

Before they hibernate, these bats feed well to build up their body weight, including a thick layer of fat under the skin. Bats usually cluster together when they hibernate, which helps keep them warm. This can result in huge clusters of bats packed tightly together, with as many as 3,000 in a square metre. The Little brown bat of North America and the Large mouse-eared bat of Europe may hibernate together like this.

Hibernating bats do not spend the whole winter asleep. Every 10 days or so they wake up and sometimes fly a short distance to another site. This probably helps rid their bodies of wastes which build up and could otherwise poison them.

AARDVARK

The Sun has set over the sparsely wooded grassland. Dotted here and there, nearly as tall as the trees, are the great mounds of termite nests. An animal the size of a pig makes its way in a zigzag path towards one of the mounds. It is an aardvark on its way to feed. A hole at the base of the mound shows it has been there before. It sets to work again, snout close to the ground, digging swiftly. It makes good progress, even though the mound is rock hard. From time to time the aardvark pauses, sits down and thrusts its snout into the mound to feed on the insects scurrying about inside.

◄An aardvark sits down by a termite mound ready to feed at night. Termites in the wet season and ants in the dry season are its favourite foods.

▼In parts of Zaire, people kill aardvarks both for food and for their hair and teeth. The hair is crushed into a powder and used as a poison. The teeth are used as good-luck charms.

Aardvarks are found in most parts of Africa south of the Sahara desert. But they avoid the driest desert regions and the depths of the tropical rain forest. The name aardvark means "earth pig" in the Afrikaans language, and the animal does look rather like a pig, although it is no relation. It has a long round snout, big ears and a bristly coat.

The aardvark eats ants and termites, but it is not related to anteaters. In fact it is not closely related to any other mammal. Its nearest relatives appear to be hyraxes and elephants. It has certain body features in common with these animals – for example, their claws are a cross between nails and hoofs. For this reason they are sometimes classed together as "primitive ungulates". Ungulates are the hoofed mammals.

THICK-SKINNED AND SHY
The aardvark eats ants and termites using its long, worm-like tongue, which is sticky with saliva. Its skin is thick and tough, which protects it from insect bites.

The aardvark has keen hearing and a well-developed sense of smell, senses it uses when foraging for food. A mat of hair around the nostrils helps keep out the dust. The animal can also close

its nostrils when digging to prevent dirt and insects getting in.

Aardvarks are shy and secretive creatures, whose way of life is not well known. They spend the day asleep in a tunnel-like burrow. They dig several burrows within the home territory and may rest in a number of them during the night.

The young are born in a deeper and longer burrow system. They emerge above ground after about 2 weeks and go out foraging with their mother. They begin to dig their own burrows at 6 months old, but usually stay with the mother until she mates again.

AARDVARK:
Orycteropus afer

Habitat: open woodland, scrub and grassland.

Diet: ants and termites, sometimes fruit.

Breeding: 1 young born after pregnancy of about 7 months.

Size: head-body 105-130cm; tail 45-63cm; weight 40-65kg.

Colour: yellowish-grey coat, head and tail off-white, often stained brownish by soil.

Lifespan: up to 10 years in captivity.

ELEPHANTS

In the blazing red of an African sunset, a herd of elephants makes its way down to the river bank. In the middle of the herd, close to their mothers, are two young babies. Suddenly the leader stops. She puts up her trunk and fans out her ears. She senses danger. The elephants halt and bunch up. From some thorn bushes two lionesses appear. The leading elephant gives a squeal of rage, tucks up her trunk and charges. The lions scatter. No other animal stays in the path of a charging elephant.

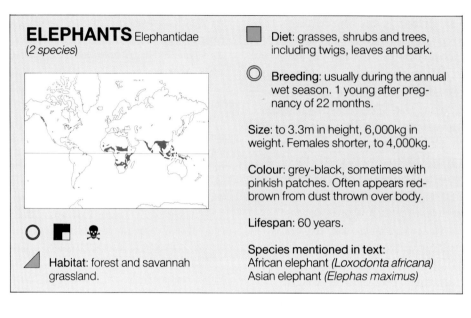

ELEPHANTS Elephantidae
(*2 species*)

Habitat: forest and savannah grassland.

Diet: grasses, shrubs and trees, including twigs, leaves and bark.

Breeding: usually during the annual wet season. 1 young after pregnancy of 22 months.

Size: to 3.3m in height, 6,000kg in weight. Females shorter, to 4,000kg.

Colour: grey-black, sometimes with pinkish patches. Often appears red-brown from dust thrown over body.

Lifespan: 60 years.

Species mentioned in text:
African elephant (*Loxodonta africana*)
Asian elephant (*Elephas maximus*)

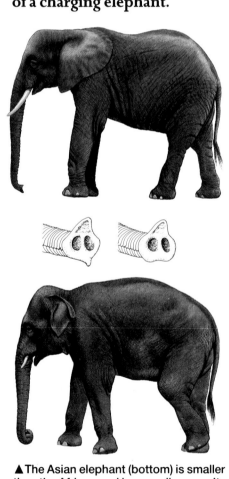

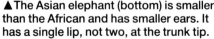

▲ The Asian elephant (bottom) is smaller than the African and has smaller ears. It has a single lip, not two, at the trunk tip.

▶ Elephants have a good sense of smell. Trunks are held high to catch scents.

The African elephant is the biggest living land animal. The slightly smaller Asian species is rare now as a wild animal, and only about 50,000 are left.

GIANTS OF THE LAND

The biggest African elephant ever measured stood 4m tall, about as high as a bungalow. It was a male (bull) elephant. These often reach 3.2m tall, and nearly 6 tonnes in weight. Females (cows) are shorter, and weigh up to 4 tonnes. The biggest African elephants are those from savannah country. Those from forests near the equator are usually smaller, and have rounder ears.

Since elephants are so big, they have problems keeping cool. Their ears give a large surface from which heat can be lost. The elephants also use them as fans.

GIANT APPETITES

Elephants have an appetite to go with their size. An adult needs about 150kg of plant food a day. This is equal to about six small bales of hay. But much of the food is of poor quality. Bacteria in the gut help the elephant break down its food. Even so, nearly half passes through the elephant without being digested. Elephants have to spend about 16 hours out of every 24 feeding. Water too is drunk in large amounts. An elephant needs about 80 litres a day (equal to 140 pint bottles of milk).

TRUNK CALLS

An elephant gathers all its food and water with its trunk. This is a combined nose and upper lip. The trunk is full of muscles which can move it in all directions with precision or strength. It can be used to pick a single leaf or berry, using the "lips" at the tip. Or instead, it may be used to rip a branch from a tree before lifting it to the mouth. Water is always sucked into the trunk, then squirted into the mouth and swallowed. Another use for the trunk is as a snorkel when bathing.

▲ Where their numbers are high, elephants can cause enormous changes to an area by uprooting trees to feed on their tops.

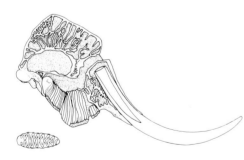

▲ In the elephant's huge skull 24 chewing teeth grow in sequence. Of these only four are used at a time. When worn, they are lost and replaced from behind.

The trunk is also important in making sounds, and helping elephants to "keep in touch". Elephants greet one another by putting the trunk tip to the other's mouth. Mothers reassure their babies (calves) by touching and guiding them with the trunk. Sniffing and touching with the trunk tells an elephant much about its surroundings.

LIVING TOGETHER

Adult bull elephants live alone, or sometimes in small groups. They join the females only for mating. Cow elephants live in herds accompanied by their calves. Bulls leave the herd as they become adult, but cows stay with their mother. The herd is usually led by the oldest and largest cow, the matriarch. She, by example, shows when and where to move. She also decides how to react to threats. She may charge an enemy, or lead the herd away. An elephant's lifespan is nearly as long as a human's. The leader has had time to learn many useful things. By following her behaviour, other cows in the herd can gain experience for the time when they may have to lead a herd. The matriarch is often too old to produce young.

BIG BABIES

The elephant has the longest pregnancy of all mammals. At birth, the newborn baby weighs 120kg – more than most adult humans. It sucks milk from its mother using its mouth, not its trunk. In the first months the trunk is almost useless. The calf takes milk until about 2 years old, but eats plants after only a few months.

Elephants grow fast until they are about 15 years old. After this growth

◄In Asia people have used elephants for thousands of years. A few are still used for work in some timber forests. They can move logs over a tonne in weight and can work where tractors cannot reach.

The elephant's most important teeth are the huge grinding cheek teeth. Without these it cannot eat properly. An old elephant which has worn down its last teeth will starve.

ELEPHANTS AND PEOPLE

Although elephants are so big, people can tame and train them. Working elephants are usually females, as these are better tempered than males. People have used Asian elephants much more than African ones for working, but the African general Hannibal crossed the Alps with 57 African war elephants on his way to attack Rome in 218 BC. Tame elephants, often painted or with bright costumes, take part in some Asian festivals. In some places light-coloured ("white") elephants are especially respected.

HEADING FOR EXTINCTION?

Hunting for ivory to make ornaments is perhaps the greatest danger facing elephants. Each year, about 100,000 African elephants are killed, most of them illegally, for their tusks. Also, as human numbers increase, farms are built where elephants used to roam freely. When crammed together, elephants destroy habitats. Occasionally they must be culled. In Africa there may still be a million elephants, but their numbers are falling fast.

may slow down, but elephants, unlike many mammals, go on growing throughout life. Their tusks too continually grow.

WORLD'S BIGGEST TEETH

The elephant's tusks are simply enormous front (incisor) teeth. The tough material of which they are made is known as ivory. The longest tusk on record was 3.5m long. The heaviest pair known weighed a total of 211kg. Most are much smaller, but, even so, a big bull elephant carries a great weight in tusks. Cows have smaller, more slender, tusks. In Asian elephants the tusks of cows are so small they hardly stick out beyond the lips. The tusks are occasionally used in feeding, or may be used to threaten or fight a rival. But most of the time they are used very little.

▲Bull elephants sometimes fight one another for the chance of mating with a cow who is on heat.

Fighting consists of charges and shoving matches. Sometimes the trunk and tusks are used in wrestling.

Usually the smaller elephant gives way once it has tested its strength. Only rarely is one of the animals hurt.

ZEBRAS

A long column of zebras crosses the dry plain, each animal following the ones in front. They are in search of water. Suddenly a leopard drops to the ground from the branch of a tree, just missing a foal that is lagging behind its mother. There is a moment of panic. Zebras dash in circles, creating a confusing mass of black and white. The foal escapes. As the disappointed leopard stalks off, calm returns. The zebras plod on towards the next river.

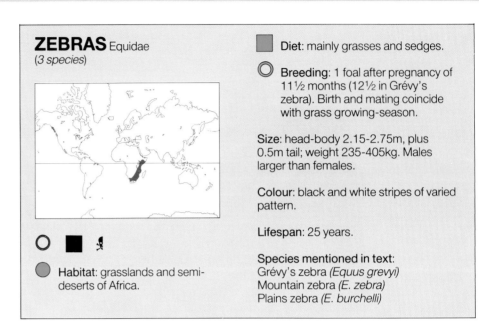

ZEBRAS Equidae
(3 species)

○ ■ ☠

● Habitat: grasslands and semi-deserts of Africa.

■ Diet: mainly grasses and sedges.

○ Breeding: 1 foal after pregnancy of 11½ months (12½ in Grévy's zebra). Birth and mating coincide with grass growing-season.

Size: head-body 2.15-2.75m, plus 0.5m tail; weight 235-405kg. Males larger than females.

Colour: black and white stripes of varied pattern.

Lifespan: 25 years.

Species mentioned in text:
Grévy's zebra *(Equus grevyi)*
Mountain zebra *(E. zebra)*
Plains zebra *(E. burchelli)*

A zebra is a striped horse. There are three species of zebra. Apart from stripes, and the fact that they all live in Africa, the species have little in common, and are only related genetically.

WHY BE STRIPED?

There are various ideas about why it is useful to a zebra to have stripes. One theory is that the stripes are mainly for use among zebras, as a bright signal that allows them to follow one another's movements. Zebras certainly seem to be attracted by stripes. Perhaps at times there are other uses for stripes, such as camouflage.

MIGRATING MULTITUDES

The most numerous of the zebras is the Plains zebra, found from South to East Africa. In many areas its broad black stripes and rather dumpy body are a familiar sight. The Plains zebras of some areas, such as the Serengeti and Botswana, make long migrations to make use of seasonal growth of grass. At this time many thousands of zebras may move together, but for most of the year the typical herd is a

▶A herd of Plains zebras drinks at a waterhole in Etosha National Park in Namibia.

◄Each zebra has a unique pattern of stripes. This may help them recognize one another. This zebra is unusually marked.

male (stallion) and his group of females (mares) and their young (foals).

THREATENED ZEBRAS

The Mountain zebra is found in mountain grasslands of south-west Africa. It has narrower stripes than the Plains zebra and a fold of skin, the dewlap, under the throat. It has a "grid-iron" arrangement of stripes over the rump. It lives in small herds. Populations are small. They are protected in national parks, but this species is listed as vulnerable.

Grévy's zebra lives in northern East Africa. It is the largest zebra, and has the narrowest stripes. It has a tall mane and big rounded ears. It lives in small herds in thorn scrub country. Once fairly common, it has been hunted for its beautiful coat in recent years. It is now endangered.

▲The three species of zebra The Mountain zebra (1) has a sleek coat and narrow hoofs. The neck dewlap and rump pattern are distinctive. The Plains zebra (2) is striped across the belly. Grévy's zebra (3) has a mule-like head and a very obvious mane.

215

RHINOCEROSES

An African Black rhinoceros wallows in a muddy pool, her tiny calf beside her. Suddenly sounds of movement come from a thicket not far away. The mother rhino stands up and charges towards the thicket. An animal scurries away. She stops, turns, and trots back to the calf.

RHINOCEROSES
Rhinocerotidae (*5 species*)

○ ■ ☠

● **Habitat:** grassland, swamp and forest.

■ **Diet:** grass, leaves and shoot ends of shrubs.

◐ **Breeding:** 1 calf after pregnancy of 8-16 months.

Size: head-body 2.5-4.0m; weight 800-2,300kg.

Colour: greyish skin, hairless except in Sumatran rhino, which has sparse long reddish hair.

Lifespan: 45 years.

Species mentioned in text:
Black rhinoceros (*Diceros bicornis*)
Indian rhinoceros (*Rhinoceros unicornis*)
Javan rhinoceros (*R. sondaicus*)
Sumatran rhinoceros (*Dicerorhinus sumatrensis*)
White rhinoceros (*Ceratotherium simum*)

There are five species of rhinoceros. The Black rhino and the White rhino both live in Africa. They differ little in colour, and both have two horns, but they can be told apart by the shape of their faces. The Black rhino is a browsing animal, feeding on leaves from bushes. It has a long pointed upper lip which helps it pull food into its mouth. The White rhino is a grazer, and has a wide muzzle. It crops many blades of grass at once.

The other three species of rhino live in Asia. The Indian rhino has an armour-plated look, with big folds of skin above the legs. This, and the African White rhino, are the two biggest species. Males grow to 1.85m tall and 2.3 tonnes in weight, and females to 1.7m and 1.7 tonnes. The Javan rhino is smaller and has less obvious body folds. The Indian and the Javan rhino have only one horn.

The smallest rhino is the Sumatran, which has two horns, and has a thin coat of reddish hair. Javan and Sumatran rhinos browse from bushes and saplings. Indian rhinos pull in shrubs and tall grass with the upper lip, but can fold the tip away to graze short grass.

HORNS AND HAIR
Rhino horns are unusual in that they lie along the middle of the snout and, unlike the horns of sheep, cattle and antelope, they do not have a bony centre. They are not firmly attached to the skull. Rhino horns grow from the skin, and are made of the same chemical as hair and claws. They are hard and solid, but are made up of many fibres. African rhinos sometimes have front horns 1.6m in length.

Except in the Sumatran rhino, hair is only visible as eyelashes, ear fringes and tail tassels. These animals do not need fur to keep warm.

SENSES
Rhinos rely mostly on their sense of smell to explore their surroundings.

▲Rhino courtship and mating may take several hours. Courtship is rough, with long chases and "fights" – sparring with the horns – between male and female.

They have rather poor vision. They cannot pick out a person standing still more than 30m away. Their hearing is good, and they turn their tubular ear flaps towards sounds in which they are interested. Rhinos can make many sounds, from roars and squeals to bleats which sound too gentle for such massive animals.

Partly because of their poor vision, perhaps, some species are apt to make sudden charges at intruders. The Black rhino has a reputation for aggression, and the Indian rhino too may make apparently unprovoked attacks. Most rhino charges are not carried through. African rhinos attack with their horns, but the Asian species may bite a supposed enemy. These are the same methods that male rhinos use when fighting each other.

SOLITARY LIFE-STYLE
Most rhinos live alone. A calf may stay with its mother for 2 or 3 years. Sometimes several rhinos are found together around a good feeding site. But most rhinos prefer to be by themselves.

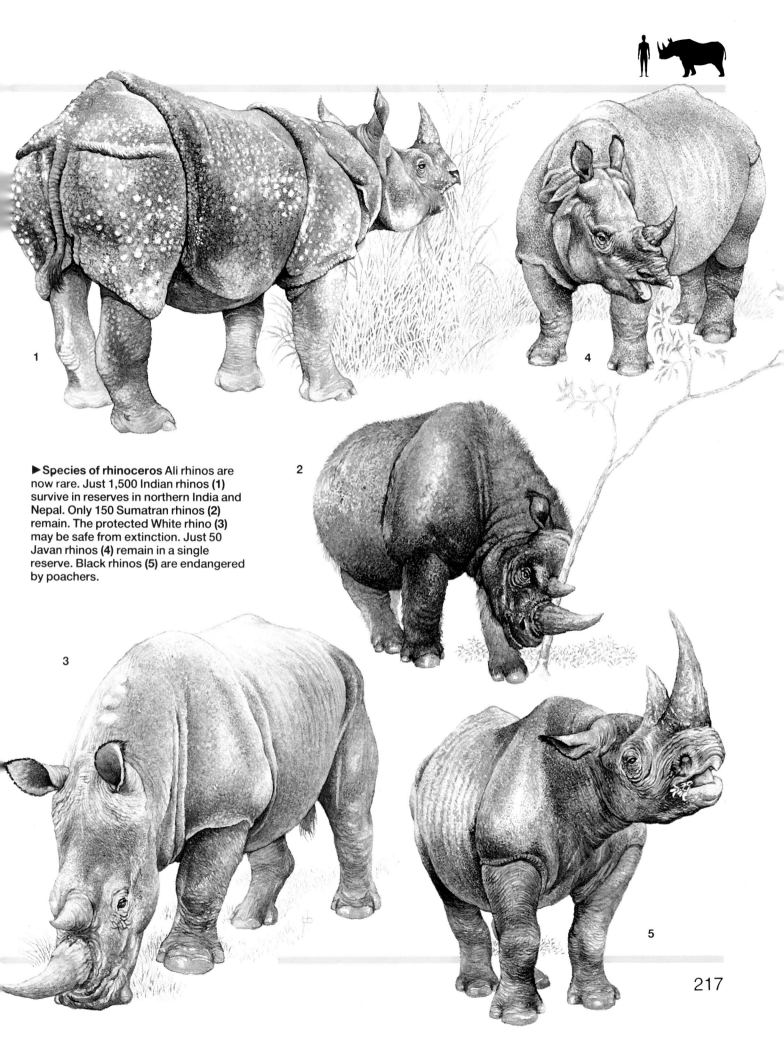

▶ **Species of rhinoceros** All rhinos are now rare. Just 1,500 Indian rhinos **(1)** survive in reserves in northern India and Nepal. Only 150 Sumatran rhinos **(2)** remain. The protected White rhino **(3)** may be safe from extinction. Just 50 Javan rhinos **(4)** remain in a single reserve. Black rhinos **(5)** are endangered by poachers.

217

The exception is the White rhino, which may form small herds of six or seven animals. Even so, adult males are usually solitary.

Adult males often claim an area for themselves, keeping out other males. These may be repelled by ritual fighting, such as sparring with horns, or wiping the horns on the ground. Sometimes a real battle begins, and the animals wound one another. Usually, the rituals are enough to keep the males spread apart. They also mark the edges of their territories with special piles of dung and urine.

LIFE HISTORY

Rhinos have long lives. They may be able to breed at 5 years old, but females bear a calf only every 2 or 3 years. Males may not be able to defend an area and breed until they are about 10 years old. Baby rhinos are small compared to their parents, weighing only about 40kg in the case of the Indian rhino, but they are still as heavy as most 12-year-old children. Rhino mothers usually find a quiet spot in which to give birth. They may leave tiny babies hidden while they feed elsewhere, but after a few days most baby rhinos move with their mother. Baby Indian and White rhinos tend to run in front of the mother, baby Black rhinos usually run behind.

SURVIVAL IN QUESTION

Some 40 million year ago, rhinos of various kinds were abundant in most warm regions of the world. Now these animals are in danger of extinction. They are hunted for their horn, which is believed to have medicinal properties. It is also used to make handles for daggers which are status symbols in parts of Arabia.

◀African White rhinos are usually peaceable and rather timid, in spite of their size. These grass-eaters are more often found in groups than other rhinos.

HIPPOPOTAMUSES

In a deep pool in an African river the fish swim lazily. A small crocodile drifts by. Suddenly a huge animal springs across the bottom of the pool in a slow motion gallop, lightly touching the bottom with its toes. Then it floats to the surface, where just its eyes, nose and ears peek above water. It is a hippopotamus. On land the animal is heavy and cumbersome. Buoyed up by the water it is almost weightless and moves easily and gracefully.

HIPPOPOTAMUSES
Hippopotamidae (*2 species*)

● ■ ☠

Habitat: lakes, wallows and rivers during day, grassland at night. Pygmy hippo in swamp forest.

Diet: mostly land vegetation, especially short grasses.

◎ Breeding: 1 young after pregnancy of 190-240 days.

Size: Pygmy hippopotamus: head-body 1.5m; weight 180kg. Hippopotamus: head-body 3.45m; weight 3.2 tonnes. Males larger than females.

Colour: blackish grey, lighter or pinkish below.

Lifespan: 45 years.

Species mentioned in text:
Hippopotamus (*Hippopotamus amphibius*)
Pygmy hippopotamus (*Choeropsis liberiensis*)

▶The hippo's lower tusks are up to 50cm long. They are used in fights between rival males. Adult males are often scarred.

The most familiar hippo is the larger of the two species. It is found in slow-moving rivers and lakes. It lives over much of Africa south of the Sahara where water and grassland are close to one another. The second species is the Pygmy hippo found in the forests of West Africa. This is a much rarer animal. It is tiny compared to its grassland cousin, and much more difficult to observe. Few details are known of its habits.

The common hippo has eyes, ears and nose at the very top of the head, so it can hear, see and breathe in air while mostly submerged. The nostrils and ears can be closed when under water. In the Pygmy hippo the eyes are further to the side of the head.

DAY-TIME LAZY-BONES
The common hippo spends most of the day in water. It seems to prefer slow-moving rivers, but also lives in lakes, and sometimes in estuaries. This aquatic habit takes the weight off its feet, and also prevents water loss through the skin. Water escapes through hippo skin four times as fast as through a person's in dry air. Hippo skin is smooth, with few hairs. Glands in the skin secrete a pink fluid which protects the skin from sunburn. Beneath the skin is a layer of fat 5cm

▶Hippos feed on land but often get rid of waste food (defecate) in water, so adding fertilizer to the water. Some kinds of fish stay close to hippos, either to graze on tiny plants that grow on the hippos skin, or to feed on the dung.

thick, which keeps the hippo warm in cool water.

Day is a lazy time for the hippo. It rests, swims a little, submerges for up to 5 minutes, and yawns repeatedly.

NIGHT-TIME GRAZERS
At night the hippo emerges from the water. This is when it does all its feeding. For 6 hours or so, the hippo crops grass with its huge lips. Where possible it feeds on patches of short grasses, or hippo lawns, close to

◄A baby Pygmy hippo weighs about 4kg at birth. Pygmy hippos are less aquatic than common hippos, and feed on roots, shoots and fruit found on the forest floor and in swamps.

water, but sometimes has to travel several kilometres to find food. Hippos sometimes make long overland journeys to new bodies of water.

The strongest male in an area mates with all the females in it. He keeps rivals away by displays of yawning to show the teeth, by charges, and by loud grunting calls. As a last resort he will fight. Another way in which males stay spread apart is by marking the edge of their territory with dung. As the animal defecates it wags its short flat tail. This scatters the dung and makes an effective scent mark.

Sometimes males are solitary, but most hippos live in groups of 10 to 15. Most hippo babies are born in the rainy season, when the grasses are growing well. Pygmy hippos live alone, or in pairs.

CAMELS AND LLAMAS

A group of six camels is huddled in the middle of the desert. It is early winter in Central Asia. The wind is blowing across the vast empty plain. There are flurries of snow. The camels' thick woolly coats are caked with snow that fell earlier. Some are sitting, with their legs tucked under their bodies. They are chewing the cud, waiting for the snowfall to stop. Then they will set off to search for patches of grass and shrubs to eat. Their double humps are plump, a sign they are still feeding well.

There are six species in the camel family. Wild camels still live in the Mongolian steppes. These are the two-humped Bactrian camels. Most Bactrian camels, though, are domestic animals, used to carry goods or people. Arabian (one-humped) camels are also used by people. No truly wild ones remain. They were tamed thousands of years ago. They are used by people all over northern Africa and the Middle East.

The other members of the camel family are all South American. Two are wild. The smallest is the graceful vicuña, which lives high in the Andes. The larger guanaco lives lower on the mountains, and also down to sea level on some grasslands. The other two species are the llama and alpaca. They are both domestic animals. It is believed that people bred them from the wild guanaco starting 5,000 or more years ago.

DESERT SURVIVORS
Camels are able to survive in some of the harshest deserts. They wander widely, and feed on a variety of plants. They eat thorn bushes, dry vegetation, and even saltbushes. Most animals will not eat saltbush, but camels seem

CAMELS AND LLAMAS Camelidae (6 species)

● ■ 🧍

● **Habitat**: steppe and desert. Mountain grassland.

■ **Diet**: grasses; also shrubs and salty plants (camels).

◎ **Breeding**: 1 young after pregnancy of 330-410 days.

Size: smallest (vicuña): head-body 1.2m, shoulder height 0.91m, weight 45kg; largest (Bactrian camel): head-body 3m, shoulder height 2.1m, weight 450kg.

Colour: mainly brownish fur, but domestic forms may be white, dark or parti-coloured.

Lifespan: 20-45 years.

Species mentioned in text:
Alpaca (Lama pacos)
Arabian camel (Camelus dromedarius)
Bactrian camel (C. bactrianus)
Guanaco (Lama guanicoe)
Llama (L. glama)
Vicuña (Vicugna vicugna)

to thrive better with some salty food. Camels can withstand long periods without water. They often graze far from oases, and have been known to go as long as 10 months without water. In such cases, a camel loses much weight and strength. Once it finds water, a thirsty camel may drink as much as 140 litres within a short time with no ill effects.

Camels do not store water in their bodies. They are just very good at keeping what they have got. They produce little urine, and dry faeces. They hardly sweat. Instead, they allow their body temperature to rise by as much as 8°C on a hot day, and cool down at night. This rise and fall in temperature would make most mammals ill, but not camels. Camels can sweat if they really need to. The inside of their large nose helps trap moisture rather than letting it escape from the body in the breath. Any moisture dripping from the nose runs down a groove to the split upper lip. The nostrils can be closed to keep out

desert dust. The fur in the ear-flaps also keeps out dust.

KEEPING COOL
The camel's fur coat acts as insulation from the heat of the Sun. The way the camel folds its legs right under its body when it is resting cuts down the amount of surface exposed to the Sun. The camel's humps are filled with fat. This is mainly a reserve of food, as is fat in most animals, but it is concentrated on the back. Here it also serves as a barrier to the Sun's rays, without wrapping the whole camel in a layer of fat.

KEEPING WARM
Camels are not always in hot surroundings. Even in the Sahara the desert nights can be freezing. In Central Asia it can be bitterly cold all winter. The woolly coat of a camel protects it against cold. The Bactrian camel has a very thick winter coat. In spring the coat is shed in lumps, giving the animal a ragged look.

▲**Members of the camel family** The
Bactrian camel **(1)** and the Arabian
camel, or dromedary **(2)** have two-toed
feet with pads which spread the weight
on sand or snow. The llama **(3)** has been
an important beast of burden in South
America for nearly 5,000 years. The
alpaca **(4)** is raised for its wool. The
vicuña **(5)** is from the high Andes.

HIGH LIFE

The guanaco can also live in desert conditions, but the speciality of the South American members of the camel family is living high in the mountains. The vicuña lives in alpine grasslands at 3,700 to 4,800m above sea level. The llama and the alpaca also live high in the Andes, as do some guanacos. These animals all have blood which is especially good at taking up oxygen in the thin air. They also have woolly coats that keep out the cold.

HERD LIFE

In camels and in the vicuña and guanaco, the herd usually consists of a single adult male with a harem of females. There may be 5 or 6 females in a vicuña herd, and up to 15 in a camels', plus their young. The male does not tolerate rivals, and young males are pushed out of the herd as they grow up. In the vicuña the male defends a particular area in which the herd feeds. He may stand on a mound, keeping watch on his group, and ready to give the alarm.

Camels nearly always produce a

▼With their long necks, Arabian camels feed from bushes or from the ground.

►An alert guanaco stands on the pampas. The guanaco can often get enough water from its food without drinking. In Argentina, it is hunted for its pelt.

single baby. The newborn is able to walk and go with the herd after only a few hours. It lacks the hard pads of skin that adult camels have on their knees on which they rest on the ground. It is adult at about 5 years old. Llama and guanaco babies grow up faster. They are able to run almost the moment they are born. They feed on milk for only 3 months. Some are able to breed at 1 year old.

SPITTING AND BLOWING

All members of the camel family chew the cud. They bring the stomach contents up for a second chewing. They can also use this mechanism as defence against any animals (including people) that annoy them. Their ears go back as they bring up part of the stomach contents and spit the foul-smelling liquid over the enemy.

Male camels have another type of display which they use against rivals. In the mouth is a piece of skin which the camel can fill with air and blow out

►Even in thin mountain air, the vicuña can run at 47kph.

like a pink balloon, at the same time giving a "roar".

VITAL AND VALUABLE

The camel family has been vital to people. All species are marvellous beasts of burden in difficult conditions. A camel can carry 100kg of luggage 30km in a day. A llama can carry a 60kg burden nearly as far, high

In the early morning snow, Bolivian llama drivers prepare their animals for a day of high-altitude transport. The llama may be brown, black, white or blotched. As well as carrying goods and giving wool, llamas provide meat and leather, and their dried dung is used as fuel.

in the mountains. As well as working, camels provide wool and meat. They are also milked, and can give 6 litres a day for up to 18 months. They can be ridden, raced, used in warfare, and also used as wealth.

The llama was the mainstay of the civilization of the ancient Incas. When the Spanish reached South America in the 15th century AD, over 300,000 llamas were being used in the silver mines alone. Thousands of others carried goods. The llama has good wool, but the smaller alpaca is bred especially for its wool. Some animals grow wool almost to the ground. The llama is becoming less important as a pack animal, but the alpaca is still important for wool production. There are about 3,000,000 alpacas in Peru.

The finest wool of all comes from the vicuña. However, instead of trying to conserve this valuable animal, and harvest the wool, people have killed it for a single fleece. Numbers dropped from several million in the 1500s to less than 15,000 in the late 1960s. But now the vicuña is fully protected and the population is growing again. Now there are over 80,000.

DEER

It is autumn. In a woodland glade a Red deer stag is surrounded by hinds. He lifts his head and roars. From beyond a ridge a rival replies, and then comes trotting over the hill. The two stags walk in the same direction for a while, gauging each other's size. Then they turn towards one another and their antlers clash. They push back and forth in a trial of strength. The first stag is just the stronger. The other stag breaks away and runs, but is chased by the victor.

Deer live in North and South America, Europe, North Africa, and over most of Asia including many islands. There are no deer in Africa south of the Sahara desert. Nor are there deer in Australia and New Zealand except for those introduced by people.

Deer range in size from smaller than an Alsatian dog to the moose that towers over an adult human, but most are medium-sized animals. The majority of deer are coloured in a shade of brown. Some kinds are spotted. The dull colours are good camouflage for animals such as deer which are good to eat and often hunted by others. Deer mostly feed on grasses and low-growing plants, but some kinds feed on leaves and twigs from bushes and trees. They all chew the cud.

WHAT MAKES A DEER?

Deer look similar to other plant-eaters, especially antelopes, and have graceful, elongated bodies, slender legs and necks, and short tails. They have long heads with jaws that bear many chewing teeth to deal with plant food, and also large noses providing a keen sense of smell. Their sense of hearing is also good, and the large ear-flaps are very mobile. The large round eyes are set on the side of the head, giving a good all-round view to warn of approaching enemies.

The feature which sets deer apart from all other animals, however, is the possession of a pair of antlers. These are carried only by the males (except in reindeer). Antlers are made entirely of bone, unlike the horns of cattle or antelope, which have a horny covering over a bony core. In some deer the antlers are just simple spikes. In many they are branched. The way the antlers

▶A Red deer stag roars to lay claim to his harem. The thick neck and mane develop for the breeding season.

▼▶American species of deer The Southern pudu (*Pudu pudu*) (1) is the smallest deer, and comes from forests in South America, as do the Red brocket (5) and the huemul (*Hippocamelus antisensis*) (4). The Swamp deer (3) is the largest South American deer and lives on wet grasslands. The Pampas deer (*Ozotoceros bezoarticus*) (2) lives on dry plains. The White-tailed deer (6) lives in small herds in North and Central America.

DEER Cervidae (*36 species*)

Habitat: mostly woodland and forest; some found on tundra or open grassland.

Diet: grasses, or shoots, twigs, leaves and fruit of shrubs and trees.

Breeding: 1 or 2 young after pregnancy of 24-40 weeks.

Size: smallest (pudu): head-body 0.8m, shoulder height 0.38m, weight 8kg; largest (sambar): head-body 2m, shoulder height 1.4m, weight 270kg (but see Moose).

Colour: mostly shades of grey, brown, red and yellow. Some adults and many young spotted.

Lifespan: 10-20 years.

Species mentioned in text:
Chital (*Axis axis*)
Fallow deer (*Dama dama*)
Indian muntjac (*Muntiacus muntjac*)
Mule or Black-tailed deer (*Odocoileus hemionus*)
Père David's deer (*Elaphurus davidiensis*)
Red brocket (*Mazama americana*)
Red deer (*Cervus elaphus*)
Reeve's muntjac (*Muntiacus reevesi*)
Roe deer (*Capreolus capreolus*)
Rusa deer (*Cervus timorensis*)
Sambar (*C. unicolor*)
Sika deer (*C. nippon*)
Swamp deer (*C. duvauceli*)
Tufted deer (*Elaphodus cephalophus*)
Wapiti (*Cervus canadensis*)
Water deer (*Hydropotes inermis*)
White-tailed deer (*Odocoileus virginianus*)

1   2

3

4

5

6

227

branch is slightly different for each species, so is a good means of identification. In a few species, such as the Fallow deer, the antlers have flattened sections with a hand-like (palmate) appearance.

The main function of antlers seems to be for fighting and display between the males. As males mature the antlers become bigger and, in some cases, more complicated in branching. They show well the maturity, strength and condition of a male. Thus they are good signals which another male can interpret before deciding on a challenge for supremacy.

RUTTING

In the breeding or rutting season, in species such as the Red deer and wapiti, males (stags) fight for a group or harem of females (hinds). Fights mostly take place between well-matched males. Smaller animals give up their challenge on hearing the herd master's voice or seeing his size. Fighting mainly consists of pushing matches with antlers locked, which may go on for many minutes. Losers are usually allowed to run away without harm, but sometimes bad injuries are caused by antlers. Fighting and guarding a harem takes up much energy, and males become very tired by the end of the rutting season. They need a period of rest and building up before they are again ready to mate.

RENEWABLE WEAPONS

During this rest period the antlers are shed. All deer replace the antlers regularly, unlike the permanent horns of antelope. The bone of each antler dissolves away at the base, and the antlers drop off, usually within a day or two of each other. A bony stub is left on each side of the skull. The deer begins the process of growing a new set. This involves making large amounts of new bone. Many deer gnaw cast antlers, so getting back some of the substances they need.

While the antlers are growing they are covered with skin and hair. This covering is known as "velvet". So much chemical activity goes on below the velvet that it can feel hot to the touch. When the antlers have grown to their full size for the year, the blood supply to the velvet is cut off and the skin dies and begins to shrivel. The deer may help get rid of the dead skin by rubbing its antlers against a tree.

HERDS

For much of the year typical deer live in single-sex herds. A group of females and young keep together. Males may be found singly, or else in a "bachelor herd". The intense rivalry between males occurs only in the breeding season.

The size of herds varies according to species and the habitat they live in. The Red deer is basically a woodland

▲Fallow deer prefer open woodlands. Originally from the Mediterranean, they have been introduced to Britain, and more recently to Australia.

◄Two male Black-tailed deer struggle for supremacy. Their branched antlers lock together.

►Out of the breeding season, Red deer stags live together in herds without fighting. These stags are "in velvet", in the process of growing new antlers.

animal, and there it lives in herds of about 20. In open country the herds are often larger, up to 100 strong. The chital, a deer that feeds on grass and lives in grassland and light woodland in India, may have herds of more than 100. At the other extreme is the Roe deer of Europe and Asia, and the Red brocket of South America, each of which often inhabits dense woods and forests. These deer mainly browse, eating shoots, twigs and leaves. They are solitary animals, except when breeding.

SIGNALS

Many species of deer have light-coloured rumps or tails. When the animals flee, these marks are easy for

▲ The wapiti is found in western North America and Asia. It is closely related to the Red deer, but larger. Its antlers can be more than 1m long.

others in a herd to follow. Other signals are also used. Mothers and young sometimes bleat to keep in touch with one another. Many deer "bark" when they are alarmed. Males in the breeding season can be noisy too. Their sounds range from a bellowing roar in the Red deer to a whistling scream in the Sika deer.

Deer have sensitive noses, so scent signals are especially important to these animals. Many species have special glands between the toes, which leave behind their owner's scent imprint. Glands in slits just in front of the eyes produce strong-smelling secretions. These the animals deposit on twigs and grass stems.

REARING THE YOUNG

Most deer produce a single young (calf). This stays hidden for a few weeks, emerging only when the mother visits to suckle it. After this period it moves with its mother and herd. It suckles for several months. A young deer may still be following its mother while she is rearing her next calf. Babies often have a spotted coat, but this pattern disappears long before adulthood. A few kinds of deer, including the Fallow deer, chital, and

Sika deer, are spotted as adults.

The Water deer of China is unusual in that it often gives birth to triplets. Even bigger litters have been recorded. This solitary swampland deer is also unusual in having no antlers in either sex. The males have tusk-like canine teeth, as do the males of the muntjac and Tufted deer, both of which have very small antlers.

DEER AND PEOPLE

Deer have been hunted by people for their flesh (venison), skins and antlers since prehistoric times. Deer are still hunted, but in some places farms have been started to produce venison. In parts of Asia deer damage crops and are considered a pest.

Some 70 years ago, Père David's deer was nearly exterminated. This is a large species with spreading hoofs, native to the river plains of northern China. When Europeans first visited China in the 13th century, the only specimens left were in the Emperor's hunting park in Beijing. The last one there died in 1920. The species was saved because a few had been brought to Woburn in England. These bred, and now some have been taken back to China.

▲The Rusa deer of Indonesia shows the large ears, big eyes and wet nose typical of deer.

▼European and Asian species of deer
The Roe deer (1) is found over much of Europe and Asia. Spotted deer include the chital (2) and Sika deer (4) from Asia. Reeve's muntjac (3), and the Tufted (5), Père David's (6) and Water deer (7) are all from Asia.

GIRAFFE AND OKAPI

Two female giraffes feed on a thorn tree. A kilometre away a lone male crops another tree. He is disturbed. He stops feeding and watches a movement in the distance. The females stop feeding and watch him. Uneasy, the male moves away from his tree. The females, and then three more giraffes, follow him to a safer place.

The giraffe family consists of two species, the giraffe and the okapi. The giraffe lives in most of Africa south of the Sahara. The okapi is found in a small area of rain forest in Zaire, but is locally common. Although a large animal, it was unknown to Europeans until 1901. Little is known of its behaviour in the wild.

The giraffe is the tallest animal. The biggest ever measured was 6.09m high to the top of the horns. The males (bulls) are heavier and much taller than the females (cows), which rarely exceed 4.5m in height.

CHOOSING DINNER

The two sexes also have different styles in eating. Male giraffes stretch up high into a tree for their food. Females more regularly feed at around their shoulder height. So not only does the giraffe feed above the level of most other animals, but the food available is divided between the sexes.

The giraffe is a browser, picking leaves and shoots off trees and shrubs. It may also eat seed pods, flowers, fruits and climbing plants. The giraffe has very mobile lips which it uses to

▲Young bull giraffes hold ritual fights to discover which is stronger. They use their necks for wrestling, and their horns and heads as butts. Only the strongest adult bulls mate with the females in an area.

▼The okapi is a secretive, solitary animal. It feeds on leaves of young tree shoots. Its face and tongue are like the giraffe's. It has poor sight, but good senses of hearing and smell.

GIRAFFE AND OKAPI
Giraffidae (*2 species*)

○ ■

● **Habitat:** open woodland and savannah (giraffe); dense forest (okapi).

■ **Diet:** leaves, bark and shoots. Some flowers, seeds and fruits.

◎ **Breeding:** 1 calf after pregnancy of 453-464 days.

Size: (giraffe) head-body 3.8-4.7m, height to 5.5m, weight 550-1,930kg, males larger than females; (okapi) head-body 1.9-2m, height to 1.7m, weight 210-250kg.

Colour: (giraffe) red-brown to almost black patches of variable size separated by network of lighter fur; (okapi) dark velvety purplish-brown, with white stripes on rump and legs.

Lifespan: 15-25 years.

Species mentioned in text:
Giraffe (*Giraffa camelopardalis*)
Okapi (*Okapia johnstoni*)

pull food to its mouth. It can stretch out its tongue about 45cm to gather food. The canine teeth are shaped like a comb, and are used to strip leaves from a branch. The animal often feeds from thorn trees, which have spines several centimetres long. It can pick leaves from between these, but will even chew thorns if they are taken into the mouth.

LONG NECK AND GIANT HOOFS
Many features of the giraffe's anatomy are very odd. Each giraffe has its own individual coat pattern, like human finger-prints. There are, though, different types of colour and pattern according to the part of Africa the giraffe lives in. The enormously long neck has only seven bones in it, like the neck of other mammals, but each

one is greatly elongated. The body is comparatively short in length. Tangling the long legs is avoided by moving both legs on the same side of the body together. This produces a loping movement. When the animal raises or lowers its head, blood drains or rushes to the brain. To cope with this the blood vessels are specially elastic to help pump blood, and strong valves in the veins prevent backflow.

A giraffe is born with small horns. As it gets older, particularly if it is a bull, these grow thicker and heavier, and many bony lumps appear on the skull as well. The giraffe also has soup plate-sized hoofs. These it uses as weapons; with a powerful kick, a giraffe can kill a lion. The skin is thick and tough for defence. Adults have few enemies, but about half the young (calves) die in their first year, killed by lions, leopards or hyenas.

The giraffe has good hearing and sense of smell, but closes its nostrils when poking its head into a thorn tree. Its most acute sense, though, is sight. It can see clearly for many kilometres across the plains.

CALVING
A pregnant giraffe gives birth to her baby in a special calving area within her home range. The baby can stand soon after birth. After a week or two the calf may join up with other calves and form a "nursery group". The group is left alone during the middle of the day while the mothers go off to feed. A newborn giraffe is 1.8m tall. In its first year, it may grow 8cm a month. Giraffes are adult at about 5 years old, but males may be 8 years old before they manage to breed.

◄This male reticulated giraffe, feeding at full stretch, belongs to a race from northern Kenya and Somalia. To pump blood to its head it has a heart 60cm long and weighing more than 11kg.

GOATS AND SHEEP

High in the Rocky Mountains two horned male sheep face one another. These rams stand a little apart, lower their heads slowly, then rush at each other. They crash into one another head-on, with an enormous bang that echoes round the mountain. They back away, then launch themselves again, banging their enormous horns together with a jarring crash. Again and again they do this, until one accepts defeat and retreats. Neither animal has been injured by this head-banging.

Although it is easy to tell a domestic sheep from a domestic goat, it is not always so easy with the wild species. Females may be very similar. Males show more differences. In goats the males have chin beards and usually smell strongly. Goats have anal scent glands, and the males may also spray themselves with urine. Males have sharp scimitar-shaped horns with knobbed ridges. Goats have long flat tails with a bare underside.

Male sheep do not have chin beards but may have a throat mane. Sheep, unlike goats, have scent glands between the toes, in the groin and in front of the eye, but no anal gland. Male sheep (rams) do not have the offensive smell of goats. Rams have large, rather blunt horns which curl in a spiral. Sheep have short tails and often have a rump patch.

AGILE CLIMBERS
Goats and sheep tend to live in different types of country. Goats specialize in cliffs, while sheep live in the open, rolling dry lands close to cliffs. But both types of animal include agile climbers. This group of animals has made use of some of the most difficult, dangerous land, and eats

GOATS AND SHEEP
Bovidae; tribes Caprini, Rupicaprini, Saigini (*24 species*)

○ ■ 🐾

◤ **Habitat:** often steep terrain, from hot desert and moist jungle to snowy wastes.

■ **Diet:** grasses, leaves and bark of shrubs, other plants.

◎ **Breeding:** 1 or 2 lambs or kids after pregnancy of 150-180 days.

Size: head-tail 1.1-1.86m, weight 25-140kg.

Colour: usually shade of brown, some blackish, white or golden.

Lifespan: 10-15 years.

Species mentioned in text:
Argalis (*Ovis ammon*)
Barbary sheep (*Ammotragus lervia*)
Bighorn sheep (*Ovis canadensis*)
Chamois (*Rupicapra rupicapra*)
Chiru (*Pantholops hodgsoni*)
Goral (*Nemorhaedus goral*)
Himalayan tahr (*Hemitragus jemlahicus*)
Ibex (*Capra ibex*)
Japanese serow (*Capricornis crispus*)
Mainland serow (*C. sumatrensis*)
Markhor (*Capra falconeri*)
Mouflon (*Ovis musimon*)
Mountain goat (*Oreamnos americanus*)
Saiga (*Saiga tatarica*)
Snow sheep (*Ovis nivicola*)
Thinhorn sheep (*O. dalli*)
Wild goat (*Capra aegagrus*)

▼▶**Goats or goat antelopes** Goral (1), Japanese serow (6), chamois (7) and Mountain goat (9) have both sexes similar in size and looks. They have short, sharp horns. In many other species males are bigger and have beards and manes. A male Himalayan tahr (2) may weigh 108kg. The male urial (*Ovis orientalis*) (3) and male Barbary sheep(4) have spiral horns and a throat mane. The Wild goat (5) and ibex (8) have long curved horns. The argalis (10) has huge horns.

▲The Mountain goat has a thick coat with a layer of fat beneath to keep it warm in bitter cold.

some of the toughest plants.

There are 24 species of goats and their relatives. Some are rather odd looking, such as the serows, chamois, goral and Mountain goat. More "typical" in appearance are the tahrs and the true sheep and goats. There are also two bigger species of "giant goat", the Musk ox and takin.

SIMILAR TO GAZELLES

On the borderline between the goats and the gazelles are two species, the saiga and the chiru. The chiru lives high in the plateaux of Tibet in small groups. Only the male has horns. The same is true of the saiga. This animal once lived across a wide area, from Poland to the steppes of Central Asia, in large numbers. It was hunted to near extinction, but is now protected and out of danger.

The saiga migrates long distances across the steppes, and huge herds form at this time. The saiga is a fast runner, reaching speeds of up to 60kph. It has a large bulbous nose, which helps to warm the air it breathes. It also has a good sense of smell.

The chiru and saiga look and behave like gazelles, and this is what the majority of scientists now believe them to be.

STURDY AND SURE-FOOTED

The serows are rather clumsy and slow compared to goats, but they are sure-footed as they go up and down the steep rocky slopes of their home areas. They live where there is shrub or tree cover. The Mainland serow is found from India south to Sumatra and east to southern China. The Japanese serow is found in much cooler conditions, including snow, in Japan and Taiwan. Both species of serow are browsers.

The goral is a smaller but similarly shaped animal, with a slightly shaggy coat, living over a wide area of Asia from India to Thailand and north to Siberia. It usually lives in dry climates on very steep cliffs. The goral climbs and jumps well. It feeds morning and evening and may rest on a sunny ledge for much of the day.

GOATS OF THE SNOWS

The Mountain goat lives in western North America. It is found in rocky areas high in the mountains, often above the tree line. It climbs steep cliffs and along the edges of large glaciers. The Mountain goat is sure-footed, but moves slowly most of the time. It eats grasses and lichens and

▼A domestic sheep cleans her new-born lamb. The domestic sheep's dense woolly coat is not found in wild sheep.

▶A group of Thinhorn sheep stay alert as they rest and chew the cud on a pasture high in the mountains of Alaska.

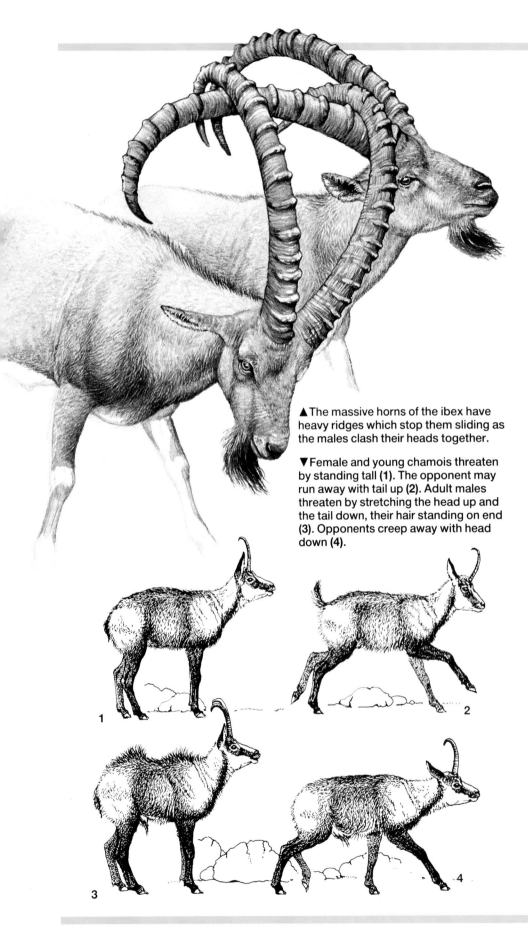

▲The massive horns of the ibex have heavy ridges which stop them sliding as the males clash their heads together.

▼Female and young chamois threaten by standing tall (1). The opponent may run away with tail up (2). Adult males threaten by stretching the head up and the tail down, their hair standing on end (3). Opponents creep away with head down (4).

1

2

3

4

may browse on bushes. Because it lives where the snowfall is heavy, the Mountain goat has developed a stocky build and a thick white woolly coat. The thick legs look as though they are in pantaloons. They have very large hoofs with hard rims and softer centres which give a good grip.

The most nimble of the "near-goats" is the chamois. This lives in the cold snowy mountains of Europe and Asia Minor. The chamois comes down the mountain to spend winter in woodland, where it feeds on buds, young tree shoots, lichens and small grass patches. Summer is spent high on the mountains, feeding on grasses and herbs.

The chamois can make use of tiny areas of good footing to leap up and down the most unlikely looking rock faces at speed. A whole herd will throw itself down a cliff which, to a human, looks almost impossible to climb. Even the babies are agile. The kids are born in May and June on rocky, inaccessible areas. They can follow their mother almost immediately, and within a week are at home jumping about the crags.

Old male chamois are usually solitary, but females live in herds of up to 30. Males fight viciously during the breeding season, using their hooked horns. Unless a loser submits by flattening himself on the ground, he may be gored to death.

BEARDLESS GOATS
Tahrs live on tree-covered mountain slopes and cliffs. They have no beards and a naked muzzle. The horns are rather flattened. Males do not smell like true goats. The Himalayan tahr has a thick shaggy mane around its shoulders. Other species live in southern India and in Oman. Tahrs are wary animals. A few animals in the herd of up to 40 are always on watch.

The Barbary sheep is native to North Africa. It is found in mountainous areas which are barren and rocky.

It seems able to survive without drinking water. In some respects it is more like a goat than a sheep, and it has a long flat tail. But it fights like a sheep, by clashing heads together. The horns of big male Barbary sheep are large. Males also have a body weight twice that of females.

TRUE GOATS

Six species of wild goat are found from the Pyrenees to central China. They are mainly browsers, but also graze. The ibex exists in a number of slightly different forms in various mountain ranges. The horns of the Siberian ibex are the longest, growing to 1.4m.

The horns of the markhor grow equally long, but they are twisted. The markhor lives in the mountains of Central Asia and is the largest goat. Males can be 1m high at the shoulders and weigh 110kg.

The Wild goat from which our domestic animals were bred still exists in western Asia and the eastern Mediterranean. It was first tamed in western Asia approximately 8,500 years ago. Its eating habits prevent the regrowth of trees in some parts of the world.

GRAZING IN HERDS

Six species of sheep live from the Mediterranean across Asia to Siberia and in the west of North America. Most live by grazing. They are herd animals which rely on keeping together to escape enemies.

The mouflon is a small sheep found in Asia Minor and the Mediterranean. This is probably the species from which tame sheep were bred. Some of the old-fashioned breeds like the St Kilda sheep still have much the same size and colouring as the mouflon. It is chestnut brown with a light saddle. The mouflon is hardy and can live in cold or desert habitats. Domestic sheep have been bred for various characters, including a long woolly fleece, and there are now many breeds, mostly with white coats.

MOUNTAIN SHEEP

The largest wild sheep is the argalis, which lives in cold desert and mountain habitats in Central Asia. It has a light brown coat with a white rump patch. A male can be 1.25m tall and weigh 180kg. The horns curve in a spiral and can be 1.9m long and 50cm round, weighing up to 22kg.

The Snow sheep lives in the mountains and Arctic wastes of Siberia. The Thinhorn sheep lives in similar conditions in Alaska and western Canada. The Bighorn lives in mountainous and dry desert areas from Canada to Mexico. In the Rocky Mountains it occupies the same areas as the Mountain goat, yet the two species have very different life-styles. The Bighorn is migratory, moving seasonally across wide areas of woodland, while the Mountain goat ruthlessly defends a territory when food becomes scarce on the cliffs in deep snow.

▼ The chamois moves lower down the slopes in the winter, but is still likely to encounter snow in its mountain home. These animals are at 2,100m in the Swiss Alps.

KANGAROOS

KANGAROOS Macropodidae and Potoroidae
(60 species)

Habitat: inland plain and semi-desert to tropical rain forest and hills.

Diet: grasses, other low-growing plants, shoots of bushes.

Breeding: 1 joey after pregnancy of 27-36 days, plus a period in the pouch of 5-11 months.

Size: smallest (Musky rat kangaroo): head-body 28cm, plus 14cm tail, weight 0.5kg; largest (Red kangaroo): head-body 1.65m, plus 1.07m tail, weight up to 90kg. In larger species, males bigger than females.

Colour: mainly shades of brown or grey; some have contrasting facial markings or stripes on body or tail.

Lifespan: up to 20 years in the wild, 28 years in captivity.

Species mentioned in text:
Eastern grey kangaroo (*Macropus giganteus*)
Lumholtz's tree kangaroo (*Dendrolagus lumholtzi*)
Musky rat kangaroo (*Hypsiprymnodon moschatus*)
Red kangaroo (*Macropus rufus*)
Wallaroo or euro or Hill kangaroo (*M. robustus*)
Western grey kangaroo (*M. fuliginosus*)

Two grey kangaroos sip water from the edge of a small river. They turn and move slowly up the bank. Suddenly alarmed by a flock of birds landing to drink, they begin to move fast. They thump their back legs down hard and spring into the air. Each bound sends them higher and faster, until they are in full flight, travelling at 50kph in jumps 4m long.

The kangaroo family is large. There are about 50 species. The larger species are called kangaroos, the smaller ones wallabies. There are also 10 small species known as rat kangaroos and bettongs. Kangaroos are marsupials, animals of which the female has a pouch where she keeps the young.

HOW THEY HOP
The whole group have long back legs and travel fast by hopping. The long tail works as a counterbalance to the weight of the body as they jump. When moving slowly, kangaroos may use the front legs and tail as a tripod to

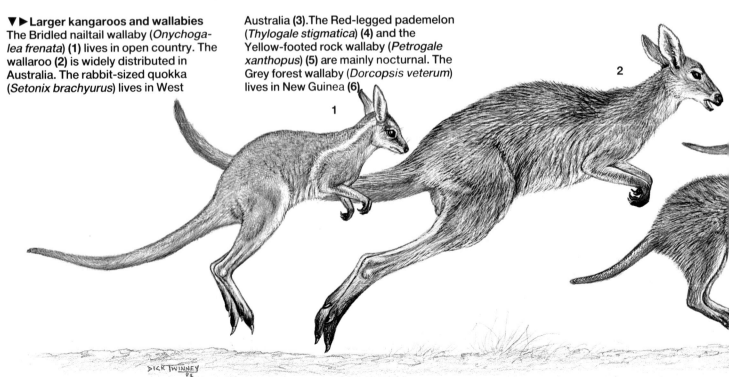

▼►Larger kangaroos and wallabies
The Bridled nailtail wallaby (*Onychogalea frenata*) (1) lives in open country. The wallaroo (2) is widely distributed in Australia. The rabbit-sized quokka (*Setonix brachyurus*) lives in West Australia (3).The Red-legged pademelon (*Thylogale stigmatica*) (4) and the Yellow-footed rock wallaby (*Petrogale xanthopus*) (5) are mainly nocturnal. The Grey forest wallaby (*Dorcopsis veterum*) lives in New Guinea (6).

take the weight, then they swing the back legs forward. Next, the back legs support them while they move their front legs and tail.

The long and narrow back foot has four toes. Two of these are large. The other two are small and joined together. They make a kind of comb which a kangaroo uses to keep its fur in good condition.

Kangaroos are plant eaters. They have good chewing teeth in the back of the mouth. As with elephants, their teeth move forwards as they grow older and the front teeth wear down. Kangaroos have large stomachs where there are bacteria which help break down the tough plant food. Most kangaroo species feed at night.

WIDE VARIETY

The big Red kangaroo lives mainly on open plains. It has a thick woolly coat which helps keep out both heat and cold. During the heat of the day it rests in the shade of a bush, feeding when it is cooler. It needs little water, but even in a dry brown landscape it will find newly sprouting grasses and herbs to eat.

▲ Male, female and joey (young in pouch) of the largest marsupial, the Red kangaroo, which lives in grassland.

▼ Kangaroos and wallabies, as plant-eaters, are the Australasian equivalents of African hoofed mammals.

Wallaroos are also desert animals and can exist on even poorer food. The Eastern and Western grey kangaroos live in wooded country. They eat the grasses that grow between trees and they need to drink more often.

Many smaller wallabies like to live in scrub or dense thickets. In some parts of Australia much of this kind of vegetation has been cleared for farms or ranches, and this is one reason why some of the small kangaroos have become rarer. Another reason is that they have suffered from introduced rabbits competing for food and living

▲ The back legs of tree kangaroos are fairly short, but the tail is long and provides a good balancing limb.

▼ Small- and medium-sized kangaroos
The Lesser forest wallaby (*Dorcopsulus macleayi*) (1) lives in New Guinea. The Musky rat kangaroo (2). Lumholtz's tree kangaroo (3). The Desert rat kangaroo (*Caloprymnus campestris*) (4). The rare boodie (*Bettongia lesueur*) (5) burrows. The Rufous hare wallaby (*Lagorchestes hirsutus*) (6). The Long-nosed potoroo (*Potorous tridactylus*) (7) and the Rufous bettong (*Aepyprymnus rufescens*) (9) are now rare. The Banded hare wallaby (*Lagostrophus fasciatus*) (8) survives only on coastal islands.

places, and also from being hunted by introduced cats and foxes.

Some kangaroos live in hot wet forests, such as are found in northern Australia and New Guinea. Tree kangaroos (such as Lumholtz's tree kangaroo) climb, and have some of the brightest coloured fur among marsupials. They are agile, making big leaps from one tree to another. But on the ground they are rather slow and clumsy.

SOCIAL AND FAMILY LIFE

Many of the smaller kangaroos live alone, but the Red and grey kangaroos live in groups (called "mobs"). From 2 to 10 move around together, but larger numbers may come together where food is good. In the largest species the males may be twice the size of the females. In Red kangaroos and wallaroos the males and females are different colours.

Kangaroos, like other marsupials, have a very short pregnancy, about a month long. Even in the biggest kangaroos, the baby weighs less than 1g at birth. The baby has big arms and small legs. It crawls by itself to the mother's pouch, where it attaches to one of the four teats. Here it suckles and grows. After several months it takes trips outside the pouch. Even when it leaves the pouch completely (up to a year after birth) it suckles for a few months more.

KOALA

From October to February the eucalyptus forests of eastern Australia echo with strange night-time calls. Long, harsh, indrawn breaths are followed by bellowing growls. No sooner has one call died away than it is answered by others from different parts of the forest. It is the koala's breeding season, and these are the cries of the male koalas.

KOALA *Phascolarctos cinereus*

● ■

Habitat: eucalyptus forest up to 600m above sea level.

Diet: eucalyptus leaves, from a small number of preferred species.

Breeding: 1 young, in summer, after pregnancy of 34-36 days.

Size: head-body to 85cm male, 75cm female; weight 12kg male; 8kg female. (Animals in northern part of range are considerably smaller.)

Colour: grey to reddish-brown, white on chin, chest, and under forearms.

Lifespan: 13 years, 18 in captivity.

The koala might look like a teddy bear, but it is not related to the bears at all, and is certainly not as friendly as it looks. It will defend itself fiercely with its sharp claws if attacked.

THE COMPLETE SPECIALIST
The koala is a marsupial, a pouched mammal, and one of the most specialized animals in Australia. It lives only in the eucalyptus forests of the east coast, and it eats hardly anything but eucalyptus leaves. Not only that, but with 350 eucalyptus species to choose from, the koala feeds mainly on just 5 or 6. It is a low-quality diet, not very

▼ Even the koala's liver is special. It deals with the poisonous chemicals that occur in some eucalyptus leaves it eats.

rich in energy, so the koala is not very active. It spends almost its entire life in the trees, sleeping for up to 18 hours a day and spending the rest of its time eating. Young leaves are bitten off, then ground to a paste with the large cheek teeth. An adult koala weighing about 9kg will munch its way through up to 1kg of leaves in a day. The animal's intestine is long, to help it digest this mass of leaves.

RAISING A BABY
For most of the year koalas live alone. Their feeding areas may overlap, but the animals do not mix very much, even when there are several of them in a small area of forest. In the breeding season, each breeding male (usually over 4 years old) has several mates. His territory overlaps theirs, and throughout the mating season he is on the move, visiting his mates, calling and bellowing, and chasing rival males from his territory.

In midsummer the female produces a single baby, and like all marsupials it crawls straight into the pouch. There it stays for about 6 months until it is fully developed and ready to cope with the outside world.

The weaning process that follows is very unusual. At first, the baby koala is fed on partly digested leaf pulp

that has already passed through the mother's body. This processed food is easy to digest, but it has another important function. Along with the pulp, the young koala receives a supply of microbes from the mother's gut. These are helpful "bugs" that remain in the youngster's body and enable it to digest tough eucalyptus leaves for itself.

▶ ▼ Once it has left the pouch, a young koala rides about on its mother's back for another 4 to 5 months. The adult is a good climber. It can grasp thin branches with an unusual grip – two fingers at one side of the branch, three at the other.

PLATYPUS

The dog sniffing around near the river bank suddenly gives an excited bark. It makes a short dash and pounces on a small furry creature, which has the bill of a duck and the flat tail of a beaver. This odd-looking creature is a platypus – unfortunately for the dog, a male. The platypus wriggles this way and that and then manages to jab the dog with the spurs on its hind legs. They deliver a powerful venom. Startled and in pain, the dog drops the platypus, which escapes into the river.

The platypus is the only mammal besides certain shrews that is venomous. But only the male is able to produce and deliver the poison, which can kill a dog and cause agonizing pain to human beings.

The platypus is also most unusual among mammals because it reproduces by laying and hatching eggs. When the young hatch, they feed on their mother's milk, like all mammals do. The only other mammals to lay eggs are the echidnas, which together with the platypus make up the animal order of monotremes.

The platypus is found in eastern Australia. It lives in burrows in the banks of rivers and lakes, spending much of its time in the water. Once hunted nearly to extinction for its fur, the platypus is now protected and thriving.

SLEEK SWIMMER
The platypus moves awkwardly on the land on its short legs. But in the water it is swift and graceful. Its body, covered with short thick fur, becomes beautifully streamlined, and it propels itself with its broad webbed forefeet. It steers with its partly webbed hind feet and flat tail.

When walking on land, the platypus

folds back the webbing on its forefeet. This exposes thick nails, which the platypus uses for digging its burrows.

FEEDING AND BREEDING
When the platypus dives into water, it closes its eyes and ears. Under water the platypus's soft, rubbery and skin-covered bill becomes its eyes and ears. The bill is very sensitive to touch, which helps the animal find its food as

▼ The female platypus digs a breeding burrow where she will lay her eggs and raise her young. The young suckle her and remain in the burrow for up to 4 months.

▲ The platypus is often called the duckbill. But unlike a duck's bill the bill of the platypus is soft and flexible.

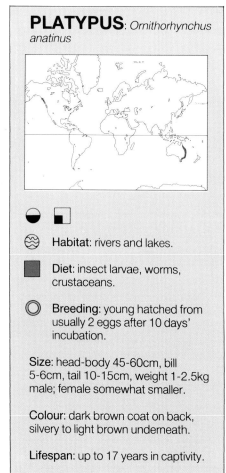

PLATYPUS: *Ornithorhynchus anatinus*

◐ ■

〰 Habitat: rivers and lakes.

■ Diet: insect larvae, worms, crustaceans.

◎ Breeding: young hatched from usually 2 eggs after 10 days' incubation.

Size: head-body 45-60cm, bill 5-6cm, tail 10-15cm, weight 1-2.5kg male; female somewhat smaller.

Colour: dark brown coat on back, silvery to light brown underneath.

Lifespan: up to 17 years in captivity.

▲ The platypus feeds mainly on the river bottom. It uses its sensitive bill to sift through the mud and gravel for insect larvae and small shellfish.

it searches for food on the river bed.

The platypus scoops up insect larvae and crustaceans in its bill, then stores them in its two cheek pouches, located just behind the bill. The platypus has no teeth, but inside the cheek pouches are horny ridges which help grind the food into smaller pieces.

It is thought that platypuses mate in the water after the female slowly approaches the male and he then chases her and grasps her tail. Some days later the female starts to dig a long breeding burrow. She makes at the end a cosy nesting chamber, lined with grass and leaves. There she lays up to three soft, leathery eggs and keeps them warm.

In about 10 days the young hatch and crawl to the mammary glands on the mother's belly and start to suck the milk-soaked fur there.

GLOSSARY

Adult A fully developed animal that is mature and capable of breeding.

Aggression Any behaviour in which one animal threatens another.

Albino An animal whose hair, skin and eyes contain no colour pigments. This makes the coat white and the eyes pink.

Amphibian An animal of the class Amphibia. Members of this class generally have a larval stage that is dependent on water and an adult stage that lives on land. They have smooth scaleless skins.

Amphibious Capable of living both in water and on land.

Anal gland A gland opening into the anus or close beside it. Many mammals have scent glands close to the anus or the tail.

Antarctic The bitterly cold region in the far south of the world, around the South Pole.

Aquatic Living for much, if not all, of the time in or near the water.

Arctic The bitterly cold region in the far north of the world, around the North pole within the Arctic Circle.

Arid Dry. Usually refers to land on the fringes of deserts.

Big cats Members of the genus *Panthera*, including the lion, tiger, cheetah, jaguar and leopard.

Bill Also called beak; the horny part of a bird's mouth with which it gathers food.

Blubber The thick layer of fat beneath a whale's skin.

Brood The group of young raised in a single breeding cycle.

Browse To feed on shoots, leaves and bark of shrubs and trees.

Buck The male of the deer, rabbit, mouse and other species of mammal.

Camouflage Colour and patterns on an animal's coat that allow it to blend in with its surroundings.

Canopy The more or less continuous leafy layer of the trees in a wood or forest.

Carcass The dead body of an animal.

Carnivore In general, a meat-eater. Specifically a member of the mammal order Carnivora, which includes the cat, dog, bear and raccoon families.

Carrion Meat from a dead animal.

Cetaceans Members of the order Cetacea, which includes whales (Baleen and Toothed), dolphins and porpoises.

Class The division of animal classification above order.

Cloaca In reptiles and amphibians, the chamber, opening to the outside of the body, into which discharge both liquid and solid waste, and also eggs and sperm during reproduction.

Clutch The group of eggs laid by a female at a single laying.

Colonial Living, especially breeding, in colonies.

Competition The contest between two or more species over such things as space and food.

Coniferous forest Forest of trees with needle-like leaves, which are usually borne all year.

Conservation Preserving and protecting living things, their habitat and the environment in general.

Courtship The period when an animal tries to attract a mate or renew its bonds with a mate from previous years.

Creche A kind of nursery den in which several mothers leave their young.

Crest A raised structure running along the back of the body or head. A set of long feathers on the head of a bird.

Crustaceans Members of the group of jointed-legged animals that includes shrimps, crabs, krill and wood lice.

Cud Food that is brought back into the mouth, by plant-eaters such as cows, from the first part of the stomach to be given a thorough chewing. It then passes to the second part of the stomach.

Deciduous forest Forest of trees that shed their leaves seasonally, usually in winter.

Diet The food an animal eats.

Digit A finger or a toe.

Display A pattern of things done by one animal that gives information to other animals. It may be seen or heard. Greeting, courtship and threatening may involve displays between animals.

Doe The name of a female mammal, such as a rabbit or mouse, whose male is called a buck.

Domestication Taming a wild species and gradually altering it by selective breeding to make it more useful to humans.

Dorsal Along the back.

Echo-location The method dolphins, porpoises and other toothed whales use to find food. They send out high-pitched sound signals and listen for echoes, which the prey will reflect back. Bats also use echo-location.

Ecology The study of living things in relation to their environment.

Edentates An order of mammals that includes the anteaters and armadillos. The word edentate literally means toothless, though only the anteaters are completely lacking in teeth.

Endangered species One whose numbers have dropped so low that it is in danger of becoming extinct.

Environment The surroundings of a particular species, or the world about us.

External fertilization Joining of eggs and sperm outside the female's body.

Extinction The complete loss of a species, either of a local population or from the whole Earth.

Family In classification of animals, a group of species that share many features in common and are thought to be related.

Feral animals Those that have escaped from captivity and returned to live in the wild. Also, descendants of those animals.

Fertilize To introduce sperm to eggs during reproduction.

Fledging The time when a young bird first takes to the air; a fledgling is a bird that has just begun to fly.

Flight feathers The large feathers on the wings, which are divided into the primaries and secondaries.

Foraging Going in search of food.

Game birds Birds such as pheasants, grouse, guinea fowl and turkeys, which are hunted for sport or food.

Genus The division of animal classification below family and above species.

Gill A structure in aquatic animals through which exchange of oxygen and carbon dioxide takes place.

Glands Organs that produce a special chemical (secretion) that may be passed (secreted) to the outside world.

Grazer A plant-eater that feeds on grasses and gathers its food from the ground, rather than from tall plants.

Habitat The surroundings in which an animal lives, including the plant life, other animals, physical conditions and climate.

Harem A breeding group of two or more females that is attended by just one male.

Hatchling An animal that has just emerged from its egg.

Helper An animal that assists in raising offspring that are not its own. This practice is notable in jackals, for example.

Hibernation A winter period during which an animal is inactive. In hibernation the body processes, such as the beating of the heart, slow down as the body temperature falls.

Home range The area where an individual animal normally lives.

Incubation The period during which a bird sits on a clutch of eggs to keep them warm so that they will develop and eventually hatch.

Insectivores Animals that live chiefly on insects. An order of mammals including hedgehogs, shrews and moles.

Internal fertilization Joining of eggs and sperm inside a female's body.

Invertebrates Any animals without a backbone, for example insects, worms, crabs and slugs.

Juvenile A young animal that is no longer a baby, but is not yet fully adult.

Krill Shrimp-like creatures (crustaceans), which form the main food of Baleen whales.

Lagomorphs Animals belonging to the order Lagomorpha. They include rabbits and hares.

Larva An early stage in the life-cycle of an animal after it has hatched from the egg. Usually it has a very different form from the adult, for example a frog tadpole, or an insect grub or caterpillar.

Mammals Animals whose females have mammary glands that produce milk, on which they feed their young.

Mangrove forest A type of forest that grows on the muddy shores of the sea in deltas and estuaries in the tropics.

Marsupials An order of mammals whose females give birth to very under-developed young that are usually raised in a pouch. The koala, wombat and the possums are marsupials.

Metamorphosis A change in the structure of an animal as it goes from one stage of its life history to the next.

Migration The long distance movement of animals. It is typically seasonal and for the purpose of feeding or breeding.

Molluscs Soft-bodied animals, usually with protective shells, including land snails, cockles, mussels and limpets.

Moult The period when a bird sheds old feathers and grows new ones.

Monotremes The echidnas and the platypus, called monotremes because they have a single opening at the rear of their body. They are unique among mammals in that they lay eggs.

Nocturnal Active during the night.

Nomadic Wandering; having no fixed home territory.

Omnivorous Having a varied diet, eating both plants and animals.

Order The division of animal classification below class and above family. For example, all the frog and toad families belong to the order Anura.

Placenta A structure attached to the inside of the female's reproductive system through which an embryo receives nourishment.

Plankton Minute creatures that live in the sea.

Plumage The feathers of a bird. Many birds develop a more striking plumage in the spring and summer breeding season, in order to attract their mates.

Polygamous An animal that has more than one mate; most often this applies to males.

Population A separate group of animals of the same species.

Pouch A flap of skin, usually like a pocket, which covers the teats of female marsupials and in which the young are raised.

Prairie A type of open grassland found in North America and Canada.

Predator An animal that hunts and kills other animals, its prey.

Preening In birds, running the bill through the feathers to keep the plumage clean and airworthy. The action also distributes oil onto the plumage from a preen gland just above the tail.

Pregnancy The period during which the young grows in the body of a female mammal.

Prehensile Able to grasp, as in a hand, foot or monkey's tail.

Prey The animals that are hunted by a predator. The word is also a verb, so an eagle is said to prey on rabbits.

Primaries The long outer flight feathers on the wings, with which a bird propels itself through the air.

Primates The order of mammals that includes monkeys, apes and humans.

Race The division of animal classification below sub-species; it refers to animals that are very similar but have slightly different characteristics.

Rain forest A type of forest found in the tropics and sub-tropics that has heavy rainfall throughout the year. Such forests usually contain a large number of different species. Some rain forest grows in temperate regions, as in the Pacific north-west of the USA.

Raptor Another name for a bird of prey such as an eagle or a hawk.

Ratites Ostriches and their relatives, such as emus, cassowaries and rheas.

Regurgitate To bring up food previously swallowed. Many sea-birds feed their young by regurgitation.

Resident An animal that stays in the same area all year round.

Rodent A rat, mouse or other animal belonging to the order Rodentia.

Roosting Sleeping or resting.

Savannah Tropical grassland, particularly in Africa.

Scavenger An animal that feeds on the remains of carcasses that others have abandoned.

Scent glands Special organs or areas of skin that produce chemicals which have a distinctive smell. The scent may not be detectable by humans. Scents are an important means of communication in many animals.

Scent marking Marking territory by smearing objects with scent from glands in the body or by means of urine.

Scrape A hollow in the ground made by an animal in which it lays its eggs.

Scrub Vegetation in which shrubs are the most common plants. It occurs naturally in some dry areas, or results from human destruction of the forest.

Secondaries The shorter inner flight feathers on a bird's wing. They provide the lift that keeps the bird in the air.

Sibling A "brother" or "sister". In some animals the young remain with their parents and look after their younger siblings.

Simians Monkeys and apes; higher primates.

Solitary Living alone, not in a group.

Species The division of animal classification below genus; a group of animals of the same structure that can breed together.

Sperm The male sex cells.

Steppe The temperate grassy plains of Eurasia. Called "prairie" in North America and Canada.

Sub-species The division of animal classification below species and above race; typically the various sub-species live in different places.

Sub-tropics The two warm regions bordering the tropics to the north and south of the equator.

Talons The sharp curved claws with which many birds of prey catch the animals on which they feed.

Temperate A climate that is not too hot and not too cold. Temperate zones lie between the sub-tropics and the cold high-latitude regions in both hemispheres.

Terrestrial Living on land.

Territory The area in which an animal or group of animals lives and which it defends against intruders.

Tropics Strictly, the region between latitudes 23° north and south of the equator. Tropical regions are typically very hot and humid.

Tundra The landscape at high latitudes where the very cold climate prevents the growth of trees. A similar habitat occurs at high altitudes on mountains.

Ungulates Mammals that have hoofs. Most of these animals are large and feed entirely on plant material.

Vertebrate An animal with a backbone.

Waterfowl Birds such as swans, geese and ducks, belonging to the order Anseriformes.

Wintering ground The region where migrant birds go, outside the breeding season; usually in warmer, lower latitudes.

INDEX

Scientific names

The first name of each
double-barrel Latin name
refers to the *genus*, the second
to the *species*.

FURTHER READING

Alexander, R. McNeill (ed) (1986), *The Encyclopedia of Animal Biology*, Facts on File, New York

Bellairs, A.d'A. and Cox, C.B. (eds) (1976), *Morphology and Biology of Reptiles*, Academic Press, London

Berry, R.J. and Hallam, A. (eds) (1986),*The Encyclopedia of Animal Evolution*, Facts on File, New York

Carr, A. (1963), *The Reptiles*, Life Nature Library, New York

Clutton-Brock, J. (1981), *Domesticated Animals from Early Times*, Heinemann, London; University of Texas Press, Austin

Cochran, D.M. (1961), *Living Amphibians of the World*, Doubleday and Co., Garden City, New York

Corbet, G.B. and Hill, J.E. (1980), *A World List of Mammalian Species*, British Museum and Cornell University Press, London and Ithaca, N.Y.

Englemann, W.-E. and Obst, F.J. (1981), *Snakes: Biology, Behavior and Relationships to Man*, Edition Leipzig, Leipzig

Ferguson, M.W.J. (ed) (1984), *The Structure, Development and Evolution of Reptiles*, Academic Press, London

Goin, C.J., Goin, O.B. and Zug, G.R. (1978), *Introduction to Herpetology* (3rd edition), W. H. Freeman and Co., San Francisco

Grzimek, B. (ed) (1972), *Grzimek's Animal Life Encyclopedia*, vols 10, 11, 12, Van Nostrand Reinhold, New York

Halliday, T.R. and Adler, K. (eds) (1985), *The Encyclopedia of Reptiles and Amphibians*, Facts on File, New York

Harrison, C.J.O. (1978), *A Field Guide to the Nests, Eggs and Nestlings of North American Birds*, Collins, London

Harrison Matthews, L. (1969), *The Life of Mammals*, vols 1 and 2, Weidenfeld and Nicolson, London

Herrins, C.M. and Middleton, A.L.A. (eds) (1985), *The Encyclopedia of Birds*, Facts on File, New York

Macdonald, D. (ed) (1984) *The Encyclopedia of Mammals*, Facts on File, New York

Moore, P.D. (ed) (1986), *The Encyclopedia of Animal Ecology*, Facts on File, New York

National Geographic Society (1987), *Field Guide to the Birds of North America* (2nd edition), NGS, Washington

Nowak, R.M. and Paradiso, J.L. (eds) (1983) *Walker's Mammals of the World* (4th edition), 2 vols, Johns Hopkins University Press, Baltimore and London

Porter, K.R. (1972), *Herpetology*, W.B.Saunders Co, Philadelphia

Skutch, A.F. (1975), *Parent Birds and their Young*, University of Texas Press, Austin

Slater, P.J.B. (ed) (1986), *The Encyclopedia of Animal Behavior*, Facts on File, New York

Tyne, J. van and Berger, A.J. (1976), *Fundamentals of Ornithology* (2nd edition), Wiley, New York

Winn, H.E. and Olla, B.L. (1979), *The Behavior of Marine Mammals*, vol 3, Cetaceans, Plenum, New York

Young, J.Z. (1975), *The Life of Mammals: their Anatomy and Physiology*, Oxford University Press, Oxford

Zeuner, F.E. (1963), *A History of Domesticated Animals*, Hutchinson, London; Harper and Row, New York

ACKNOWLEDGEMENTS

Picture credits

Key: *t* top. *b* bottom. *c* center. *l* left. *r* right.

Abbreviations: A Ardea. AH Andrew Henley. AN Agence Nature. ANT Australasian Nature Transparencies. BCL Bruce Coleman Limited. BH Brian Hawkes. FLPA Frank Lane Picutre Agency. GF George Frame. J Jacana. LLR Leonard Lee Rue III. MF Michael Fogden. NHPA Natural History Photographic Agency. NP Nature Photographers. NSP Natural Science Photos. OSF Oxford Scientific Films. PEP Planet Earth Pictures. RWV R W VanDevender. SA Survival Anglia. WWF World Wildlife Fund for Nature.

10*t* NP/Bisserot. 10*b* R W V. 12*t* OSF/G I Bernard. 13*b*, 14*b* David M Dennis. 15 NHPA/R J Erusin. 16–17 NP/G E Janes. 17 MF. 20 NSP/C Mattison. 20–21 MF. 22–23 J. Gibbons/University of South Pacific, Fiji. 25 NHPA/S Dalton. 29 A/F Gohier. 31 MF. 33*t* RWV. 33*b* NHPA/K Switak. 36*t*, 36*b* MF. 38 NHPA/J Shaw. 39*t* MF. 39*b* RWV. 40 Anthony Bannister. 41 NHPA/S Dalton. 44*t* NSP/C Banks. 44*b* ANT/D B Carter. 45 SA/Alan Root. 48 David Hosking. 51 BCL. 53 BH. 54 NP/M P Harris. 55 FLPA/C Carvalho. 56 J. 58–59 A. 61*t* B Davidson. 61*b* David Hosking. 62 LLR. 63*t* William Ervin. 63*b* BH. 66–67 BCL/Gordon Langsbury. 69 NHPA/Joe B Blossom. 70 J. 74 AN/Gohier. 75 J. 78–79 AH. 80 NP. 84–85, 86 A. 88. AN/Gohier. 89 A. 90 BCL. 91, 92 A. 94 BCL. 95 BCL/George Laycock. 96 A. 97 BCL/Pekka Helo. 98 BCL. 99*t*, 99*c*, 99*b* SA. 101 LLR. 102 BCL. 103 SA. 104 A/P Morris. 105 A. 107 NHPA. 108*t* A. 108*b* SA. 109 NHPA/Nigel Dennis. 110 BH. 111 SA/D & M Plage. 112 MF. 113 FLPA. 118–119 NHPA. 120 SA/J & D Bartlett. 121 William Ervin. 124 SA/J & D Bartlett. 125 Aquila. 126*t*, 126*b*, 128 Bio Tec Images. 129 MF. 130 OSF/Rodger Jackman. 131 GF. 132 Anthony Bannister. 133 BCL. 134 Tony Morrison. 135 BCL. 138–139 OSF/G I Bernard. 140 A. 141 GF. 142–143 BCL. 144 Fiona Sunquist. 145 WWF/Andy Purcell. 147*t*, 147*b* GF. 149 A. 150 OSF. 151 R O Peterson. 152 J W Lentfer. 153*t* FLPA/C Carvalho. 153*b* BCL/B & C Calhoun. 154 LLR. 155, 156 OSF. 157*t* A. 157*b* BCL. 158/, 158*r*, 159 J. 160/, 160*r* BCL. 161*t* OSF. 161*b* FLPA. 163 BCL. 164 J. 165 BCL. 166 N Lightfoot. 168 R M Laws.

168–169 A. 170 J. 172 AH. 173 W N Bonner. 174–175 FLPA. 179 AN. 178–179 Mel Wursig. 181 D Gaskin. 182, 183 Sea Mammal research Unit, Cambridge. 184 Fred Bruemmer. 186 A. 187 AN. 189 Ken Balcomb. 190–191 PEP/James Hudnall. 194 BCL. 195 AH. 196 J. 197 Peter Veit. 198 OSF. 199*t* MF. 199*b* A. 201*t*, 201*b* J. 202 OSF. 203 NHPA/S Dalton. 204 A. 206 WWF/Sylvia Yorath. 207*t*, 207*b* ANT. 207*r* J. 208 SA/Alan Root. 209 BCL/M P Price. 210–211 A. 212 WWF/Mark Boulton. 213 BCL. 214 SA/J & D Bartlett. 215, 216 J. 218–219 AN. 221*t* AN/Lanceau/220–221*b* SA/Alan Root. 224*t* AN/Gohier. 224*b* PEP/P Scoones. 224–225*b* AN/Gohier. 225*t* BCL/H Jungius. 227 BCL. 228–229 J. 229*b* AN. 230 William Ervin. 231 John MacKinnon. 232 J. 233, 235 LLR. 236 BCL/Eric Crighton. 236–237 LLR. 239 BCL. 241 NHPA/P Fagot. 242 ANT. 244/, 244*r* AH. 245 AN/Ferrero. 246 E Beaton. 247 G Mazza.

Artwork credits

Artwork in the book has been prepared by:

Norman Arlott	Malcolm McGregor
Rob von Assen	Sean Milne
Priscilla Barrett	Milne and Stebbing Illustrations
Trevor Boyer	Denys Ovenden
Ad Cameron	Mick Saunders
Stephen Cocking	Chloe Talbot-Kelley
Jeanne Colville	Laurel Tucker
David Dennis	Dick Twinney
Simon Driver	Ian Willis
John Fuller	
Robert Gillmor	
Peter Harrison	
Hayward Art Group	
Richard Lewington	
Mick Loates	
Michael Long	